A
DOCTOR'S
PRESCRIPTION
FOR LIFE

A
DOCTOR'S
PRESCRIPTION
FOR LIFE

Frank A. Pedreira, M.D.

Sterling House

ISBN 1-58501-007-3

Trade Paperback
© Copyright 1999 Frank A. Pedreira, M.D.
All rights reserved
First Printing—2000
Library of Congress #98-87119

Request for information should be addressed to:

CeShore publishing Co.
The Sterling Building
440 Friday Road
Department T-101
Pittsburgh, PA 15209
www.ceshore.com

Cover Art: Michelle Vennare-SterlingHouse
Typesetting: Tracy Lynn Reedy

Printed in Canada

For
The Honor of God
and
In Memory of All Those Who
Never Had a Chance at Life

Contents

Chapter 3: The Abortion Dilemma

Acknowledgements

I wish to thank Pastor Eddy Swieson who initially encouraged me to write this book. He has been a loyal friend and ongoing source of inspiration to me in pursuing this project. It is impossible for me to overestimate the personal sacrifice and dedicated labor that Vance and Linda Kauzlarich have made in typing and preparing the manuscript for publication. Vance brought the book into the computer age, even though he left me behind. My wife, Anita, performed a huge labor of love by reading and listening to me read the entire book many times. She has an uncanny ear for the English language and a discerning sense of what works. In this, as in all things, she has sacrificially given of herself and enriched me in the process. My son, Dr. Mark Pedreira, a professor of English literature and a rhetorician, did what no son should ever be subjected to do. He agreed to edit my book and did so most skillfully, concentrating his considerable talents on the core chapters of Abortion and Euthanasia. That the process went so smoothly is a testimony of our love for each other and his enduring patience. Each of my children, Tracy, David, and Christina and my son-in-law, Timothy, offered valuable advice and encouragement along the way. More importantly, they demonstrated their confidence in me and affirmed me when I most needed a psychological boost. My sister Elaine went beyond the call of sisterly duty when she actually gave me her personal copy of *The Chicago Manual of Style*. Moreover, she lent her considerable professional expertise in advising me about the complexities of the book publishing world. In this same vein, my friend, Mary Ott, an English literature major in her college days, generously emptied her library of grammar and rhetoric books, thus immeasurably relieving my perpetual state of language confusion. She is, in no way, to be blamed for the mistakes that have crept into the text. I am also indebted to Janice Lester, the medical librarian at my local community hospital. She graciously assisted me in my medical literature search and enthusiastically followed the progress of the manuscript. In addition, I am grateful to my medical partners, Edward Feroli and Gordon Mella, for supporting me in this work and constantly encouraging me through the process. Gordon actually read the book in its unedited state, an obvious labor of love and a sign of his solidarity with me. My thanks also go to my secretary, Sylvia Fowell, for typing most of the correspondence generated by this work. As always, she has represented me well. In a very personal sense, I am deeply indebted to my mother who first taught me to believe in myself, and then never stopped believing in me. Her love and affirmation have followed me all the days of my life. Finally, my thanks and gratitude are extended to Cynthia Shore Sterling, my publisher, who also believed in me and took a chance on this controversial and emotionally charged book. The final edit of the book by her staff rounded out its many rough edges. I am grateful for so much generous help. At the same time, I willingly and cheerfully assume full responsibility for all the imperfections in my work.

Preface

The concept for this book was conceived in the preparation for and the delivery of a series of lectures given at the Christian Covenant Church in Rockville, Maryland. Dr. Eddy Swieson, the pastor of the church, invited me to give a monthly seminar on a variety of topics relating to life and health. The emphasis was to focus on life issues that impacted on physical, emotional, and spiritual health. Accordingly, the series was entitled "Forum on Life's Issues."

In the course of the Forum, I decided to specifically address the topic of life. In a series of presentations, I attempted to define life and death, probe the origins and meaning of life, consider the value and dignity of each human person, and discuss, from a medical and Christian perspective, the issues of abortion, euthanasia, and suicide. These presentations formed the basis for the topics covered in this book.

With the encouragement of Dr. Swieson, I subsequently began to collect material and develop an outline for future publication. This volume represents the fruit of that labor. My intention had always been to direct this work to Christians, to help them sort out all the disparate voices currently addressing the topics discussed. The goal was to help each Christian believer examine these complicated life issues from a biblical, Christian perspective. From the onset, I elected to focus on abortion and euthanasia, and to frame the debate about life as it centered on the Scriptural concepts of the sanctity and meaning of life, moral absolutes and truth. In addition, the book was also written with the purpose of examining the sources of the conflict these issues engender and with the intention of devising a strategy to combat the daily abuses of life we encounter in this country.

The first chapter of the book explores the origins of life from the perspective of faith and science. It contrasts the dehumanizing view of science on the evolution of man with the encouraging hope implicit in our creation, establishing the Scriptural basis for the ethical value of the sanctity of life.

Further, it considers the possible determinations as to the moment human life begins and personhood is conferred on that life. The second chapter discusses the biblical perspective on the nature of God and man as it is expressed in the creedal truths of the Christian Faith. It distinguishes between the Christian belief that upholds the ethical value of life with the arbitrary concepts of self-determination and self-autonomy implicit in the currently popular form of atheism called secular humanism. The third and fourth chapters address the most serious contemporary assaults on life — abortion and euthanasia. The third chapter addresses the topic of abortion in its many ramifications. The chapter begins by defining abortion and framing the debate within the contradictory views held about it by our society. Subsequently, the issue is considered from the standpoint of law, medicine, ethics, moral philosophy, and public opinion. Included in the chapter are sections devoted to abortion and feminism and abortion and Christianity. Problem areas such as mother's health, rape and incest, and fetal malformation and/or genetic disorders are candidly discussed. The chapter concludes with a look at medical advances that further complicate the issue. The Fourth chapter considers the problem of euthanasia. After presenting a historical perspective on the topic, the varying faces of euthanasia are defined and discussed. Complicated issues such as pain and suffering, the terminally ill, natural and unnatural euthanasia, physician-assisted suicide, and patient rights are discussed from the standpoint of medical ethics, constitutional law, and biblical, orthodox Christian faith. The proper role of medicine in the debate is considered from its varying perspectives. Finally, a concluding section addresses the contemporary problems of living wills, the right to refuse treatment, and the inherent right to choose life. The fifth and final chapter is entitled "Reclaiming the Land" and examines what Christians can do to reclaim our nation for life. Rather than advocating specific methods of pro-life activism, it offers advice to Christians on how to present our case to a largely secular world. It decries violence and belligerent confrontation and proposes instead a biblical model on how God would have us wage war against the twin evils of abortion and euthanasia. Utilizing a scriptural foundation for Christian dissent, it explores current ungodly attitudes in Christian activism that mimic the world's approach to disagreement and result in a negative witness for our cause. Finally, the chapter calls the nation to individual and corporate repentance and encourages pro-life advocates to not abandon the cause of life to those who devalue it. It concludes by cautioning that evil must neither be accommodated nor appeased and prevails upon all Christians to uphold the righteous biblical standard of the sanctity of life, laboring on behalf of the most vulnerable members of our society, the fetus and the terminally ill.

In this regard, it is striking that, as of this writing, we have reached the 25th anniversary of the Roe v. Wade Supreme Court decision. It is a milestone that no pro-life advocate welcomes or celebrates. Twenty-five years ago, the Supreme Court had hoped to end the divisive public debate over abortion and establish legal guidelines that would impose order on a controversial and nationally disruptive issue. Good intentions aside, the public argument and debate continues as heated as ever, and we remain a country divided.

There has been some change in the general strategy adopted by those actively engaged in the conflict. Abortion activists have assumed a defensive posture and desperately are trying to hold on to ground presumed already won. Abortion opponents, on the other hand, have turned their creative energies towards state legislation and have methodically chipped away at the unsteady edifice of Roe. In the meantime, almost unnoticed, 35 million fetuses have been aborted — a gruesome reminder of the evil initiated by the infamous Roe decision.

In addition, in the short time interval since the book was completed, a growing number of people on both sides of the argument have tried to seek out a middle ground of compromise. Specifically, some antiabortion activists and abortion rights supporters have attempted to find common cause in the often raucous debate on life. In many respects, they are touching on several of the issues I have covered in this book and seem to be seeking to address the problems that contribute to the demand for abortion, while hoping to protect and help the women caught in the trap of an unwanted pregnancy.

Others are declaring that the abortion war is all but over. David Garrow, a professor at Emory University, recently reviewed three books on the abortion conflict that has gripped this nation (N.Y. Times Book Review, January 25, 1998). He exults that the "constitutional legacy" of Roe v. Wade is "alive and well at age 25" and that the abortion "war" is ended. In his view, the law has taken the initiative from the Pro-Life movement and the struggle has become merely political. On the other hand, feminists increasingly are concerned that political attention is shifting from the woman to the fetus and in this, Garrow concedes, the political conflict is far from concluded.

In many respects, Garrow appears to be on target. Many in our country seem to be losing their sense of moral outrage over our national assault on life. On January 16, 1998, the Republican National Committee rejected an abortion litmus test for Republican candidates and appeared to move towards an abortion-neutral position. The United States Supreme Court also sidestepped the abortion debate this year by refusing to hear the State of Ohio's appeal of a 1995 Ohio Court ruling striking down its ban on late-term abortion. And true to form, the American Academy of Pediatrics (AAP), an organization presumably dedicated to the health and well-being of all children everywhere, tabled a 1997 resolution by its state chapter leaders to ban partial-birth abortions. This action prompted many Academy members to conclude that political correctness in the abortion debate was more important to the AAP than the protection of the increasingly vulnerable and endangered fetus. If nothing else, the AAP demonstrated consistency. It has, since the beginning of the abortion debate, resolutely maintained a pro-choice stance.

There is yet further evidence of an emerging national malaise and moral ambivalence regarding abortion. In 1997, both the House and Senate passed bills banning partial-birth abortion. In a startling move from its long-avowed position of neutrality over abortion, the American Medical Association, one day before the Senate vote, endorsed the resolution. Predictably, President Clinton vetoed the bill, marking the second time he kept the procedure legally viable by vetoing congressional legislation to ban its use. On this occasion, the public outcry seemed muted. As anticipated, amidst little national protest, Pro-Life Senate advocates fell three short of the number needed to override the Presidential veto. Further, the N. Y. Times recently documented additional striking evidence of national moral ambiguity over the issue of abortion (January 17, 1998). Statistics from the Communicable Disease Center in Atlanta, Georgia, were cited demonstrating that abortion has become a common means of birth control among young, single women in their early 20s and that personal beliefs not withstanding, moral principles were often sacrificed on the altar of expediency. It was also clear that an increasing number of young women choosing abortion were relatively untroubled by the moral issues at stake. In this, they mirror the moral uncertainties of our secularized and confused society.

In this same vein, the past year has been a particularly eventful one regarding euthanasia. On June 26, 1997, the United States Supreme Court ruled that there was no constitutional right to assisted suicide with the help of a physician. Many were quick to point out that while the Court decision did not guarantee Americans a right to physician-assisted suicide, it did not bar the door for further state legislation. The Supreme Court ruling would prove not to be the last word on this matter. The citizens of Oregon, within four months of the Court ruling, voted to block an attempt to repeal their 1994 law which approved physician-assisted suicide. In turn, within just a few months of the Oregon vote, the Justice Department of the United States, after a review of the Oregon law, concluded that Federal drug officers could not punish physicians who assisted patients to die. This, despite the fact that the head of the Federal Drug Enforcement Agency (DEA) had told Congress a year before that the DEA had the authority to punish physicians who prescribed a controlled substance for any illegitimate purpose, including assisted suicide. Clearly, the United States Supreme Court, in inviting the nation to pursue an honest debate on euthanasia, opened the door to serious mischief on the part of its proponents.

Many in our country have, over the years, proposed the Dutch experiment with euthanasia as a model for our nation. A commentary in the Journal of the American Medical Association of June 4, 1997, by Dr. Herbert Hendin, an eminent New York psychiatrist, and two Dutch colleagues, Dr. Chris Rutenfrans, a member of the Department of Justice, The Hague and Dr. Zbigniew Zylicz, a physician working in hospice care in the Netherlands, found the model to be seriously flawed. They carefully documented the fact that the Netherlands, as previously predicted by many, is rapidly moving down a slippery slope as they extend physician-assisted suicide to an expanding number of patients. Grave moral offenses repeatedly include ending life without the sick patient's request or intention, and the administration of drugs, particularly opioids, with the explicit intention to kill. The authors concluded that the Dutch government had been unable to regulate euthanasia and had allowed serious moral lapses to infiltrate the process. Distinct lines between the terminally and chronically ill had been crossed. Even more distressing, patients with psychological illness had often been encouraged to end their lives.

Further, Dr. Hendin and his associates rightly point out that by so quickly embracing life termination, Dutch physicians had failed to develop competency in palliative care, especially for the alleviation of pain and suffering. Rather than being proposed as a model, the Dutch experiment, more appropriately, should be viewed as flawed, dangerous, and morally bankrupt. It is far easier to propose death than to grasp and confront life. In truth, we ought not to emulate them, rather, we ought to diligently avoid making their mistakes. The United States Supreme Court, in their 1997 decision, recognized the inherent danger in easy access to legally sanctioned life termination. They required all states to ensure that any laws regulating assisted suicide not obstruct their provision for adequate palliative care. In this, the Court specifically addressed those states whose laws severely restrict the appropriate use of opioids in the management of severe pain. In the care of the terminally ill, suffering patient it ought always to be permissible to provide relief from pain, even in the face of foreseeable consequences. On the other hand, it is morally indefensible to use these agents with the intent to kill. The Court wisely implied a distinction between these two courses of action.

As we approach the next millennium, the cause of life continues to be in jeopardy. It remains to be seen whether this country has the moral courage and the stamina to withstand the agents of death that assail us daily. Certainly, the struggle is not for the timid. We can be assured that the problem will not go away on its own initiative. Laws cannot effectively legislate what the heart doesn't want. Tragically, the soul of our country is at stake and the next chapter on American freedom remains to be written.

Frank A. Pedreira
Gaithersburg, Maryland
May 17, 1998

In The Beginning

INTRODUCTION

> *"I am determined to be wise" - but this was beyond me.*
> *Whatever wisdom may be, it is far off and most profound*
> *- who can discover it? So I turned my mind to under-*
> *stand, to investigate and to search out wisdom and the*
> *scheme of things and to understand the stupidity of*
> *wickedness and the madness of folly.*

Ecclesiastes 7:23-25

The writer of Ecclesiastes was determined to find the meaning of life, but found instead that the subject was too much for him. He knew the questions to ask, he just had trouble coming up with the answers. Most of us can sympathize with him. Life is a mystery and complicated. But having acknowledged that much doesn't let us off the hook. How will we find the answers to the questions life presents to us? The problem is real and personal. The following story illustrates my point.

Shortly after Roe.v.Wade was enacted as national policy (1973), I was visiting my mother in New Jersey. My family and I had just arrived after an arduous four-hour automobile trip, much of it in bumper to bumper traffic on the New Jersey Turnpike, and I was settling down on the sofa for a brief nap before dinner. My sleep was abruptly disturbed when my mother called out to me, "Frank. Look who's here to visit you. Marie and her friend." Marie's family and ours were long-time friends. I had known her all of her life. She was now 23 years old, a beautiful young woman and steadily dating a young man I had never met before. When Marie and her friend entered the living room, I knew something was wrong. Her face was pinched, and she barely managed a smile in greeting me; he looked pale and frightened. She got right to the point, barely controlling her emotions. "I'm two months pregnant and John and I agree that I should have an abortion." With that she began to sob. John quickly assured me that they planned to marry, but weren't prepared to have a baby at that time.

I didn't say anything at first, but my heart went out to them both, and my face must have reflected what I was feeling. Slowly her head came up and she asked me through her tears, "Well? What do you think?"

I replied by asking her a question: "What's in your belly?"

She looked surprised but quickly answered, "A baby, of course."

"Is it a human person?" I asked them both, adding, "at this moment?"

They looked at each other with a startled expression on their faces. "Of course!" they blurted out simultaneously.

"Then," I asked, "if you abort this baby who's a human person at this moment, what will you be doing to it?"

Marie looked shocked and slowly said, "Killing it."

"What's another name for killing someone?" I asked as gently as I could manage.

This time, John answered first, "Murder."

"Right," I responded – "and is this wrong?"

"Yes," Marie sobbed, "and it's a sin."

"Well," I then asked, "what are you going to do?"

A visible weight seemed to lift off both of them as they smiled, hugged each other, and replied, "We're going to have a baby." John then made a face and said with a chuckle, "I sure hope it looks like Marie."

Marie and John subsequently married and had their baby. The little girl was beautiful and did indeed look like Marie. Nineteen years later, the baby, now grown up and the joy of her parents, got married to a fine young man. A little more than a year later, I received an announcement of the birth of her baby. Wouldn't you know it? Another girl and the new parents tell me they are thrilled and so very happy. I put the announcement card down and thought about the significance of three generations — grandmother, mother, and baby — together giving testimony to the celebration and wonder of life. And all because Marie and John, given a hard choice to make, came up with the right answer.

Today, as in any age, people face the myriad of questions life poses: "Why am I here?" "Does my life count for anything?" Recently, the dialogue has expanded, and we wrestle with issues almost too deep for us. "When does life begin?" and "What determines the value of a person's life?" The questions are too serious to ignore, but the problems they pose for us and our society seem to grow larger daily.

In this first chapter, we will consider the scriptural understandings of the origin of life, contrasting it with the current secular theories of science. In addition, we will review the prevalent opinions regarding when life is conferred on the developing fetus, and the moral and legal implications these opinions hold for each of us. Finally, we will provide a biblical framework upon which these questions can be resolved.

The Origin of Life

> *"Who has measured the waters in the hollow of his hand,*
> *and marked off the heavens with a span,*
> *enclosed the dust of the earth in a measure,*
> *and weighed the mountains in scales,*
> *and the hills in a balance?"*

Isaiah 40:12

The Perspective of Faith

The origin of life is a matter usually left to theologians, and for good reason. Jews and Christians hold that God created the universe "ex nihilo" — "Divine will constituting nature from nothingness."[1] The universe itself is not eternal, but was brought into existence out of nothing by God's free choice and continues to exist because He wills it to exist. All beginnings are rooted in Him and our days are numbered from this primordial event.

> *"In the beginning God created the heavens and the earth."*

Genesis 1:1

Further, Rabbinic and Christian theology hold that God is at once separate from and far above the universe (transcendent), while very near to man and the soul of the universe (immanent).[2] These truths form the basis of what Christians and Jews believe about God and his creation and are the teaching of scripture.

Scripture consistently testifies to God's creative work in the formation of the earth and all living creatures.

> *"The earth is the Lord's and all that is in it, the world, and*
> *those who live in it: for he has founded it on the seas, and*
> *established it on the rivers."*

Psalm 24:1,2 (NRSV)

Scripture also speaks of God's order and meticulous design in establishing the natural laws of the universe. God, in speaking to Noah after the flood, says:

> *"As long as the earth endures, seed time and harvest, cold and*
> *heat, summer and winter, day and night will never cease."*

Genesis 8:22

Yet, for all of God's sovereign majesty, the Bible reveals him to be very near to human beings, the perfection of his creation.

> *"When I look at your heavens, the work of your fingers, the moon*
> *and the stars that you have established; what are human beings*
> *that you are mindful of them, mortals that you care for them."*

> Psalm 8:3,4 (NRSV)

A View Through the Telescope

Dr. Robert Jastrow, in his book <u>God and the Astronomers</u>, writes that three lines of scientific evidence "the motions of the galaxies, the laws of thermodynamics, and the life story of the stars" pointed to one conclusion; all indicate that the universe had a beginning.[3] While many physicists would disagree, some have argued that not enough evidence supports the fact that matter was pre-existent before creation and that it is simpler to conclude that God created the universe as we know it from nothing.

The British mathematical theorist, Edward Milne, stated that our picture of the universe is incomplete without God.[4] Albert Einstein, while he never could accept the idea of a personal God, nonetheless acknowledged the necessity of a Prime Mover who willed all things into being. He argued that the precision and order of the universe required God.[5] Dr. Jastrow, a self-professed agnostic in religious matters, has written, "Now we see how the astronomical evidence leads to a biblical view of the origin of the world."[6]

These speculations are daring and startling. Scientists live by their reason, not by faith. However, the bulk of scientific evidence today clearly does support the notion that the universe had a sudden beginning (the "Big Bang"). Jastrow concludes the final chapter of his book with this charming story:

> *"For the scientist who has lived by his faith in the power of*
> *reason, the story ends like a bad dream: he is about to con-*
> *quer the highest peak; as he pulls himself over the final rock,*
> *he is greeted by a band of theologians who have been sitting*
> *there for centuries."* [7]

THE STORY OF MAN

While scientists generally have been reluctant to hypothesize about the origins of the universe, they have shown little reluctance to enter the debate about the origins of man. The basic question to be answered remains, "How did man get here?" Essentially, there are two views that are prevalent on the origins of life: evolution and the teaching of scripture.

Evolution

Evolutionary biologists hold that plants and animals have changed from generation to generation and are still changing today. This theory was first formulated by Charles Darwin who, as a young naturalist, made observations onboard HMS Beagle, a ship sent by the British Admiralty on a surveying voyage around the world. Darwin concluded that plants and animals develop through natural selection of variations that increase the organism's ability to survive. He subsequently published two seminal works: "On the Origins of the Human Species by Means of Natural Selection" and the "Descent of Man."

His theory involved three basic ideas: (1) living things change, producing new descendants with new characteristics; (2) this process accounts for all living things now in existence, as well as those extinct; and (3) all living things have a common origin and, thus, are related. Two essential components of Darwin's theory are biological variation and natural selection. Implicit in his theory is the belief that all life had its origins in the primordial seas that covered the earth in its beginnings.[8]

Contained within this hypothesis is the understanding that all human beings exist as a result of blind, capricious chance. Having left God out of the equation of life, it is easy to understand how one is left with a question that Somerest Maugham, the English novelist (1874-1965), succinctly probed.

> "If one puts aside the existence of God and the possibility of survival as too doubtful to have any effect on one's behavior, one has to make up one's mind what is the meaning and use of life?"[9]

It clearly is apparent why Maugham was disillusioned. The question he posed is appropriate for all men everywhere. Science, in ignoring God, has dehumanized man. What is the significance of our existence if we randomly evolved from single-celled organisms living in the primordial seas? Blind chance is an uncomfortable ancestor for most of us. If our life has any meaning and if there is any value to be ascribed to each individual person, we need a surer anchor on which to rely.

The Teaching of Scripture

> "Have we not all one father?
> hath not one God created us?"

> Malachi 2:10

While scripture does not preclude the possibility of evolutionary change occurring at different levels and stages of life, it clearly teaches that the creation of the universe and man was not accidental, but the result of God's purposeful and intentional action. Jews and Christians may differ among themselves as to how they are to interpret the early chapters of Genesis, but they resolutely hold fast to the fundamental teaching of the Bible that "God created man in his own image."

"The Shorter Catechism" asks the question, "How was man made?" and provides the proper biblical answer: "God created male and female after his own image, in knowledge, righteousness, and holiness with dominion over the creatures."[10] The Jewish Talmud teaches that human beings were created in the image of God, and in that respect they are pre-eminent above all creatures and represent the culminating point in God's work of creation.[11] The "Catechism of the Catholic Church" adds that because man is created in the image of God, he occupies a unique place in creation, in that, in his own nature, he unites the spiritual and material worlds.[12]

Therefore, our faith teaches us that we are not here by blind, arbitrary chance. God has created us and we occupy a special place in his creation. The following words of scripture constitute the basis for the Judeo-Christian concept of the Sanctity of Life.

> "So God created man in his own image, in the image of
> God he created him; male and female he created them."

Genesis 1:27

Since the Bible teaches that we have been created in God's image, He has become the measure of our worth. Accordingly, every human life is sacred. This notion of the sanctity of life has been the ancient tradition of the Church and, until recently, the bulwark of western civilization. Because God made us in His image, we are free to properly value ourselves. Since our worth is God-derived, our real merit can never be determined solely by the quality of our life or our productivity. Thus, understanding the significance of the Genesis creation story helps us to better understand and appreciate ourselves.

Further, the biblical account of creation emphasizes that "man" (used to denote both genders) was made differently from everything else. God fashioned Adam from the dust of the earth and established a special and personal relationship with him.

> "The Lord God formed the man from the dust of the
> ground and breathed into his nostrils the breath of life,
> and man became a living being."

Genesis 2:7

When God created the universe, the earth, and all other living creatures, he spoke each thing into being. But God formed man from the dust of the earth. Thus, man, in a special sense, has the fingerprints of God upon him.

Then, the scriptures inform us, God "breathed into his nostrils the breath of life." The poet Phillip James Bailey has captured the moment in verse:

> *"Let each man think himself an act of God.*
> *His mind a thought, his life a breath of God."*

If every human life is a deliberate, loving act of God, every assessment of our worth must give way to that fact. The dehumanizing estimate of science must yield to the encouraging words of scripture. Therefore, we are not our own to do with as we please. People are not expendable. Life can never be sacrificed on the altar of convenience or personal preference.

Further, God has implanted, in each one of us, an instinct to preserve our life. Recently, while visiting a nursing home, I met Miriam, an enthusiastic and bright elderly woman who resented the confining nature of her institutional life. She told me she was "tired of the way she had to live" as a prisoner of other people's schedules and expectations. Moreover, she disliked her physical limitations and lamented the loss of her freedom. Tearfully, she confided in me that suicide "had crossed her mind." But, because she was convinced that this would be a sin against God, herself, and her family, she chose to live and was determined, with the Lord's Grace, to finish all the days allotted to her with dignity.

In Western society, we see an almost universal condemnation of suicide. John Locke wrote, "Men are God's handiwork and are made to last during His, and not one another's pleasure."[13] Thus, under natural as well as divine law, everyone is required to maintain his life. In this regard the Jewish Talmud teaches:

> "Man was first created a single individual to teach the
> lesson that whoever destroys one life, Scripture ascribes
> to him as though he had destroyed a whole world; and
> whoever saves one life, Scripture ascribes it to him as
> though he had saved the whole world."

> Sauh.IV.5[14]

Therefore, suicide, whether self-inflicted or physician-assisted, is a grave offense against God because it destroys His special act of creation — man. Self-determination cannot stand against that fact. Sadly, until fairly recently, it was scarcely an issue in our society. We need, once again, to recapture these truths in our country so that we can save man from himself and live up to God's estimate of our worth.

WHEN DOES LIFE BEGIN?

In the Talmud the question is posed: "At what time is the embryo endowed with a soul?"[15] We might rephrase the question and ask: "When does a person become fully human?" The answer is at the heart of the abortion debate.

Does life begin when the baby is viable outside the uterus?

Paul Veyne, in <u>A History of Private Life: From Pagan Rome to Byzantium</u>, writes: "The birth of a Roman was not merely a biological fact. Infants came into the world, or at any rate were received into society, only as the head of the family willed. Contraception, abortion, the exposure of freeborn infants, and infanticide of slaves' children were common and perfectly legal practices."[16] The fetus was not considered human.

Since the first century, the Christian Church has upheld the dignity of every person and affirmed the immorality of every procured abortion. Today, society universally condemns exposure of newborn infants and infanticide, yet abortion remains a subject of intense and heated controversy.

However, it remains true that viability outside the uterus does not address the basic question: "When does human life begin?" The issues of viability and personhood are not the same. In fact, viability outside the uterus is an ever changing proposition. The highest rate of neonatal mortality is among newborns who weigh less than 1000 grams (2 pounds 2 ounces) at birth and whose gestation is less than 30 weeks. As late as 1970, few babies who were less than 28 weeks gestation (7 months) had any chance of survival. Today, thanks to remarkable advances in neonatal care, newborns weighing as little as 500 grams (1.1 pound) have survived, and the limits of viability outside the uterus have moved closer to 23–24 weeks.

In my private medical practice, I have been honored within the past few months by being chosen to be the pediatrician for a set of quadruplets. The babies were born at 25 1/2 weeks gestation and weighed between 1 pound 4 ounces and 2 pounds 14 ounces. They were cared for in my hospital's pediatric neonatal intensive care unit (NICU), and required assisted ventilation, oxygen, and constant cardio-respiratory monitoring. Thanks to the superb care of the neonatologists and the intensive care nursing staff, all of the babies lived. After three months of hospital care, the quads are being sent home, one at a time. This is particularly special for me because the father, Fred, was my patient during his childhood and his mother, Jean, was the Lord's instrument in helping me to rediscover my faith in a time of personal crisis. Imagine my joy when Rebecca, the youngest of the quads (quad D) came to my office, the first to be released from the hospital. Jonathan, Rachel, and Jeremy are soon to follow. In my own practice lifetime, the limits of viability have changed dramatically. None of these babies would have survived in 1969, the year I entered private practice. Today, in my hospital's NICU, few babies born at 25 weeks or older die.

With this in mind, we legitimately can ask the question, "Is God to be held captive to man's technology?" Is it conceivable that the Creator has a shifting frame of reference in defining life dependent on man's changing technological advances? Clearly not. Viability outside the uterus is a totally unsatisfactory way of defining human life.

It is interesting to reflect on the fact that the "Paterfamilias" in ancient Rome had the autonomy under law to determine whether his child would live or die. Today, pro-choice, militant feminists, under the guise of the concepts of self-autonomy and self-determination, are claiming that same right for women in deciding whether or not to abort their baby. Christians, on the other hand, believe that each person is unique and that God has a special plan for everyone He has created. There are no unwanted pregnancies in God's economy. Man is not always inclined to welcome the conception of new life, but God has, by His will, created every human being for a specific purpose. These truths, in part, form the basis for the Christian's celebration of life in each new birth. The apostle Paul writes: "For by him all things were created: things in heaven and on earth, visible and invisible, whether thrones or powers or rulers or authorities; all things were created by him and for him (Colossians 1:15,16)."

Does life begin sometime between conception and birth?

While this appears to offer a safe ground, it has the potential to become the refuge of cowards. Justice Blackmun's opinion in "Roe v. Wade" (1973) considered pregnancy in its three periods, or trimesters. During the first trimester (first three months), the woman was granted essentially an unrestricted right to abortion. During the second trimester (fourth through the sixth months), the states were granted the right to regulate abortion, since abortion posed a greater threat to the woman's health. Only in the third trimester (seventh through the ninth months), was the state's interest in protecting the fetus deemed great enough to severely restrict abortions, except when necessary to save a woman's life. Further, Blackmun's opinion held that the states could not define when life began.[17] The implication is clear. If a state should decide that life begins at conception, every fetus would enjoy the same rights as every newborn baby.

A scriptural example serves to underline the fallacy in our current judicial opinion. The biblical passage correlates to an episode recorded in the first chapter of the Gospel of Luke. Mary is visited by the angel, Gabriel, and is told that she will conceive and bear the Messiah of Israel, the Chosen One of God. When she protests that she is a virgin, the angel assured her, "The Holy Spirit will come upon you, and the power of the Most High will overshadow you. So the holy one to be born will be called the Son of God" (v.35). And as proof that nothing is impossible with God, the angel continues, "Even Elizabeth your relative is going to have a child in her old age, and she who was said to be barren is in her sixth month" (vv. 26-37). We can only imagine the turmoil that was raging in Mary. How was she to explain this to Joseph? What would she tell her parents? How would her neighbors react? "Why me?" Yet, with all of the uncertainty of the moment, the text tells us that immediately after the visitation, Mary hurried to visit her kinswoman, Elizabeth.

From the perspective of our discussion, the events that follow are nearly as startling as the visitation. The Gospel informs us that upon entering Zechariah's home, Mary greeted Elizabeth. What happened next was wonderful. The baby in Elizabeth (the future John the Baptist), somewhat less than 24 weeks intrauterine age, leapt in her womb in response to the newly fertilized egg (the future Jesus) in the womb of Mary. Life greeted life. Life exulted in life. Under our law, both fetuses were abortable. Under our law, neither was defined as human; neither was viable outside the uterus. Is God trying to tell us something?

Does life begin at conception?

This view reflects the clear teaching of scripture and the historical position of the Christian Church. From the first moment of conception, every fetus is a human being in the process of formation. The ability to survive outside the uterus does not add to or subtract from his personhood. Justice Blackmun is right — the state has no right to define when life begins because a higher authority has already decided the matter. The fetus ought to have the rights of every person, among which is the right to life. No state or court has the legitimate authority to violate that right.

Abortion is a serious offense against God and man. It is gravely contrary to the dignity of man and the holiness of God. Moreover, abortion violates the fifth commandment and is contrary to moral law. The fetus, because it is human and alive, has the right to life and must be defended and cared for like every other human being. At the moment of conception, God is present and accomplishing his purposes in every fetus:

> *"All the days ordained for me were written in your book before one of them came to be."*

> Psalm 139:16

SUMMING UP

Briefly, we have considered the biblical basis for the sanctity of life. To say that we have been created in the image of God conveys more than a theological truth; it says something about who we are. It hardly seems believable that we now have to defend this ancient Judeo-Christian truth from assault, but secular, atheistic humanism has captured the minds of many in our country. Cut adrift from the traditional and safe mooring of faith in God and the authority of the scriptures, society is wandering aimlessly trying to find the meaning of life. In the next chapter, we will see how our understanding of the origins of life and the beginning of personhood tie in with the biblical perspective on the nature of God and man as expressed in the creedal truths of the Christian Faith.

The Value and Dignity of Life

"It is difficult to make a man miserable while he feels worthy of himself and claims kindred to the great God who made him."

Abraham Lincoln

BELIEF UNDER ATTACK

Western civilization for centuries has held that human life is sacred. Since 1973, and the United States' Supreme Court decision of Roe v. Wade, this ethical value has been under attack. The widespread acceptance of abortion in our country, and throughout much of the western world, opened the floodgates to a major assault on the philosophical premise that human beings are special in the eyes of the Creator and that they have eternal value.

Central to the view held by opponents of this position is the belief that man is the center of all things and that God does not exist. This currently popular form of atheism is called secular humanism. Humanism has several core beliefs. One is that man has the capacity to improve and find self-fulfillment without supernatural assistance. Denying the existence of God, secular humanists contend that man alone is responsible for his life and that all people have the right of self-autonomy and the right to determine for themselves which decisions would best serve them and others. Foundational to this belief system is a strong reliance on human reason and the liberating power of science. Consequently, assessments of value are necessarily self-determined and centered on the situation at hand. Universal values and moral absolutes are eschewed. Present experiences are the gauge with which future questions are assessed. Thus, experience becomes the standard of measuring individual and collective worth.[1]

11

Thomas V. Morris, a contemporary Christian philosopher, in his book, *Making Sense of it All*, has correctly framed the central issue in the debate: "Is there a God or not? Is the most basic truth about ultimate reality a personal truth, or is it an impersonal truth? Are human persons small anomalies blindly thrown up by natural processes for a temporary, transient existence in an otherwise hostile universe, or *could it be that we may have both eternal value and everlasting existence?*" (emphasis mine)[2] Clearly it does make a difference what you believe. Christians have a different world view than that of secular humanists. We believe that all of human history has been, and will always be, under God's sovereign control; they do not. We believe that man was made in the image of his Creator; they do not. We believe that God personally involves himself in the lives of men and women; they do not. We believe that all life exists because God wills that it do so; they do not. We believe that all humans are on a journey, that this life is only one point of the human experience, and that life and death are different only in degree, not in kind; they do not. We believe, as Harry Blamires writes, that all life is "contained within eternity" [3]; they do not. Christians, in short, have a supernatural perspective of life. Small wonder, then, that it has become increasingly difficult for Christians to communicate with the many nonbelievers and secularized people we daily encounter. The Christian comes to understand the full meaning of life through the doctrinal truths of the Christian faith, recognizing our Creator God as sovereign and His authority over us as absolute. For those who do not believe, religion threatens a loss of control. They prefer to live their lives with the notion that they are free to do whatever they want and that they do not have to answer to a higher authority. Therein lies the dilemma. From this perspective, it is easy to understand why Peter Singer, a liberal bioethicist and ardent animal rights advocate, has concluded:

> *"If we can put aside the obsolete and erroneous notion of the sanctity of all human life, we may start to look at human life as it really is: at the quality of life that each human being has or can achieve…"* [4]

Leo Roston, noted author and political scientist, has written that the purpose of life is not to be happy, but "to matter, to be productive, to have it make a difference that you lived at all."[5] Both Singer and Roston apparently believe that the only real basis for evaluating the worth of human life is on its quality. While it undeniably is a good thing to achieve and to enjoy a high quality of life, is human life solely to be measured by its productivity? Do only productive human beings have value? What about handicapped people and bedridden, incapacitated people and mentally deficient people and senile people? Let's examine the biblical understanding of the value and dignity of life.

A VIEW FROM THE TOP

*Life has value and dignity because God knew us
before we were yet formed.*

Psalm 139 teaches us that God has invested even the anticipation of life with
honor. Carefully reflect on the words of the psalmist:

> *"For you created my inmost being; you knit me together in
> my mother's womb. I praise you because I am fearfully and
> wonderfully made; your works are wonderful. I know them
> full well. My frame was not hidden from you when I was
> made in the secret place. When I was woven together in the
> depths of the earth, your eyes saw my unformed body. All the
> days ordained for me were written in your book before one of
> them came to be."*

(Psalm 139:13-16)

The psalm teaches us that God knew us before we were formed, had a
direct hand in our formation, protected us while we developed in our mother's
womb, and has a plan for each man and woman. We are not "small anomalies
blindly thrown up by natural processes for a temporary, transient existence in
an otherwise hostile universe." We are not the accidents of nature. No one is
unplanned or unwanted in God's mind. To the contrary, God anticipated our life
and has invested it with eternal value; we are special in His sight.

*Life has value and dignity because God has invested
even the fetus with favor.*

Psalm 22:10 says, "From my mother's womb you have been my God." How is
this possible unless every unborn baby is fully human? Jesus said, "God is not
a God of the dead, but of the living" (Matthew 22:32). Now, if David could
say, "From my mother's womb you have been my God," and if Jesus taught
that God is a God of the living, it follows that the fetus is not only alive but
exists in a personal relationship with its Creator. And since only human beings
are in personal relationship with God, it follows that the fetus is fully human,
though in the process of intrauterine growth and development.

Further, note that the Bible doesn't say, "From the 24th week of intrauterine gestation, you have been my God." Instead it says, "From my mother's womb."
In other words, "From the moment life began in my mother's womb, you have
been my God." From this perspective, the Bible disagrees with the United States'
Supreme Court.

Further biblical evidence of God's call on humans while still fetuses
comes when the Lord speaks to Rebekah, the wife of Isaac.

"Two nations are in your womb, and two peoples from within you will be separated; one people will be stronger than the other, and the older will serve the younger."

(Genesis 25:23)

In this passage God reveals to Rebekeh that He has sovereignly chosen Jacob, who would be the second born of twin boys. Here, the ancient law of the rights of the firstborn (primogeniture) would be set aside, and God would intervene in choosing Jacob, who would eventually become Israel, the father of the Jewish nation. What is more important to this discussion is that the call on Jacob's life came before his birth. God prophetically spoke about the baby, yet in his mother's womb, in anticipation of what he would become at a later point in his life.

Similarly, the Lord called Jeremiah as a prophet to the nations even before he was formed in his mother's womb (Jeremiah 1:4,5). The prophet Isaiah also was called before his birth (Isaiah 49:1), as was the apostle Paul who wrote that God had set him "apart from birth... to reveal his Son in me so that I might preach him among the Gentiles" (Galatians 1:15,16). Therefore, our worth and our call are established on the person of our Creator God who made and established all things. We have divinely derived value and dignity because God has willed it so.

Life has value and dignity because God, in Christ, became a man, entering into our humanity.

It is at this point that the Christian faith departs from Jewish teaching. The apostle and evangelist John captures the core truths of the Christian Faith in the first few words of his Gospel.

(1) "In the beginning was the Word" (John 1:1)

The Divine Word had no beginning, but was already there at the beginning of things. The Word was not created but was there before creation. Creatures have beginnings and endings. They exist in time and have a reference point in history. But the Word is eternal, without beginning or end. While Genesis records, "In the beginning God created the heavens and the earth" (Genesis 1:1), John says the Word was there — not as part of the created order of things, limited in time and space, but eternally there with the Father.

(2) "And the Word was with God" (John 1:1),

The Eternal Word was with the Father and exists in intimate relationship with Him. Clearly distinct in person, yet one in purpose and identity, the Word was with God before time began (John 1:2).

(3) "And the Word was God" (John 1:1).

Though personally distinct from the Father, the Word is not a creature but God himself. The Word is not identical to the Father God, but perfectly the same in character, purpose and desire so that when we look at Jesus, we see the Father. In this sense, Jesus reveals to his disciples, "Anyone who has seen me has seen the Father" (John 14:9). The Word and the Father are One, and the Word is the only One who can reveal to us what the Father is like. If you would see God, look to Jesus.

(4) "Through him all things were made" (John 1:3);

All things were created by the Word. His creative work is revealed in the first chapter of Genesis. It is of Him that the author of Hebrews writes, "but in these last days he has spoken to us by his son, who he appointed heir of all things, and through whom he made the universe" (Hebrews 1:2). The Apostle Paul further instructs us, "He is the image of the invisible God, the firstborn over all creation. For by him all things were created, things in heaven and on earth, visible and invisible, whether thrones or powers or rulers or authorities; all things were created by him and for him. He is before all things, and in him all things hold together" (Colossians 1:15-17). Jesus, the "firstborn," in preeminence and sovereignty, was the Father's agent in making all things; everything that was created was created through Him. Out of nothing, Jesus created the heavens and earth. "By the word of the Lord were the heavens made... for he spoke, and it came to be" (Psalm 33:6,9). The Logos — the Word and the mind of God — was a person, the creator of all that has been made. J. I. Packer captures the powerful truth of this thought when he writes, "The Word of God is [thus] God at work." [6]

(5) "In him was life" (John 1:4),

Jesus is the source and the essence of life. He breathed life into Adam and gave life to all the plants and animals. There is no life in what was created until, by His Word, He imparted life to all that He had made. And as Paul reminds us, all things exist as He wills. In other words, He holds life together (Colossians 1:17). Thus, life is not inherent in the thing made, but in the Word, in whom there is life. Jesus brings clarity to this thought when He says, "I am the way and the truth and the life" (John 14:6). It also is striking that John begins his Gospel by writing, "In him was life" (John 1:4), and ends it by telling us that his aim in writing was that all people might believe "that Jesus is the Christ, the Son of God, and that by believing you may have life in his name" (John 20:30).

(6) John concludes his introduction to the Gospel by declaring "The Word became flesh and made his dwelling among us" (John 1:14).

In view of all that I have written, it should come as no surprise when I say, along with many others, that the greatest miracle the world has ever seen is the miracle of the Incarnation. Theologians, mystics, and simple believers have all marveled at the words of John: "The Word became flesh and made his dwelling among us." The Divine Word, who existed before all things and was himself God, took on human flesh and became man. This, more than anything else, demonstrates God's incredible love for us and the divine favor that rests on every human being. Without the Incarnation, our history has no meaning. Thus, this revealed truth is central to a Christian world view; when God became man, in the person of Jesus Christ, He exalted man for all time and eternity. True, God humbled himself when He took on human flesh and was "made in the likeness of man" (Philippians 2:7). But, in doing so, He lifted up the dignity and worth of all human kind. Because God became man, all men are linked together with God. The Incarnation dignifies our humanity and blurs all distinctions based on social status, wealth, and productivity. St. Augustine of Hippo has written, "the Son of God became the Son of Man so that the sons of men could become the sons of God." [7]

Life has value and dignity because God, in Jesus Christ, chose to die for us, that we might be saved.

John Stott has written that "Christianity is a rescue religion." [8] God has done for us what we could not do for ourselves. That is the essence of Grace. The cross of Jesus is the central event in all of history. The death of Jesus, as a sacrifice for sin, is the central truth of the scriptures. Paul presents a summary of the Gospel message and its purpose when he writes, "God made him who had no sin to be sin for us, so that in him we might become the righteousness of God" (2 Corinthians 5:21). The life and death of Jesus were pure gifts to us, the undeserving. We deserve God's wrath and judgment, but Paul writes, "The wages of sin is death, but the gift of God is eternal life in Christ Jesus" (Romans 6:23). Later, Paul would add, "For God was pleased to have all his fullness dwell in him, and through him to reconcile to himself all things, whether things on earth or things in heaven, by making peace through his blood shed on the cross" (Colossians 1:19,20).

This is the heart of the Gospel message. Jesus died on the cross as our substitute and sinbearer. He took our place so that we might become the friends of God. In the light of this truth, who can ever doubt God's love for us or our value and worth in His eyes?

Several years ago I was conducting monthly healing services with a Baptist pastor in a Roman Catholic Church, with the support and active participation of the Roman Catholic priest and pastor. During one of our evening services, my friend the Baptist minister preached a salvation message. At the conclusion of the sermon, before any invitation was extended to the congregation, an elderly woman struggled up the center aisle, barely able to walk and hunched over at the waist. She told us that she hadn't been to church in over 30 years, having abandoned her faith in a time of family crisis and loss. She went on to add that she had an inoperable brain tumor, and several neurosurgeons had told her she would die within six months. A neighbor had convinced her to come to the service for prayer. At this point, her eyes brightened and she said, "Now I know why I came tonight. God wanted me to hear this message so that I would come back to Him. I want to receive Jesus." People began to weep, and audible sobs were heard throughout the church. The pastor and I led her in a brief prayer in which she asked forgiveness for her sins and confessed Jesus as her Savior. With that, she turned and began to hobble back to her seat.

I could barely get the words out. "Wait a minute." I asked, "Don't you want anything else?" "No," she replied. "I already have everything I need." "But what about your brain tumor? Don't you want any prayers for your healing?" She thought a moment and said, "Oh, all right. I don't mind." We prayed a simple brief prayer over her and subsequently for many others in attendance; I don't recall thinking about or praying for her in the ensuing month before the next healing service.

The next month, I preached the message. Before I finished speaking, the same woman came up the center aisle and approached the pulpit. This time, however, she appeared to walk straighter and with much less difficulty. She asked me if she could make a brief announcement. Without a word, I handed her the microphone. She told the congregation that she had started to feel so much better after the last prayer service that she decided to return to her personal physician for a reevaluation. He concurred that her neurological exam was improved and ordered a repeat brain CT scan. The radiologist subsequently reported back to him that the repeat scan revealed an inexplicable 25 percent reduction in brain tumor mass. With a smile on her face, the woman quietly said to me and those assembled, "I need one more prayer!" It brought down the house. People were standing and clapping and crying. We prayed with her and she returned to her seat. After the service, unlike the previous month, I thought about and prayed for her often. The thirty days before our next service moved very slowly for me.

The next month before we could sing our first hymn, the woman briskly walked up the aisle, erect and without any visible gait disturbance. She didn't ask permission; she took the microphone from my hand. I had the feeling that I was the warm-up act, and she was the main event. Sobbing and laughing at the same time, she told us that immediately following the last service, she began to feel much better — so much so that she was convinced that she had been cured. She returned to her doctor who examined her and, without a word of explanation, called the radiologist and ordered another brain scan. "Well," she cried, "can you believe that the scan was normal and didn't show any brain tumor?" There was no sermon that night for God had already spoken. We sobbed along with her and ended by praising God for his mercy and goodness.

Later, from the perspective of time, I recalled the Gospel account of Jesus healing the paralytic who was brought to him on a mat by his friends (Luke

5:17-26). Jesus, sensing that the real need of the paralytic was to deal with the unrepentant sin in his life, said to him, "Friend, your sins are forgiven." The Pharisees and the teachers of the law objected, thinking to themselves, "Who is this fellow who speaks blasphemy? Who can forgive sins but God alone?" Jesus, knowing what they were thinking, asked, "Why are you thinking these things in your hearts? Which is easier to say, 'Your sins are forgiven,' or to say, 'Get up and walk?' But that you may know that the Son of Man has authority on earth to forgive sins…" He then said to the paralyzed man, "I tell you, get up, take your mat and go home." Luke concludes the story by telling us that immediately the man got up, picked up his mat, and went home praising God. The paralytic clearly got more than he bargained for. So did the woman in our story; she was forgiven, accepted, and healed all in one package. She also went home praising God and those of us who witnessed it all, reminiscent of the story in Luke, were filled with awe and said, "We have seen remarkable things today."

At times when I feel discouraged or burdened, I remember this: God loves me, and nothing can ever separate me from His love. I am very important and special in His eyes. The cross of Jesus is all the evidence I need to assure my heart in this matter. At moments such as this, I often recall the story of my encounter with the woman who had an inoperable brain tumor — forgiven, accepted, and healed — the message of the cross.

But, in a larger sense, the story addresses the basic premise of the Christian Faith, that the Cross underscores the great value that God has placed in all human life. The vulnerable, dependent fetus as well as the debilitated, dying elderly person are precious in the eyes of our Creator. God invests all of life, from the moment of conception to the dying moments at life's end, with value and dignity. The life and death of Jesus are a testament to how He views us.

Life has value and dignity because God, in Jesus Christ, rose from the dead and conquered sin and death.

If the cross of Jesus is the central event in all of human history, the resurrection of Jesus Christ from the dead is the cornerstone of the Christian faith. The atoning death of Jesus and His resurrection are the two fundamental truths of the Gospel, and without the resurrection there would be no Gospel. The apostle Paul wrote, "if Christ has not been raised, our preaching is useless and so is your faith" (1 Corinthians 15:14).

Few events in the history of antiquity have been as well documented as the fact of the resurrection of Jesus. First, all four Gospels record the event with amazing consistency. All categorically agree that Jesus rose from the dead. Second, all four Gospels testify to the empty tomb; the body of Jesus is not there. Third, the Gospels record at least nine distinct appearances of the risen Lord. He first appeared to Mary Magdalene (John 20:10-18), then to Peter (1 Corinthians 15:5) and to the two men going to Emmaus (Luke 24:13-15), later to ten disciples gathered in the upper room (excluding Thomas) (John

20:19-23), and then to the eleven (including Thomas) one week later (John 20:24-29), again to his disciples by the Sea of Tiberias (John 21:1-14), "to more than five hundred brethren at one time" (1 Corinthians 15:6), finally to James (1 Corinthians 15:7), and lastly, Paul on the road to Damascus (1 Corinthians 15:7). Never have so many witnessed an event that subsequently was so ardently disputed. Yet, the record is clear. Paul writes, "This is what we preach, and this is what you believed" (1 Corinthians 15:11).

Fourth, an amazing change occurred in the lives of those who saw the risen Christ and those who would subsequently accept his resurrection as fact. The Acts of the Apostles, the letter to the Hebrews (Chapter 11) and the history of the Christian Church provide a stirring record of those who were martyred for the faith. Timid followers became bold preachers of the Word and living epistles of the resurrected Jesus.

History records that they went to their death singing praises to the Lord; having been persecuted and mistreated — "the world was not worthy of them" (Hebrews 11:38). Tertullian, an early Church father, wrote ,"the blood of martyrs is the seed of the Church."[9] St. Jerome (342-420 A.D.) would subsequently add, "the Church of Christ has been founded by shedding its own blood, not that of others; by enduring outrage, not by inflicting it. Persecutions have made it grow; martyrdoms have crowned it." [10] This happened, Kenneth Scott Latourette informs us, "in spite of the general policy of the Church officials" who discouraged any from seeking martyrdom. [11]

The courage of the victims who were convinced that Jesus had indeed risen made a great impression on pagans and contributed, in part, to the early growth of the Church. Peter, Paul, James, and thousands of unrecorded others were forever changed because of the truth of the resurrection (Acts 4:32-37), and so are all who believe today.

But the resurrection does more than inspire courage, it also inspires hope. Job, who lived centuries before Christ, asked this question of his friends, "If a man dies, will he live again?" (Job 14:14). Job did not understand the concept of resurrection, but he prophetically anticipated it. In life, death is the only certainty; it is inevitable, and the thought of it fills many with dread. Jesus confronted the grief and fear of Martha, the sister of Lazarus, when he said to her, "I am the resurrection and the life. He who believes in me will live, even though he dies, and whoever lives and believes in me will never die. Do you believe this?" (John 11:25,26). The apostle Paul reassures us that all who confess Jesus as Lord and Savior will also share in His resurrection; he writes, "If only for this life we have hope in Christ, we are to be pitied more than all men" (1 Corinthians 15:19). He further adds these magnificent words of hope:

> *"Listen, I tell you a mystery: We will not all sleep, but we will all be changed - in a flash, in the twinkling of an eye, at the last trumpet. For the trumpet will sound, the dead will be raised imperishable, and we will be changed. For the*

perishable must clothe itself with the imperishable, and the mortal with immortality. When the perishable has been clothed with the imperishable, and the mortal with immortality, then the saying that is written will come true. 'Death has been swallowed up in victory. Where, O death, is your victory? Where, O death, is your sting?' The sting of death is sin, and the power of sin is the law. But thanks be to God. He gives us the victory through our Lord Jesus Christ."

1 Corinthians 15:51-57

All believers enjoy victory in the Lord Jesus Christ, victory over condemnation for sin and the finality of death. Consider how much our God loves us that He has provided the way for everlasting life with Him. Just as the grave could not hold Jesus; in Jesus, the grave will not hold us.

Several years ago, a friend asked me to visit her former husband in the hospital. Though they had been divorced for years, they remained friends. The man, whom I shall refer to as John, had lived a desolate life. For over 30 years, he was either drunk or drying out. At the time of my visit, he was dying of liver cirrhosis and was slipping in and out of coma. John was a self-professed atheist, although he had been raised in a Christian home and at one time attended church. During his hospitalization, in one of his lucid moments, he asked his former wife, "Do you know that doctor you're always talking about? You know, the religious one? Do you think he might come to talk to me?" My friend told me she thought John would be able to hear the beating of her heart after he finished asking about me. She assured him that I would be glad to talk to him, and she called me that night.

I asked my wife, Anita, and two friends to accompany me to the hospital. While I entered his room, they remained in the waiting room praying for my meeting with John. As a physician, I was prepared to see a man near death, but John's appearance startled even me. He had been a big, muscular man in his youth. Now he weighed less than 90 pounds and looked skeletal. His skin was a lemon-yellow color, and his breath was fetid. At first, as I approached his bed, I thought he was dead. Then I noticed the faint movement of the sheet that covered him. John slowly opened his eyes. I introduced myself and asked if he could hear me. It took great effort for John to squeeze out a few words, "I have denied God for over 30 years, and I don't believe in death-bed conversions."

"Fine," I replied, "but God believes in you and loves you very much."

"What makes you think so?" he asked.

I took a deep breath and hoped Anita and my friends were still praying. "John," I asked, "have you ever heard the parable Jesus told about the workers in the vineyard?" Surprised by the question, John answered a hesitant, "No." "Well," I said, "it seems a man owned a vineyard and needed laborers to work in it. He hired some men early in the morning after agreeing to pay them a certain amount for the day's wages. Others, he hired at 9:00 AM, still others at noon and 3:00 PM after telling them he would pay them whatever seemed right. When the evening came, the owner gathered the workers and proceeded to pay them their wages, beginning with those hired last. When he paid the latecomers a full day's wages, those hired first anticipated more. When they received the wages they had agreed on, they began to grumble against the vineyard owner. The owner answered them by saying, 'Friends, I'm not being unfair to you. I paid you what we agreed before you started work. Don't I have the right to be generous with my money?' "John," I asked, "Do you understand this parable?"

"I'm not sure," he answered, "You tell me what it means."

"Well," I said, "it means that as long as you have a breath in your body, God's invitation to you is always open. It's only too late after you die. John, if we accept His call, we all get the same wages — eternal life with Him. And Jesus is your passport to this life."

At this, tears began to run down the old man's face. "Tell me more," he whispered, "and hurry up, I don't have much time."

I briefly shared the Good News with him and reminded him what he had once believed. After I finished, John prayed the most beautiful prayer of contrition I had ever heard, then he invited Jesus into his heart. When his prayer ended, he reached for my hands with trembling fingers, brought them to his lips and kissed them.

"I'm not afraid," he wept, "I'm going home. Someday we'll meet again."

I left the room knowing I would never again see John in this life. The next day, he died.

Paul wrote, "For as in Adam all die, so in Christ all will be made alive" (1 Corinthian 15:22). Today, John, though dead to this world, is alive in Jesus. God values us so much, that He has reserved eternity for all those who know Him through His Son. This fact invests our life with great value and dignity.

Life has value and dignity because God has chosen to live in each believer in the person of the Holy Spirit.

Christians worship a triune God, a God who is at the same time three distinct persons, yet One. This is the mystery of the Trinity. By contrast, most religions of antiquity were polytheistic. At this primitive stage of religious belief, men worshipped many gods - gods of the sun, moon, sea, wind, fire, mountain, even gods of the trees and rivers. To placate them, men had to distribute favors with great care, for the gods were jealous, competitive, and capricious — much like men, having sprung from the imaginations of the human mind.

Although many polytheistic religions believed in a creator god who was more powerful than the rest, the great gift of Israel to the ancient world, and all generations since, was the understanding and proclamation of the Oneness of God. This revelation given to Israel by God through the prophet Moses is heard in the confident declaration: "Hear O Israel, the Lord thy God is One" (Deuteronomy 6:4). In the Old Testament, God often is referred to as Father.

An example of this is found in the Book of Deuteronomy, in a passage referred to as "The Song of Moses": "Is this the way you repay the Lord, O foolish and unwise people? Is he not your Father, your Creator, who made and formed you?" (Deuteronomy 32:6).

Jesus instructed his disciples to address God in a most intimate and tender way when He taught them what is now referred to as "The Lord's Prayer" which begins with the words, "Our Father." In time, Jesus would reveal His unique relationship to the Father (Matthew 11:27) and His special identity with Him (John 14:9). In his Gospel, John identified Jesus as the Word of God, the divine Logos, and confessed Him to be God (John 1:1).

Following the apostolic tradition, the council of Nicaea (325 AD) declared that Jesus was "consubstantial" with the Father (having the same essence, substance or nature).[12] The Council of Constantinople (381 AD) in formulating the Nicene Creed confesses: "the only-begotten son of God, true God from true God, begotten not made, consubstantial with the Father." [13]

The next revelation of the Godhead is found in the New Testament where the Holy Spirit is revealed as a distinct personality, yet uniquely God. In the Gospels, Jesus is introduced by John the Baptist as the One who would baptize with the Holy Spirit and fire (Matthew 3:11, Mark 1:8, Luke 3:16, John 1:33). During his earthly ministry, Jesus often spoke of the Holy Spirit. He taught that the Spirit would instruct us (John 14:36), indwell us (John 16:7), comfort us (John 14:6), and empower us (Acts 1:8). Pentecost was the fulfillment of the promised Holy Spirit (Acts 2).

The New Testament further expands on the mission and role of the Holy Spirit in the Church; He is expressed in Christian community (Acts 4:23-31), in transformed individual lives (Galatians 5:22-25), and in the supernatural gifts of the Holy Spirit given to believers to edify the Church (1 Corinthians 12:1-11). Paul first gives expression to the Trinity of God, including the person of the Holy Spirit, in the closing doxology of the second letter to the Corinthian Church (2 Corinthians 13:14). In his instructive letter to his young disciple Timothy, Paul taught that the Christian life is lived in the love, joy, power, and vitality of Jesus by the Spirit: "For God did not give us a spirit of timidity, but a spirit of power, of love, and of self-discipline" (2 Timothy 1:7). He also was careful to admonish the churches that both the supernatural gifts and the fruit of the Holy Spirit are expressed in love (1 Corinthians 13:1-7, Galatians 5:22,23).

The Council of Constantinople gave expression to New Testament revelation and teaching in the wording of the Nicene Creed; they confessed: "The Holy Spirit, the third person of the Trinity, is God, one and equal with the Father and Son, of the same substance and also of the same nature... yet he is not called the Spirit of the Father alone... but the Spirit of both the Father and the Son."[14] This, then, became the teaching of the Church, joyfully expressed in this hymn of praise: "with the Father and the Son, he is worshipped and glorified."

We stand in awe at the magnificence of our God—Father, Son, and Holy Spirit—three distinct persons in One Godhead. Yet, the scriptures provide us with a further revelation of God that is both astounding and humbling. The clear teaching of the Bible is that each Christian is a personal temple of the Holy Spirit. Paul writes, "Do you not know that your body is a temple of the Holy Spirit who is in you, whom you have received from God?" (1 Corinthians 6:19). This fact and clear teaching of our faith is unique among all the religions of the world. Not only did God humble Himself by becoming one of us in the person of Jesus, but He then chose to die for us (Philippians 2:6–11) and now by His Spirit indwells every believer. Our bodies are sacred to Him. Thus, we (body, soul and spirit) have value and dignity in His eyes quite apart from our talent, accomplishment, and potential. Our value is God - derived — His doing, and His alone. For this reason Paul writes, "You are not our own; you were bought at a price. Therefore, honor God with your body" (1 Corinthians 6:19,20). Our body belongs to God; therefore, we ought to honor Him in the way we live and die!

I have been privileged to see many beautiful cathedrals in my lifetime, both at home and abroad. Each cathedral has beauty to inspire, sacred space in which to pray and worship, and a sense of the soaring expansiveness of the human spirit. Yet, for all of the beauty worked in stone and glass in the many magnificent temples of the world, the Holy Spirit chooses to live in us. God may be approached in the beauty of a building, but He dwells in the beauty of men and women. This is the eternal plan for everyone who surrenders his heart to the Lord. Human life is sacred to God.

· · · · · · ·

In light of all that we have covered in this chapter, we can see how precious all of human life is. God has not spared Himself in giving us the full revelation of His love for us. He respects us so much that He has given us the freedom to accept or reject Him. It is in understanding, accepting, and celebrating the central truths of the Christian faith that we come to understand the magnitude of God's love for us.

Now, having secured the biblical basis for the sacredness of life and established the foundation for belief in man's value and dignity, we turn in the next two chapters to the most serious contemporary assaults on life — abortion and euthanasia. In these issues, we find a troubled and conflicted society. At the heart of the debate is the central question we have already addressed, "What is truth?" Is it centered in God or man? Is the most basic truth about life a personal truth revealed in God and His Word, or is it an impersonal truth derived from individual whim and personal opinion? In reality, how we arrive at truth will determine what we believe about life.

The Abortion Dilemma

INTRODUCTION

Life is a big deal! Have you ever noticed how people make such a fuss over a pregnant woman? And all of us, no matter how dignified we are, get silly when we see a newborn baby. I love watching parents and friends at the viewing window of my local hospital's nursery. As a pediatrician, I have shared many wonderful moments with new parents, yet after 29 years of private practice, I still get excited over every newborn I examine. In my specialty, I don't deliver babies, but care for them after they are born and throughout childhood up to 21 years of age. But as a medical student, at the Center in which I trained, I was required to "deliver" five babies before graduating. My first delivery, that was something else!

Thirty seven years ago at St. Joseph's Hospital, I was midway through the obstetric rotation in my junior year at the Upstate Medical Center in Syracuse, New York. One afternoon, I was informed that a young woman was in labor and that I was assigned to deliver her baby. I can't adequately express the conflicting emotions I felt in attending her in the few hours of labor leading up to the delivery. But at last, there was the woman on the table, with me sitting on the stool at her feet, gowned, gloved, and ready for anything. Unlike me, she appeared calm and poised, having had a relatively mild and short labor, but this was, after all, her tenth baby and she had nine healthy children at home. I recall she even tried to reassure me that "it would be over before I knew it." With one big push she propelled the baby out. I felt less like a doctor than an infielder settling under a pop fly. I almost shouted, "I've got it!"

I've forgotten the events that immediately followed. What I do remember is that it all hit me after the baby was safely in the Newborn Nursery and I went to visit the woman in the Postpartum Suite. She was happy, but very tired. I managed to behave in a professional manner until I returned to the Nursing Station. Then, I ran around trying to find people to tell about "my delivery;" I called my fiancée, my roommates, and finally my mother in New Jersey. I don't remember any pride in the sense of personal accomplishment, but rather, the overwhelming feeling that I had assisted in the delivery of a new life — a baby girl.

I became a pediatrician because I love children and have a sincere desire to care for and protect them. When I entered medical school, obstetrics was a purer and nobler discipline dedicated to assisting new life into the world and protecting the health of the mother. Sadly, the reputation of this specialty has been tainted, as a significant part of its energies has gone into terminating rather than aiding pregnancies. Tragically, this has been embraced by the American Academy of Pediatrics, the governing body of my specialty, who have officially declared their position on the abortion issue to be Pro-Choice. Rather than lead the way to a higher moral ground, my profession, ostensibly dedicated to preserving life, curiously has decided to vacate that role and to accommodate those determined to end it.

The contrast between the expected promise and joy of the hospital delivery room and the horror of the abortion ward is startling. In the former, trained medical personnel are lovingly coaching and assisting the woman in labor towards the expected and longed-for moment of birth. Husbands frequently are in attendance, helping in whatever way they can and sharing in the event. In the latter, the mood is joyless and secretive, nurses and doctors mechanically prepare the patient and then, in a detached fashion, perform the bloody and gruesome procedure that will terminate the life of the fetus. Absent from the surgical suite is the pregnant woman's husband or lover. No one coaches her lovingly through the procedure. Instead, the scene will quickly become one of horror as needles, suction apparatus, and surgical hands invade the sanctuary of the womb. The fetus reacts violently to the assault. He struggles against the needle, pushes hard away from the surgical probe, and even opens his mouth in protest, but to no avail. In an instant, his life will end in a wash of blood and gore as the life signature of God is erased by the technology of science. Embarrassingly, a few aborted fetuses will manage to be born and breathe for a few moments, as doctors and nurses place the baby in a corner to die and try to avoid looking at each other. There is no joy in this scene. A messy and thankless job has been done and the sanctity of personal choice has been honored. There are no winners in the abortion ward, only participants. Afterwards, the mother will leave as quickly as she is able, and few relatives and friends will mark the date of the event. Another terrible act is recorded by few but God, as mankind is robbed of a precious life.

DEFINING THE ISSUE

Few would disagree that the surgical procedure of aborting a fetus is a violent one, inflicting great pain on the unborn child. But the issue of how to interpret abortion, particularly the status of the fetus and the conflicting rights of the fetus and mother, has been long contested and cuts to the heart of the debate.

Questions include: Is the fetus human? Does it have rights? What are the rights of the mother? What are the rights of the father, family, and community? How do church leaders and ethicists define the nature and dignity of life? Finally, with respect to medical science: How do physicians define life? And how do new technologies complicate the definition?

Before even taking up these questions, we should first take account of the dramatic shift in values in our country during the past quarter century. A good place to begin in establishing an historic definition for the abortion debate is the era of Roe v. Wade: the 1973 Supreme Court ruling that sanctioned the right to abortion.

Turning to my family's old 1970 *World Book Encyclopedia,* when I recently tried to look up "Abortion," I was surprised to find no listing; rather, the reader is referred to the heading, "Birth Control." The article on birth control defines the subject as "that term that includes all methods used to regulate the birth of children." It goes on to explain that induced abortion has been used as a method of birth control and that abortion ends a pregnancy by "destroying the unborn fetus." It also notes that in 1970, "many countries — and most states in the United States — forbid abortion except when it is necessary to save the mother's life." The piece further states that legal abortions are performed by a physician in the hospital, while illegal abortions frequently are performed by unskilled people, often resulting in "serious illness or even death."[1]

This article was in many respects more revealing about the abortion crisis than reading a more current edition because it predates Roe v. Wade, and it underscores the dramatic downward moral spiral our country has entered in the last quarter of this century. First, it was startling that the topic "Abortion" didn't even command its own listing. But this is logical when one considers that in 1970 the medical profession performed few abortions. Second, the encyclopedia article correctly states that abortion ends a pregnancy by "destroying the unborn fetus." Abortion is a violent procedure that brutally terminates the life of the fetus under the protective umbrella of a "woman's right to choose." Third, the article correctly points out that "illegal" abortions were performed under unsanitary conditions in dismal settings; whereas, today medical science has made abortion a routine procedure. A recent article in "The American Journal of Obstetrics and Gynecology" reports that the case-fatality rate in 1972 from illegally performed abortions was 4.1 deaths per 100,000 abortions; in 1987, the rate had dropped to 0.4 per 100,000 abortions, a 90 percent reduction.[2] Fourth, abortion, legal or illegal, is still being performed as a means of birth control: "Plus ca change, plus c'est la même chose" (The more things change, the more they remain the same). Fifth, it hardly needs to be said that "most states in the United States" no longer forbid abortion; the United States Supreme Court has recognized the procedure as the legal right of all women.[3]

Most Americans know the contours of the abortion debate. In 1973, the United States' Supreme Court ruled, in the Roe v. Wade decision, that women have a right to abortion up to the point that the fetus is capable of living outside the uterus. This was generally defined as beyond the 24th week. The Court also moved that abortion can be performed at any time, if it is necessary to preserve the woman's health. This point has taken on new meaning in the matter of "partial-birth" abortions. Also known as dilation and extraction procedures ("D and X"), the technique ostensibly was developed to end late-term pregnancies in which the mother's health was endangered. In reality, as we shall see later in this chapter, it has been used to terminate unwanted pregnancies that have extended beyond the 24th week. Clearly, Roe v. Wade has had aftereffects that framers of the decision could not foresee.

As a consequence of this judicial ruling, the results have been nothing less than startling. For example, in 1963, the rate of abortions was 0.13/1000 women in childbearing years (15 to 44). By contrast, in 1980, the rate was 29.3/1000. Within 10 years of Roe v. Wade, abortion became one of the most common surgical procedures performed in the United States. Since 1973, 35 million abortions have been performed in our country, approximately 1.5 million annually.[4] Without question, Roe v. Wade would change the political, social, and moral landscape of America.

FRAMING THE DEBATE

Roe v. Wade divided our country into two groups who rarely compromise their positions. *Pro-Life* groups favor the prohibition of most, if not all abortions. The basis for this position is the belief that all life is sacred. The *Pro-Choice* groups favor permissive laws on abortion. They regard attempts to restrict abortions as an infringement of women's rights. The critical issue in the debate is a moral one: Is the fetus a person?[5] The hidden agendas are the issues of gender power and ultimate authority.

Ultimate authority is an underlying issue that frames the entire abortion debate. Many in contemporary society subscribe to a view of life that is centered on man, an atheistic philosophy that has been called "secular humanism" (as opposed to the Christian humanism of our rich philosophical and literary traditions). Secular humanism places absolute reliance on the autonomy of man and the certainty of his progressive improvement. Great confidence is placed on reason and science; individual value is correspondingly found within the context of the human, evolutionary struggle.[6]

Within the framework of this mind-set, it is easy to see that people who are man-centered and treasure their autonomy above other truths, will exalt personal choice above most other rights. They celebrate self and, in the process, choice becomes a prerogative. Absolute truth is viewed as a relic of religion and man is liberated to decide for himself what is right. In this context, pro-choice is more than a slogan. Pro-choice advocates demand open access to abortion, not because they are pro-death, but precisely because their rights and their freedom to exercise them are more important than all other rights and convictions.

By contrast, others hold to a view of life which is centered on God and forms the basis of all Judeo-Christian beliefs. The Christian faith holds that God is the ultimate authority and the center of all things; that He is a personal God and has no beginning or end; that He is the creator and sustainer of the universe and everything in it; that He is defined by love and is holy in all that He is and does. Conversely, man, while created in the image of God, is finite—limited by space and time, has a physical body with all of its limitations, has a fallen sin nature in rebellion against God and is unable to live up to God's standards. Further, we believe that God in Christ, has taken the initiative to restore man to himself in a loving relationship. Man has been given intellect and reason by his creator to be used for his betterment and the benefit of others. God has revealed ultimate truth to man through the mysteries of the created universe, the nature of man, Jesus Christ, and the Bible. God's truth also is to be found in the historical record of man, philosophical study, scientific inquiry, and the application of reason, within the context that man can never be like God or fully attain His knowledge and understanding.

Having identified this general framework for the debate, we can now address the specific issues that are part of the history of the abortion controversy. First, what have our courts ruled on abortion and how have they interpreted the constitutional issues of fetal viability and the rights of the fetus versus the rights of the mother?

THE WISDOM OF MAN

A View from the Bench

Abortion and the Constitution

Prior to the 1973 Roe v. Wade ruling, the legal regulation of abortion was left to the states, and each state responded to the issue within the context of public opinion and the political process. Because of the lack of uniformity in state legislative policy, the United States Supreme Court had little option but to consider the issue in the celebrated Roe case. The basis for the Roe ruling was grounded in a previous Supreme Court case: Griswold v. Connecticut (1965).[7] In 1965, the Griswold suit was initiated by Planned Parenthood League of Connecticut.[8] The executive and medical directors of the League were convicted of providing "information, instruction, and medical advice" to married couples regarding contraception.[9] Such counseling directly conflicted with a Connecticut statute (1879) that made it a crime for anyone to use drugs or instruments to prevent pregnancy. The statute had been unsuccessfully challenged on two previous occasions (1943 and 1961). In Griswold, however, the Court sided with Planned Parenthood, invoking the right of privacy under the Fourteenth Amendment, that mandated a strict scrutiny of laws interfering with individual privacy rights.[10]

It should be noted that before this ruling, the right to privacy, as a fundamental right, was not explicitly recognized in the Bill of Rights. In Roe v. Wade, the Supreme Court decided to recognize that this right was implied in the Constitution, allowing a woman to determine whether or not to terminate her pregnancy.[11] Not only that, the Court broadened the constitutional right to privacy through the "creative interpretation of amendments 1, 3, 4, 5, 9," as well as "14 and Article IV of the Constitution."[12] The majority opinion was written by Justice Harry Blackmun with Justices William Douglas, Potter Stewart, and Warren Burger concurring. The flaws of this privacy analysis were soon exposed after the ruling and became the source of widespread criticism among the critics of Roe.

For more than a decade, Roe v. Wade was not seriously challenged. Then, in April 29, 1989, Webster v. Reproductive Health Services was argued before the United States Supreme Court.[13] The case involved several restrictions imposed on abortion by the State of Missouri. The Missouri bill contained a preamble and two separate provisions. The preamble stated that life began at conception and that "unborn children have protectable interests in life, health, and well-being." The first provision held that state property could not be used for abortions, except when necessary to save a woman's life. This prohibition against abortion in public hospitals was applicable even if the patient paid for the procedure. The State of Missouri, under the broad interpretation of the law would thus have authority to bar abortions, even in private hospitals located on land leased from the State. The second provision required physicians to determine fetal viability when they estimated the gestational age to be at least twenty weeks. Under Roe, abortion within the second trimester (before the twenty-fourth week) was permissible, albeit with the proviso permitting state regulation to promote maternal health. The second provision was an obvious attempt to move away from a rigid reliance on the 24th week as a measure of fetal viability and to expand the notion of viability to keep pace with changing medical technology.

The Webster case originally had been argued before the U.S. Court of Appeals for the Eighth Circuit Court (1986), which struck down several provisions of the Missouri statute on the grounds that it violated the Supreme Court's decision in Roe v. Wade. The U.S. Supreme Court reversed the Court of Appeals' ruling, arguing the following: (1) the preamble to the State of Missouri bill had no operative legal effect over the Roe decision because it did not conflict with Roe; in fact, the U. S. Supreme Court argued that Roe "implied no limitations on the authority of the state to make a value judgment favoring childbirth over abortion"[14]; (2) a majority upheld the State of Missouri's restrictions on the use of public employees and facilities for performing non-therapeutic abortions; and (3) the Court, however, declined to uphold the Act's provisions regarding viability testings in second trimester abortions, unless Roe was modified. Yet, the United States Supreme Court did rule that whereas Roe had held that the state's right in regulating abortion increased as the pregnancy progressed, they now rejected this analysis and held that the state's right "to protect potential life was the same <u>throughout</u>

pregnancy" (emphasis mine). Obviously, the two views are inconsistent with each other and Webster represented an acknowledgment of that fact by the Supreme Court. It would be the Court's first major retreat from the 1973 Roe decision.

It is of considerable interest that the Court viewed the trimester analysis framework as outlined in Roe as being too rigid and too capable of producing legal mischief. However, they refused to overturn Roe, citing the doctrines of stare decisis (the strict adherence to cases previously decided). This refusal was possible because the "moderate" jurists on the Court formed a coalition to uphold Roe. Thus, the expectation of the Pro-Life movement to rid the country of abortion on demand was thwarted. Justice Scalia, while concurring in the Court's rulings on Webster, chastised them for refusing to reconsider Roe, correctly predicting that failure to do so would create legal confusion and public turmoil.[15]

While this was less than Pro-Life advocates might have hoped for, Webster was a major attack on the integrity of Roe. The ruling opened the door to a state by state attempt to move legislatures into further restricting accessibility to abortion, and paved the way for 1992's Planned Parenthood v. Casey.

In this case, United States Supreme Court again reaffirmed Roe v. Wade's basic ruling (with the principle of stare decisis) that abortion was a woman's constitutional right and that "before viability" the state had no right to interfere unduly with that right. The Court did, however, uphold the States' authority to restrict abortions after fetal viability, excepting in cases where the woman's health or life were endangered. Further, the Court stated, somewhat ambiguously, that the State had legitimate interest in protecting the health of both the woman and the fetus throughout pregnancy. Under a provision of the ruling, while the Court upheld the State statute requiring physicians to inform the woman "of the nature of the procedure," the health risks involved, and "the probable gestational age of the unborn child," they denied that a husband's interest in the life in his wife's uterus permitted the State to empower him with the authority to override his wife's right to abortion. However, they did affirm the legality of a State requiring prior parental consent in a minor seeking abortion "providing there was an adequate judicial bypass procedure."[16]

Robert Bork, the respected conservative jurist, rightly discerned that the Court's ruling would please few people actively involved in the abortion struggle. He commented that the Court's assertion of "institutional integrity" in arriving at their decision meant that it had decided it "must not overturn a wrong decision."[17] On the other hand, most of the major news networks and the newspapers hailed the decision and the Court's control by a centrist coalition of jurists. For the moment, Roe had survived another advance by the Pro-Life movement. However, the door remained open to a state by state assault and another day in court.

• The Argument About Viability

The present U.S. abortion law is based on our country's legal concepts of viability and gestational age. Yet if these concepts are examined against biblical and medical standards, they should be judged morally and biologically ill-founded. We have already established in Chapter 1 that, according to biblical teaching, viability outside the uterus is a frequently changing frame of reference. Moreover, Drs. F. K. Beller and C. A. deProsse, specialists in Obstetrics and Reproductive Medicine, have argued that a law based on this standard is likely to contribute to further confusion since the timing of gestational age, i.e., the date of the last menstrual period and estimates of egg fertilization and uterine implantation, is itself an imprecise measure. They urge a clarification in the terminology of the law.[18]

That the standard of viability is susceptible to change is undeniable. Likewise, just as gestational age is an imprecise measure, birthweight is an imperfect indicator of viability. Dr. Sheldon Korones, a Professor of Pediatrics and Obstetrics and Gynecology at the University of Tennessee, has noted that measures of viability based on birthweight have changed dramatically in the past two decades.[19] In the 1970s few newborns below 2 pounds 2 ounces to 2 pounds 10 ounces were expected to live. Today, as noted previously, babies as little as 1.1 pound have survived. Dr. Korones appropriately notes that "we are dealing with a moving target." Increasing chances of survival at lower birth weights (as well as earlier gestational age) render these measures unreliable in determining viability.[20]

Some ethicists concur with these medical findings. Roger Wertheimer, a moral philosopher and bio-ethicist, has, in principle, agreed, stating that the capacity to survive outside the mother is related to the current state of available medical technology and thus unsuitable as a standard of measure.[21] I agree. Moral and ethical imperatives can not be held captive to a changing technology. Any such standard would be capricious and would even result in medical chaos, pitting sophisticated and technologically advanced academic centers against their smaller, community counterparts. Alan Zaitchik, a liberal philosopher, however, disagrees with Wertheimer, arguing that "viability…does not mean deliverability" and that "viability is not morally arbitrary just because it is a shifting standard."[22] Most physicians, whatever their opinion of abortion, probably would not agree with Zaitchik. His arguments do little to clarify the medical issues physicians face. Philosophers may be comfortable with arbitrary standards, shifting frames of reference, and philosophical uncertainty. Doctors have to treat human patients with real problems that need to be addressed immediately and concisely within the framework of available medical knowledge and skill. Ambiguous standards would only serve to confuse doctors and anger patients who lack the resources to seek more sophisticated care.

If this all sounds academic, its critical implications can be illustrated in a medical case taken from my own practice. Recently, I saw a five-month infant named Rachel who was the product of a 24-25 week gestation and weighed 1,255 grams at birth (1 pound nine ounces)—roughly the size of babies aborted near the end of the second trimester. While she has a correctable congenital heart defect, she is otherwise healthy and to date is growing and developing well. Through the advances of medical science and the loving support of concerned parents, Rachel will lead a healthy and happy life. Obviously, there is an inherent problem using viability as the standard of the legal justification of abortion.

• The Argument About Rights

The U.S. law on abortion is also based on the issue of rights. Whose rights take precedence: the rights of the mother or those of the fetus?

The position of those who claim that the fetus is not a person is quite obvious. After all, how could the rights of a non-person possibly override the rights of a person, the mother? This is why the issue of viability is viewed by many as the foundational question in the debate about rights.

But the question of rights becomes more complicated when, as some Pro-Choice advocates have done, the fetus is recognized as a person. Then, the issue becomes: is the termination of the fetus homicide? This would seem logical, but some prominent constitutional lawyers have argued that, even if the fetus is a person, the rights of the mother can override the rights of the fetus.

For instance, Laurence Tribe, the highly respected Constitutional lawyer, argues that while he believes the fetus is a human being, he does not support the contention that abortion is homicide.[23] As outlined by D. J. Leyshon in the journal *Medicine and Law*, Tribe cites the following arguments to support his contention: (1) as "the law does not require us to put ourselves at risk to save others," so the pregnant woman is not obliged to carry the newborn fetus inside her uterus; (2) the fetus in certain situations (rape and incest) is an intruder, physically invading the mother's womb; (3) the rights of the fetus are subordinate to the rights of the pregnant woman; and (4) since the fetus is unique and "different from all other forms of human life," his uniqueness justifies a creative rule of law.[24]

It seems curious that Tribe is content to deny legal protection under the law to the extremely dependent and vulnerable fetus, whom he acknowledges to be human, while, at the same time, favoring the pregnant woman. If the fetus is a human being, it has the constitutional right to be protected against murder. The law is intended to protect all citizens, even those uniquely "different," including the sick, dependent, and vulnerable members of our society.

Whose Rights?

• A Political Debate: The Pregnant Woman and the Fetus

In the abortion debate, activists in the struggle all claim that they are safeguarding basic rights. Though the abortion debate is not drawn along strict political lines, there are nonetheless conservative and liberal positions on abortion.

Conservatives generally argue for the fetus and its right to life. They assert that the fetus is a human being and entitled to full protection under the law and that abortion is murder. In recent Republican administrations, during the tenure of Ronald Reagan and George Bush, the official position on abortion has been strongly Pro-Life, with exceptions made only in cases threatening the life of the mother or in cases of rape or incest.

Liberals, on the other hand, affirm the rights of the pregnant woman, defining personhood at viability, birth, or even later. Thus, they favor permissive abortion laws and regard all attempts to restrict abortions as infringements on the fundamental rights of women. This, in fact, is the position of our current administration under President Bill Clinton. The Clinton administration has essentially endorsed Roe v. Wade and subsequent court rulings in favor of this landmark decision. It has vetoed every attempt to defend the rights of unborn children in the name of constitutional rights of women and the legal interpretation of our high courts since Roe v. Wade.

Many people in the U.S., however, take what might be called a "moderate" position, seeking a middle ground that is a compromise between these two positions. Individuals in this group generally do not favor abortion on demand, but do not want all abortions declared illegal. They frequently vary their position depending on the issue addressed. They identify neither with the strict conservative or liberal line and are represented by members of both political parties.

To date, this political debate has argued principally over whose rights, the mother's or fetus', will take precedent. The debate rarely extends beyond this issue, although the recent controversy over partial-birth abortion has stretched the parameters of the dispute.

• The Family and the Community

Unfortunately, in the polarized debate between conservatives and liberals regarding the rights of pregnant women vs. the rights of fetuses, we have forgotten a third party, the family, and, by extension, the larger community. What rights, if any, does the family have in the decision making process? Do communities have the right to organize and fight to maintain their moral values and standards? After all, rights, by definition, only make sense in a social context. The Roe v. Wade opinion considered only the rights of the pregnant woman and her fetus, unrelated to the influence of husband, boyfriend, parents or extended family. As a matter of fact, up until recently, few people have addressed the impact of family on the problem. Yet, the issues of spousal rights and parental consent for minors have been legally contested in our courts, thus prompting increased interest in the topic. The 1992 Casey decision and the discussions that ensued among legal scholars, as well as activists on both sides of the abortion issue, have fueled the fires of this debate.

Theodoro Ooms, social worker, family therapist, and Director of the Family Impact Seminar at the Catholic University of America, has perceptively argued that since abortion is a moral decision and not solely a personal one, the effect on others always must be considered.[27] In addition, she cites "the basic principle of a political democracy" in asserting that all who will be impacted by the woman's abortion ought to be included in making a decision.[28] As would be expected, the feminist and Pro-Choice movements have been insistent in their demand that no voice be legally given to anyone but the pregnant woman. Bernard Nathenson has pointed out the irony in the fact that these same groups, having demanded that men be included in the birth process and in the care of the child, now deny them any rights regarding abortion.[29]

Both Pro-Life and Pro-Choice groups need to consider more seriously how entire families and church communities can get involved in reducing circumstances conducive to abortion. Pro-Lifers, rightly, have talked a great deal about family values; they now need to expand their vision as it pertains to abortion and family rights. Accordingly, I shall share one of my own pastoral experiences with a woman, Helen, who was persuaded to choose life rather than abortion through the involvement of her family and church community.

• A Case for Community Involvement: The Miracle of Helen

For many years, I was the co-host on a 1 1/2 hour radio program aired on a Christian radio station. The first thirty minutes usually featured a guest interview regarding a community ministry. During the remaining hour, the phone lines were opened and listeners had an opportunity to call requesting prayer, to offer a comment, or to ask a question. One afternoon, during the final fifteen minutes of the show, an obviously distraught woman called. She told us that her 18-year-old, unmarried daughter was pregnant and contemplating suicide. The girl had a troubled history of general rebellious behavior, including drug and alcohol abuse. The mother informed us that the daughter was asleep in her bed. She then said, "Wait a minute, Doctor. I'll go get her. I want you to talk to her." With that the phone went silent and the host and I incredulously stared at each other. We tried to fill the air time that elapsed, until a sleepy voice sounded on the phone. "I know what I want to do. Don't try to talk me out of it. My life's a mess. I have nothing to live for." Then, the young girl started to sob.

My pastor friend and I bowed our heads and prayed silently for a few seconds. In a deliberate manner, I softly began to talk to her, telling her that God loved her very much and that our conversation at that moment was no accident, but arranged by Him. I told her that suicide was a miserable option that would satisfy no one but the devil. I shared with her the comforting hope of the Gospel and the opportunity of new life offered by Jesus Christ. When I finished, I could sense that she was interested and attentive. She asked a few questions in a soft voice, and her sobbing stopped. However, it was also apparent to me that she needed time and space to think. I suggested that she attend a church that Sunday and gave her the name of a friend and the church he pastored in her neighborhood. She thought a minute and finally said, "O.K. I'll give it a try, but I don't know what he can do for me." Off the air, after we hung up, the radio station got her phone number. A few hours later, I called my pastor friend to alert him about the young girl who might be visiting his church.

One week later, he called me to tell me that she and her mother had attended church. What happened in the ensuing few weeks is a miracle of God. The young girl decided to live and to maintain her pregnancy, accepted Jesus as her personal Savior, joined the Church, got involved in the life and ministry of the church and subsequently was baptized.

A few months after our radio phone conversation, my nurse came out of an examining room in my office and, smiling broadly, said to me, "You're going to love what's waiting for you in this room."

"What's that?" I asked. "Never mind," she said. "You'll see." When I entered the room, a young woman holding a newborn baby gave me the biggest smile this side of heaven. Holding the baby straight up in the air, she said, "This is Helen — the baby you and God wouldn't let me abort. I also owe you both my life. Thank you so much." With that we embraced and cried. God's family was involved in that decision and the answer was LIFE!

The Ethics of Abortion

When the ethics of abortion is considered, one has to take into account and try to understand the disparate voices heard in the debate. Abortion raises considerable problems for the individual conscience, national political policy, and constitutional law. Few issues have so fragmented society. Moreover, it is apparent that many people on both sides of the debate are sincere and have strong convictions. However, it is equally clear that one side has to be right and the other wrong. Sincerity, strong convictions, and personal integrity are not at issue, truth is. While it is important to understand the things that divide us and to refrain from rhetorical excess in the debate, the central and crucial question remains, "What is morally right?"

I believe it is possible to know the difference between right and wrong, good and evil. I also believe that the difference has little to do with personal or popular opinion, or conviction. The apostle Paul wrote that what may be known about God is plain to all people because God has made it plain to them (Romans 1:19). Jesus prayed to the Father for his disciples and all who would follow them in the faith, "Sanctify them by the truth; Your Word is truth" (John 17:17). Jesus also said to the Jews who believed in him, "If you hold to my teaching, you really are my disciples. Then you will know the truth and the truth will set you free" (John 8:31,32). Thus, for the Christian, the truth is to be found in the teachings of Jesus and the sacred scripture, the Word of God. Everyone is entitled to an opinion, but not every opinion is true or carries equal value. With this in mind, we will consider the many and varied voices that frame the debate.

Abortion and Feminism

It is possible that intelligent people who are exposed to the same facts and statistics can still disagree. The moral principles we bring to the debate will help frame it. In addition, the many biases and convictions that we carry with us will influence our decision in one direction or another. Nowhere is this more apparent than in the opposing views of the Christian Pro-Life and the feminist Pro-Choice movements. It will be difficult to come up with a solution to the abortion problem unless we first understand the differences that divide us.

• Historical Feminism

The emergence of the feminist movement in the 1960s and their accomplishments in the political and social life of our country over the ensuing thirty years is almost without precedent in the history of the republic. For example, we have experienced tremendous changes in the work force, which provide some barometer of the social impact of the movement. In his book *A Nation of Victims,* Charles J. Sykes cites some statistics provided by Naomi Wolf: during a thirty year period between 1960 and 1990, the nation saw three times as many women elected to public office; twenty times as many lawyers in practice and judges on the bench; and approximately 170,000 engineers added to the work force. In addition, many more women have entered management level jobs in business and banking. The record is extraordinary and, in great part, due to the success of the feminist movement.[30]

On the other hand, feminism as a social movement in this country did not spring up *de novo* in the 1960s, but had a historical antecedent. As a matter of fact, feminism has existed throughout most of our history, and then, as now, abortion and feminism have been inseparably joined. What is not so well known is that, historically, feminism had been ardently Pro-Life. In the 19th century, American feminists viewed abortion as an evil and linked it to the oppression of women. Three issues dominated the agenda of the early feminists: the mistreatment and the subjugation of women to the male-dominated society, the dissemination of information regarding female sexuality and reproductive biology, and the unwavering view that abortion was murder. The women in the movement were bold, courageous, and undaunted by the flood of masculine scorn and invective directed towards them, and were pioneers in promoting woman's health issues, including family planning. In addition, they engaged in a variety of activities in educating the general public that life began at conception.[31]

In the early years of the suffragist movement (1860-90), several articles were written by women condemning abortion and advocating family planning and sex education.[32] Feminists sought legal restrictions on abortion and advocated their strong enforcement. They also addressed the broader social issues that led to abortion, such as poverty, rape, and drunkenness, and they were not shy in denouncing the double standards that governed the lives of men and women.[33] They forcefully pointed out that, under prevalent social attitudes, men were allowed, and even encouraged, to behave irresponsibly, and women were thereby victimized. Abortion was seen as a by-product of male sexual domination and the need for gender equality a prerequisite for ending it.[34] It is fascinating that American feminists always have identified male domination as the source of their problem and yet have taken such radically different paths towards its solution. 19th Century feminists clearly saw abortion as a male solution to undesired pregnancies. They argued that abortion was murder and that men used it as an instrument of female servitude. On the other hand, 20th century feminists have insisted that reproductive autonomy and open access to abortion are key ingredients in their struggle for gender equality and that a male-dominated society has hampered the successful fulfillment of these goals.

• Classic Feminism

The Feminist Movement that emerged in the 1960s was primarily concerned with sexual liberation and reproductive freedom. Rosalind Pollack Petchesky has elucidated the two essential premises that supported these concerns: first, the movement defined the principle of "bodily self-determination," the notion that women "must be able to control their bodies and procreative capacities;" second, that women ought to have the right of self-autonomy to make decisions about birth control and abortion since they endured the pregnancy, had the babies, and primarily were responsible for the children's care.[35] Economic and political gender equality were also dominant issues in the movement. "Equal pay for equal work" is a slogan that captured the attention of the nation. Feminists boldly asserted that discrimination in the home, workplace, and community was a form of enslavement that subjugated women to an inferior status. Attention was focused on the workplace, addressing inequities in patterns of hiring, employee treatment, and opportunities for job advancement. On-the-job childcare also was advocated in an attempt to release women into the natural workforce.

Few can deny that Western society has a long and ignoble tradition of denigrating women. What is less obvious is the claim that women have been enslaved. Sykes points out that, on the contrary, some Americans in the 1960s saw women as privileged and uniquely favored in our society, arguing that their sex, throughout history, has protected them from fighting in wars, hard manual labor, and the brutality of the harshest prison conditions.[36] Obviously, feminists disagreed and discerned the essential need to raise the consciousness of America. That they succeeded in their efforts ought to be self-evident. The movement has shaped cultural attitudes to the point that sexism, under the sanction of law, has emerged as a social evil almost comparable to racism. The zeal to achieve their goals prompted more extreme forms of feminism to emerge, notably a militant form that denigrated men, decried traditional family structure, and labeled childbearing and childrearing as demeaning. The family was defined as an "instrument of oppression and exploitation."[37] These extremist views were self-defeating for feminism as they polarized the nation and energized Christians and Jews to defend the biblical view of family and home.

• Militant Feminism

In the 1980s, this more militant and radical face of feminism emerged and captured the dominant feminist organizations in our country, such as the National Organization for Women (NOW). It is also the driving force behind the women's study programs in our universities. Perhaps this radicalization of the college curriculum will prove to have the most profound impact on our society, as thousands of young women are being exposed to anti-male and anti-sex teaching and seduced into believing that there is a national epidemic of sexual assault and violence on women. Sykes has pointed out that "rape is the central metaphor haunting the imaginations and writings of radical feminists, a symbol of the systematic violence of males against women."[38] The issue is not that rape and violence are the fantasies of militant feminism. To the contrary, rape is a terrible reality and a pervasive problem in our violent society. The psychological and spiritual damage it inflicts on young women is incalculable. Unfortunately, the problem is that the feminist movement has exaggerated date and incestuous rape statistics to a level that independent measurements of sexual violence do not support.

In part, it may all come down to how one defines rape. In some cases, there may even be a fine line between date-rape and consensual sex. In our sexually permissive society, that line is often blurred by alcohol and the compromising circumstances of the encounter. Whatever the magnitude of the problem, militant feminists have zealously moved to seek legislative decrees to outlaw date rape, to censor pornography, and to enforce political correctness in the workplace, thus highlighting the idea of women's victimization. Sykes has correctly called this a "sexual nightmare" and derisively labeled our society "the rape culture."[39]

The current group of militant feminists has also embraced various causes, among them "ecofeminism" (a sort of environmentalism with a feminine slant) and goddess worship. According to *Christianity Today*, the worship of feminine deities invaded the altar and communion table of a recent religious woman's pastoral conference.[40] This form of blasphemy is not unknown to students of the Bible. The prophet Jeremiah warned Israel that false religion was worthless and counseled against offering "cakes of bread for the Queen of Heaven" (Jeremiah 7:18). In their zeal to promote the cause of women, some militant feminists have tried to replace God, who is Spirit and neither male nor female, with a female goddess, born out of legend, superstition, and demonic suggestion. The apostle Paul may have anticipated the present situation when he wrote, "For although they knew God, they neither glorified him nor gave thanks to him, but their thinking became futile and their foolish hearts were darkened. Although they claimed to be wise, they became fools and exchanged the glory of the immortal God for images made to look like mortal man and birds and animals and reptiles" (Romans 1:21-23). In a movement where morality has been reduced to a matter of personal inclination or political expediency, feminists have embarked on a moral crusade devoid of morals.

• Feminism In Medicine

Given feminism's tremendous impact on the abortion debate, it is not surprising that feminists have made inroads in the medical profession. As more and more young women enter and enrich the field of medicine, feminists have had a larger voice in the ethics of the profession. Barbara R. Gottlief, writing in the prestigious *New England Journal of Medicine*, has recently decried the medical profession's failure to integrate abortion practice "into the mainstream of health care delivery." She accuses the Pro-Life movement of isolating abortion from the whole range of women's reproductive experiences and contends that abortion services, thus isolated and marginalized, are vulnerable to harassment and violence. Further, she accuses the Pro-Life movement of contributing to the climate of violence that surrounds the nation's abortion clinics.[41]

An editorial in the *New England Journal of Medicine* written in response to an article on adolescent pregnancy in that same journal was critical of recent political efforts to deprive young, single, pregnant women of welfare benefits. The authors perceived that the intention of the proposed legislation was to promote morality and discourage teenage pregnancies. They pointed out that these legislative efforts rarely show any interest in "making contraception or abortion more readily available to adolescents."[42] In short, the editors of the journal aligned themselves with Dr. Gottlief and the pro-choice movement.

I agree that morality cannot be legislated and that limiting the access of teenagers to health services may pose unforeseen, increased medical risks. I further agree with the authors that issues such as poverty, insufficient education, and inadequate prenatal care are critical factors that demand national attention in an effort to slow the epidemic of teenage pregnancies. However, I lament the fact that, all too often, abortion is the first solution suggested. I disagree that providing more access to abortion is a good solution to a bad problem. It is a terrible solution to any problem.

• Pro-Life Feminism

While the feminist movement has many faces and is far from united in theory and policy, most of its members agree that economic and gender equality combined with the unfettered right to abortion defines the movement. Feminists view these as core issues and central to the integrity of their cause. However, the United States Supreme Court has not held that opposition to abortion constitutes sex discrimination, nor a violation of equal protection under the law. On the other hand, the Court has held to a broad consensus concerning authentic sex discrimination issues such as equal access to jobs, equal pay, promotion opportunities, and the right to work in an environment free from sexual harassment.

In an Amicus (friend of the Court) Brief filed before the United States Supreme Court in October, 1990, by Feminists for Life of America in the case of Jayne Bray, et.al., v. Alexandria Woman's Health Clinic, et.al., the argument was posed that a majority of American women did not support the view "that equal protection under the Fourteenth Amendment requires unlimited abortion on demand."[43] Christine Smith Torre (lawyer for the respondents) et.al. cited the results of a 1987 Gallup poll which revealed that 53 percent of women and 47 percent of men believed that "the unborn child's 'right to be born'" outweighs, at the moment of conception, the woman's "right to choose" whether she wants to have a child. In another public opinion poll conducted in 1990 and cited by the brief, 44 percent of married women and 42 percent of unmarried women felt that abortion should only be permissible in cases of rape, incest, or the health of the mother. Torre, et. al. pointed out that the poll demonstrated that 53-55 percent of women think that most abortions are unwarranted.

In addition, the brief also argued that the opposition of American women to abortion was attested to by the large number of women enrolled in the membership of organizations opposed to abortion. These groups include the National Right to Life Committee, Concerned Women for America, American Life League, Women Exploited by Abortion, and American Victims of Abortion. The unifying belief of each of these organizations is the conviction that abortion is wrong and exploitative of women. Feminists for Life of America (FFLA) believe that militant feminism and its derivative groups have betrayed the cause of historical feminism. The stated purpose of their organization is to "foster respect for human life and social economic justice for women."[44] The Professional Women's Network (PWN), founded in 1984, represents professional and business women across the nation. The listed objectives of this group are: "to advocate respect for human life and the well-being of all women, regardless of race, creed, or economic status; to provide a system for women to help other women in crisis pregnancies through personal community involvement; urge passage of Pro-Life legislation that protects the preborn child and affords meaningful (financial, legal, educational) assistance to women who choose to carry their pregnancies to term; and promote public awareness of women's issues and relay accurate information about abortion."[45]

These are facets of feminism which are underappreciated and virtually unknown by large segments of our society. These groups have maintained a quiet, steady, unwavering opposition to abortion yet feel they best represent mainstream feminism and the interests of women. They, like their historical predecessors in the feminist movement, have unequivocally held that not only is abortion murder, but that it poses serious physical and emotional risks to women.

Pro-Life feminism is true to its historical antecedents and provides the best model for meeting the physical and emotional needs of women considering abortion. Historically, Pro-Life feminists have never viewed legalized abortion as a solution to the oppression of women. Rather, they have seen it as the evil consequences of their marital, social, and economic disenfranchisement. Their legitimate concerns have always been broad-based, calling for the prevention of the socio-economic circumstances giving rise to abortion and directing their energies not only towards the lives of unborn children, but also towards crisis pregnancies, poor families, and uncared-for children already born. Ironically, their long-held belief that the acceptance of women in the medical profession would thwart the advancement of abortion practices has not been realized. Nevertheless, their strong presence belies the notion that feminists today are of one mind on the subject of abortion. Indeed, Pro-Life feminism's persistent opposition to abortion is most consistent with advancing the real interests of all women in our society.

Sidney Callahan is a Pro-Life feminist and ethicist who has challenged the Pro-Choice feminist principle of autonomy, upon which the unrestricted right to abortion is based. She argues that a pregnant woman can never be a fully autonomous human being since her body is being used as a vehicle through which the baby matures and from which the baby is delivered.[46] This concept actually has its roots in the Eastern Christian Church. At the Council of Ephesus (431), the Eastern Church promoted a title for Mary, the mother of Jesus, as "Theotokos," Birthgiver of God. The intent was not to promote devotion to Mary, but to emphasize the Divinity of Jesus. A more appropriate translation would be "the Womb of God."[47]

Every pregnant woman, in a sense, is the womb through which life comes. In this sense, pregnant women are not autonomous human beings. Further, Callahan asserts that Western law demands that the human life within a woman, vulnerable and totally dependent, be protected.[48] She argues that the fetus, as an immature, dependent form of human life, needs time to develop, and that the fetus deserves protection during its interuterine phase of growth and development, adding that immaturity and dependence "are not crimes."[49] It is a distorted view of morality that would promote individual autonomy and choice over the life of a human being.

Finally, she disputes the prevailing feminist notion that a fetus is only a human being when the pregnant woman makes a place for it in her heart.[50] Rosalind Pollack Petchesky, a Pro-Choice feminist and the Director of the Women's Studies Program and Professor of Political Science at Hunter College, has built a socialist feminist theory of abortion in which she asserts that it is the consciousness of the pregnant woman that determines the "humanization" of the fetus.[51] In other words, it is not until the woman consciously makes a place for the fetus in her life that it becomes fully human. Callahan rightly condemns this point of view.

In agreement with Callahan, I would argue that it is God's will, not the will of a human person, that determines the origins of life and the definition of personhood. It is the prevailing temptation of every man and woman to consider themselves self-sufficient and to take upon themselves prerogatives reserved only for God. No matter how forcefully we protest, we have neither the authority nor the power to will life or personhood on anyone. Jeremiah's prayer to God begins, "I know, O Lord, that a man's life is not his own; it is not for man to direct his steps" (Jeremiah 10:23).

Abortion and Christianity

What follows is a review, by no means complete, of what our church fathers and some contemporary Christian ethicists have contributed to the abortion debate. Their positions on abortion are, for the most part, consistent with the teachings of Pro-Life feminists discussed above but cast within the wider net of Church theology. Yet a truthful appraisal of the Church's stance on abortion must acknowledge some disunity in the ranks, disunity which has occasionally surfaced in the guise of ugly radicalism. The Church is therefore hard put to answer the question: Where do we go from here? One way to go about answering this is to explain where we've been.

Historically, the early church was united in their stand against abortion. Since the first century, the Church resolutely has affirmed that abortion is a moral evil. Until the Reformation and beyond, that teaching remained intact. The teaching of the Fathers and many Church letters and teachings of antiquity attest to this fact. For example, the Didache (commonly known as the Teaching of the Lord, through the Twelve Apostles) is an ancient compilation of teaching written sometime between 70–80 AD. In the section consisting of an exposition of Christian morality, it says, "Practice no magic, sorcery, abortion or infanticide." Then it commands, "You shall not procure abortion. You shall not destroy an unborn child."[52] The Epistle of Barnabas was written between 70–79 AD in Alexandria by an unknown author. It was a popular epistle and considered to be orthodox in matters of faith. In it, the author, contrasting the Way of Darkness and the Way of Light, wrote, "Thou shalt not murder a child by abortion, nor again shalt thou kill it when it is born."[53] The official teaching of the Early Church was that life began at conception, and that induced abortion at any stage was considered homicide.

These early teachings of the Church fathers were a strong repudiation of ancient Greek and Roman writers, who otherwise exerted considerable influence on the patristic tradition. The writings of two representative figures, Plato and Aristotle, testify to the Pro-Choice culture that the Church fathers rebutted. These thinkers both favored allowing abortion. Plato, particularly, believed abortion was to be practiced uniformly when a woman was over forty years of age and conceived,[54] and favored exposure of deformed infants and children born into poverty, a practice performed to prevent overcrowding. As Paul Fowler, an evangelical teacher and author, points out, "the interests of the state took precedence over the rights of the newborn."[55]

The Church fathers continued to make their teachings on life a bulwark of early Christian doctrine. St. Basil the Great of Caesarea in Cappadocia was a great teacher in the early Church (330–379 AD). He wrote, "Those who give drugs causing abortions are murderers themselves, as well as those who receive the poison which kills the fetus." Basil also wrote in another letter, "a woman who has deliberately destroyed a fetus must pay the penalty for murder."[56] Michael J. Gorman, a historian who has written on abortion and the early Church, documents that many other Church Fathers opposed abortion, namely Origen, Tertullian, Cyprien (Bishop of Carthage), Ambrose (Bishop of Milan), the scholarly Jerome who translated both the Hebrew Bible and the Greek New Testament into Latin, the gifted preacher John Chrysostom, and finally the great Augustine. Thus, up through the fifth and into the sixth century, the position of the Church was resolute.[57]

Little is known about Church teaching on abortion during the Dark Ages, but we do know that abortion and infanticide continued to be condemned as heinous crimes through the late Middle Ages with severe punishments exacted on the guilty.[58] However, the prohibition of abortion was, in fact, only moderately successful because significant parts of the European population did not share in the Church's assessment of it as evil.

From 750 AD until the Reformation (1520 AD) the official teaching of the Church on abortion and infanticide never wavered, but refinements were added as new controversies arose. For example, the Church taught that it was permissible to remove a dead fetus, recognizing that it posed a threat to the mother.[59] Moreover, the concept of intention in cases of abortion gradually was introduced. Was the motive behind abortion to preserve the mother's health or to kill the baby? To this day, intention remains a key principle in matters relating to the care of the pregnant woman where the possibility of miscarriage is introduced. If the intention is to help the mother or to perform diagnostic tests essential to her proper care, the physician and the woman are not culpable should the fetus be prematurely expelled. The Church has held that in these cases, since the motive was proper and no sin was intended, no sin is incurred.

Thus, until the Reformation in the early sixteenth century, the Church consistently maintained a position of moral opposition to abortion. A summary of its teaching briefly can be stated as follows: (1) all human life is sacred because it has been made in the image of the living God; (2) the quality of being human is conferred at the moment of conception; thus, abortion is homicide and a criminal act subject to punishment; (3) the fetus, like every vulnerable and helpless human being, must be protected, nurtured and defended; and (4) only God has the right to remove the fetus from the uterus, no one else. In short, the Church continually upheld the doctrine of the *imago dei*, the doctrine of life at conception, the principle of parental stewardship, and the doctrine of God's sovereignty over His creation.

By contrast, the eighteenth century set in motion a current of belief that placed great reliance on man's mind and the natural sciences and mathematics. A product of the Age of Reason, it gave rise to the Enlightenment, a philosophical movement that critically examined previously accepted doctrines and beliefs. Religiously, this movement found its expression in Deism, a persuasion (based solely on human reason) that God, once having created the universe, abandoned it, assuming no control or influence on man or nature. In this belief system, the God of personal revelation and redemption never existed. Many, including some in the Church, were affected by these theories. Nonetheless, no substantial changes in Church teaching on abortion emerged during this time of religious turmoil.

At times, Protestant leaders have appeared cautious in addressing abortion, probably in part because the Reformation stressed the freedom of each individual and the right of personal choice. In this regard, they have been guarded against making strong moral statements that reminded them of the absolute authority of the Roman Church. Despite this fact, several early-to-mid 20th century leading Protestant theologians, including Karl Barth, Emil Brunner, Dietrich Bonhoeffer, and Helmut Thielicke, strongly condemned abortion. Karl Barth wrote: "The unborn child is from the very first a child. It is still developing and has no independent life. But it is a man and not a thing, nor a mere part of the mother's body... He who destroys germinating life kills a man."[60]

Throughout this period the Catholic Church has remained true to her patristic teachings on abortion. Accordingly, several recent pontiffs have written encyclicals uncompromisingly condemning abortion. Pius XII reemphasized that the Catholic Church did not favor the fetus over the mother. He wrote, "In the one case as in the other, there can be but one obligation: to make every effort to save the lives of both, of the mother and the child."[61] John XXIII emphasized the evil effects legalized abortion had on society, stressing the responsibility of its leaders. "Human life," he wrote, "is sacred; from its very inception, the creative action of God is directly operative. By violating his laws, the divine majesty is offended, the individuals themselves and humanity are degraded, and the bonds by which members of society are united are enervated."[62] Paul VI succinctly declared, "Respect for human life is called for from the time that the ovum is fertilized; a life is begun which is neither that of the father nor of the mother; it is rather the life of a new human being with its own growth. It would never be made human if it were not human already." He concluded, "Divine law and natural reason exclude all right to the direct killing of an innocent human being."[63] On March 31, 1995, John Paul II issued an encyclical called "Evangelium Vitae" (Gospel of Life). In it, he strongly condemned abortion, euthanasia, and capital punishment, calling our modern world "a culture of death." More than half of the document is devoted to a pastoral exposition exhorting society to a revolutionary counterculture of life. In an injunctive passage, he writes, "Abortion and euthanasia are crimes which no human law can claim to legitimize. There is no obligation in conscience to obey such laws; instead there is a grave and clear obligation to oppose them by conscientious objection."[64] Clearly, the official voice of the Catholic Church is in unison on this grave moral issue.

Likewise, several prominent contemporary Christian leaders have linked their position on abortion to the historic teachings of the Church. Their views are consistent with the Bible, traditional moral theology, and an unbroken line of Christian belief, both Catholic and Protestant, that has condemned abortion and upheld the biblical understandings of the sanctity of each human life. A few representative positions are presented in what follows.

Norman L. Geisler, in 1989, wrote a very lucid and comprehensive book on the issues of Christian ethics. It is orthodox in its treatment of various problems, candid about moral ambiguities, and fair in its presentation of conflicting opinions. He correctly points out that answers devolve from the basic premises from which we begin. For example, the conclusions we make about the permissibility of abortion will depend on whether we view the fetus as fully human, potentially human, or subhuman. If we conclude that the fetus is a human being, the obvious conclusion ought to be that abortion is ethically and morally wrong. In this view, the rights of the fetus will always outweigh the rights of the pregnant woman. If, on the other hand, we believe that the fetus is subhuman, the gravid woman should have full autonomy in determining the outcome of the pregnancy. Whether the Constitutional clause, "the right to privacy," is involved or not, self-autonomy would supersede fetal life. If we are unsure of the fetus's status and ambiguously define him as "potentially human," any decision we make is problematic and each case would have to be determined on the basis of its unique characteristics. In these situations, the decision to abort would be arrived at with moral trepidation and the rights of the woman, the fetus, and the community would have to be considered. Thus, the premise of sanctity of life or quality of life is logically derived from the basic beliefs that form our starting point. In his book, *Christian Ethics,* Geisler treats all of the above stated views fairly and comprehensively.[65] For the purpose of our discussion, I will focus on his basic belief that the fetus is fully human and that abortion is never permissible.

Starting with this premise, abortion is homicide and a violation of the Fifth Commandment and the laws that govern our society. Geisler provides a number of biblical arguments for viewing the fetus as human, most of which we have already covered. In addition, he posits the following nonbiblical arguments to support his claim. The extrabiblical evidence falls into two logical categories: scientific and social. Scientific evidence for the humanity of the newborn involves available genetic information and the documentation of intrauterine growth and development making the unmistakable human appearance of the fetus. In the social evidence section, he reasons that, since all of life has the flow of continuity from conception to birth, it is impossible to establish that one point is more or less determinant of personhood than another. From this premise, the in-utero fetus is every bit as human as the newborn baby. Second, he convincingly argues that no modern hospital would neglect a five-month gestational age infant that was prematurely born. To the contrary, every effort, many of them heroic, would be expended to save that baby. Logically, we might ask how we can allow a fetus to be destroyed at one moment, that we labor to save at another. Third, he cogently puts forth the premise that since all life has moments of vulnerability and dependency, abortion is equally as reprehensible as infanticide and euthanasia. Certainly, they all end in the same way.

Next, he rightly argues that many Christian and non-Christian moralists through the ages have declared abortion an evil. In natural law, in societal belief systems and in pagan antiquity, we find a respect for life and a prohibition of abortion. Although a universal consensus opinion was never reached on this matter in any age, history is replete with many societies, cultures, and sages that condemned the practice and punished offenders. Finally, he states that no one should be discriminated against on the basis of "size, age, location, or functional ability." To do so would be to penalize and threaten the life and well-being of the handicapped, aged and seriously ill, as well as the fetus.

Franky Schaeffer, son of noted philosopher and evangelical theologian Francis Schaeffer, together with C. Everett Koop, at that time Surgeon-in-Chief of the Children's Hospital in Philadelphia, produced a five-part motion picture documentary in 1979 entitled "Whatever Happened to the Human Race?" based on their book by that title. The films stressed the uniqueness of each person and emphasized the worth of human life on the basis of the biblical concept of the sanctity of life. The series was enthusiastically received in evangelical and charismatic circles and generally raised the consciousness of many Christians. The film personally impacted me and alerted me to the magnitude of the problem, to the extent that I began to understand more fully that my Christian profession required that I relate to the moral ills of the social community. In this sense, I became a Christian activist.

Some Christian ethicists, while affirming that abortion is a morally objectionable act, do not go as far as declaring that it must never occur. Stanley Hauerwas chooses to debate the issue, not from the usual "sanctity of life" perspective, but by stressing the need for the Christian community to articulate why abortion can never be regarded as morally acceptable. He argues that the Christian prohibition of abortion is the negative side of our positive commitment to welcome, care for, and nurture new life into our community. He correctly emphasizes the value of each life from God's perspective and states that "Christian respect for life is first of all a statement, not about life, but about God." Further, he stresses that from the Christian point of view, the birth of each child "represents nothing less than our commitment that God will not have this world 'bettered' by destroying life." He closes by reminding the Christian community that we must not only make a place for each newborn life in our hearts, but that we should also be prepared to receive and care for any child that needs it.[66]

Two of the most prominent American church leaders condemning abortion have been Archbishop John Roach and Terrence Cardinal Cooke. Writing in *The American Debate*, published in 1988, they critique Roe v. Wade in the strongest possible language. In their article, they forcefully argue for the dignity of all life, born and unborn, and decry the many philosophers and ethicists who try to define personhood in terms of functionality. They rightly point out that viewing life from its purely mechanistic and functional abilities betrays the moral dilemma gripping our society. Finally, they repudiate a society that lives in a sliding scale of values independent of morality based upon a Higher Authority. Thus, Roach and Cooke reject viability and the trimester systems established by the United States Supreme Court to distinguish between the rights of the fetus and the pregnant woman and conclude by reminding the court that the pregnant woman's assertion of self-autonomy and rights over the fetus raises uncomfortable analogies with slavery, and rights of owner over slave property. As harsh as this comparison seems, let me remind you that the court once ruled that all congressional limitation on slavery in federal jurisdiction was unconstitutional and that blacks were an inferior class of human beings who had no rights or privileges under the Constitution (Dred Scott v Sandford, 1857). The majority opinion for the court was then written by its avid, proslavery Chief Justice, Roger B. Taney. Lest we forget, the Supreme Court has been known to be seriously wrong.

While the men cited above each approach the problem of abortion from their own unique perspective and training, they all share many points of agreement. Central to their opinions is the overriding belief that the Christian's respect for life is a statement about his respect for God. While some in the Church have resolutely held Pro-Choice views and even some Christian denominations have championed the cause of choice, in few instances has the universal Church spoken on any topic with such a clear and unified voice.

• Disunity in the Ranks

Having said as much, it would be wrong, on the other hand, to assume that there is among all Christians unanimity regarding abortion. For many, every abortion is intolerable. For some, the issue is less clear. Yet, there are positive signs that consensus may be developing. For years, Roman Catholics were the standard-bearers of the Pro-Life movement. By contrast, many Protestants seemed disinterested. While some individual religious leaders spoke out against abortion, many more defended it. Several Protestant denominational churches *prior* to Roe v. Wade adopted resolutions affirming that abortion ought to be a matter of personal choice; the American Baptist Convention, the United Presbyterian Church, the United Methodist Church, and the Episcopal Church were all caught up in the question of personal freedom and choice. The response of the evangelical community was mixed and quiet.

Over the past decade, as the death by abortion statistics grotesquely mounted, a sleeping giant was stirred. Independent Bible, Pentecostal, and charismatic Churches joined the Pro-Life cause in large numbers. The Southern Baptist convention reversed its Pro-Choice position in 1980, and many individual evangelical and Protestant church members similarly joined the Pro-Life movement independent of their communions. Today, once again, a consensus condemning abortion seems to be building among many Protestant churches. Yet disagreements, even in this group, still occur. Paul B. Fowler, a noted theologian and teacher, asks a simple question: "Why can't we agree?"[67]

I offer two telling examples of the kind of dissent we face today, one by a Catholic professor of moral theology, the other by a Baptist theologian. Daniel C. Maguire, professor of moral theology at Marquette University, has written an article entitled, "A Catholic Theologian at an Abortion Clinic." In the article he recounts his visits to a clinic three blocks from his University office. After three visits, he resolves to "maintain the legality of abortion for women who judge they need them."[68] While he is determined to work to eliminate the various socioeconomic and political factors that lead to abortion, he curiously concludes that, for many women, abortion might be their least violent option. Moreover, he seems outraged at the strong Pro-Life stance adopted by many religious leaders in the Catholic Church. Finally, he makes an impassioned plea to Catholic ethicists to come out of the closet and stop avoiding the issue. He concludes, somewhat insensitively, by saying that the Catholic Church is more concerned about "embryos than… the women who bear them."[69] I don't deny the sincerity, conviction, or power of his article — only his conclusions.

Paul D. Simmons, a Baptist theologian, uses a Biblical perspective to make a case for freedom of choice.[70] He argues from two basic premises. First, he states that in Western morality people have an absolute value, whereas fetuses do not. He acknowledges that the fetus has value, but not to the same degree as the pregnant woman. He cites the biblical passage in Exodus 21:22-25 where a pregnant woman has been injured in an altercation between two men. Simmons claims that the penalty exacted by the husband and judges is different for the baby and the pregnant woman — a fine for the loss or injury to the fetus and the application of "an eye for an eye, tooth for a tooth" in the case of the woman. I agree that scriptural interpretation is somewhat problematic. However, by my reading, the text says that if the woman is injured in the fight and gives birth prematurely, but without serious injury to her or the baby, an appropriate fine commensurate to the injury is levied. But if a more serious injury, or even death ensues to either mother or baby, then the full application of the law is applied. I do not, like Simmons, interpret the text as applying different values to the mother and her baby. Second, Simmons claims that the Bible does not specifically prohibit abortion and that its silence in this matter does not permit us to judge the morality of another person's choice. I do not think the scripture is entirely silent in this matter, but rather, by inference, in upholding the value and dignity of life from its earliest moments in utero, places the fetus under the protective cover of the fifth commandment.

Obviously, the problems surrounding abortion are complex and often cause a great deal of personal, emotional pain. For those involved, the issue is much more than academic or theological. Hard decisions are hard to make. Is it any wonder that eminent thinkers often disagree and that the rest of us frequently feel confused? I would not minimize the terrible sacrifice some women go through in electing not to abort their baby. I have seen and cared for the children that these women elected to have.

Recently, I received a call from Bethany, a young, unmarried mother of two children in my practice. She had graduated from nursing school and wanted me to write a letter of recommendation for her to a local hospital. The moment was a poignant one for me because I had known Bethany from her birth and was her pediatrician throughout her childhood. Bethany was an only child, and her parents Bob and Janet adored her. She attended Christian schools and was raised in a loving and nurturing home. However, after her graduation from high school, her life took an alarming, downward spiral. She developed new and destructive friendships and soon was drinking heavily, smoking pot, and behaving in a sexually irresponsible manner. Within three years, she was pregnant twice, delivering a girl, Tiffany, and a boy, Matthew. At the age of 20, she was unmarried, unemployed, and solely responsible for her two young children, her life an emotional, physical, and spiritual mess. Initially, her parents had encouraged her to have, rather than abort, the babies. Now, they invited her and their grandchildren to move in with them. Over a period of six years, they encouraged and supported their daughter through the process and assisted in raising the children. Bathed in acceptance and love, Bethany came to her senses, reembraced her faith, and determined to move on with her life. She was accepted into nursing school, and four years later, at the age of 30, graduated with a B.S.N degree. Today, she and her children live in their own apartment, and maintain a close relationship with her parents. Bethany finally has achieved her childhood goal and is working as a nurse in a local hospital. More importantly, she has re-established her relationship with God and rediscovered a sense of self-worth and personal dignity.

I know about the sacrifices this family and others like them have made, and I refuse to trivialize the issue to make a point. Yet, the truth remains — for some, electing not to abort is a sacrifice, no matter how terrible, but for the unborn child, it is always a matter of life and death.

• The Ugly Face Of Radicalism

Unfortunately, disunity is only part of the divided front we present to the public. Violence is the other part. In their avowed "civil disobedience," some in the Pro-Life movement have gone beyond the reasonable boundaries of what the Bible allows in matters of conscience. It would, therefore, be dishonest and unworthy of all the millions of people impacted by the issue of abortion to ignore the ugly face of violence revealed by a few radicals in the Pro-Life movement.

When Michael Griffin shot and killed Dr. David Gunn in Pensacola, Florida, on March 17, 1993 and Paul Hill killed Dr. John Britton, also in Pensacola, Florida, in July, 1994, a part of the heart of the Pro-Life movement died with them. That these and other perpetrators of violence have evoked the name and cause of God in justifying their murderous and odious deeds is blasphemy and dishonorable to the body of Christ. The New Covenant holds us to a higher standard of behavior. Jesus, in his Sermon on the Mount, said to his disciples, "You have heard that is was said to the people long ago, 'Do not murder, and anyone who murders will be subject to judgement.' But I tell you that anyone who is angry with his brother will be subject to judgement. Again, anyone who says to his brother, Raca, is answerable to the Sanhedren.

But anyone who says, 'You fool!' will be in danger of the fire of hell" (John 5:21,22). These are strange and troubling words. Do they represent a style of rabbinic argumentation or are they to be taken at face value? At the very least, the standard of his teaching is that anger which drives our lives to insult and violence is anger out of control, and thus sinful.

A Pro-Life activist who is angry about abortion and the existence of abortion clinics would better serve humanity and his God by allowing his anger to lead him to renewed commitment for the cause of life and to personally motivate him to work and persevere in a righteous manner. Paul warns us, along with Jesus, that there is no place for selfish and violent anger in the Kingdom of God (Ephesians 4:31). Jesus told Simon Peter who cut off the ear of the servant of the High Priest in the Garden of Getsemane, "Put your sword away, for all who draw the sword will die by the sword" (Matthew 26:52 and John 18:10,11). The New Testament teaches that we are never to personally exact revenge on another, no matter the offense. Only the valid government of the state has the God-given authority to punish offenders. Swords (or guns) are not legitimate tools for personal vengeance, but only for civil defense and punishment in the hands of the appropriate authorities (Romans 13:1-5). Peter's motives were good, but even good motives need to be instructed by a Higher law.

Selfishly, I would like to disassociate myself from the two anti-abortion activists who killed the physicians in Pensacola, but that would be disingenuous and morally dishonest. I could say, "Well, anyone who would kill someone in cold blood is not really a Christian at heart, no matter what he calls himself." However, only God knows the condition of their hearts. We only know that a senseless and violent crime was committed by one of our own, a Christian minister; therefore, we have to assume responsibility for that, as painful as it is. Further, we need to remind ourselves of the words of Jesus: "Watch out for false prophets. They come to you in sheep's clothing, but inwardly they are ferocious wolves" (Matthew 7:15). If Christ recognized false prophets, so too must we.

Finally, I believe we must look to more positive models of civil disobedience. We don't need to look far, for Christ himself modeled how we are to act when God and government are in conflict. But Christ, and other renowned examples of civil disobedience like Gandhi and Martin Luther King, Jr., argued for peaceful civil disobedience—never violent murder.

The Public Speaks

People generally assume moral positions on social issues that reflect how they view themselves and the world in general. The broader values we hold about man and God ultimately will be applied to the social crises we regularly encounter in our national community. In this sense, we can easily understand the conflict that splits our country in the abortion issue.

Clearly, abortion divides America along many lines, legal, political, ethical, and theological. But that does not mean that Americans lack consensus on this issue. Poll takers have long pursued the opinions of Americans on this issue. Though polls are not always representative and accurate, there are a number of current polls that are both fair and reliable. Below, I present three respected polls on abortion, two of the public and one of doctors. In presenting this statistical data, I am not suggesting that we, or our opposition, can decide this complicated legal and ethical issue by fielding opinions and crunching numbers. But it is worth noting that, despite the common media perception that most Americans are pro-choice, the majority of Americans hold pro-life beliefs on a variety of abortion issues.

"Focus on the Family," a ministry led by Dr. James Dobson, child psychologist and former professor at UCLA School of Medicine, commissioned the Roper organization to conduct a poll in 1995 to determine representative U.S. attitudes about abortion. The poll is reproduced in its entirety, so that we can fairly evaluate what American people think about this issue (Reprinted with permission. Copyright 1994 Focus on the Family. All Rights Reserved. International Copyright Secured.)

If we concentrate on categories 1 through 4, which might be said to represent a pro-life position, we see that 55 percent of respondents could be categorized as pro-life; while the belief that abortion is wrong in all circumstances was held by only 19 percent of those polled, 36 percent found abortion permissible only in narrowly defined circumstances. Only 26 percent of respondents were tolerant of abortion under most circumstances. Very few of those polled (13 percent) could be categorized as favoring abortion on demand without legal restrictions.

When the differences between male and female respondents is studied, we find that 60 percent of women selected pro-life positions, as opposed to 50 percent of men. Conversely, 26 percent of both men and women could be defined as Pro-Choice. On the basis of this poll, we can conclude that women are more Pro-Life than men. Perhaps the Pro-Life feminists are on to something.

In a poll conducted by Gallup in 1979 and reported in "Redbook" magazine, the data are very similar to that presented in the Roper Poll: 18 percent felt that abortion was not permissible under any circumstances (versus 19 percent), and 54 percent (versus 55 percent) found abortion permissible under certain limited circumstances. Only 25 percent (versus 26 percent) felt there should be no legal restrictions on abortion.[71]

Most national polls seem to reflect a consensus that abortion is not morally wrong in cases of maternal health, rape and incest, and genetic deformity and retardation. Approximately 75-80 percent of citizens would allow abortion in these cases. On the other hand, less than half of poll respondents feel that an unwed mother, unemployed welfare mother, large family, and failed contraceptives are reasons for abortion. Mary Ann LaManna, a sociologist at the University of Nebraska, points out that only 25 percent of people support abortion as defined in Roe v. Wade.[72] Obviously, the majority of Americans do not favor abortion, finding it permissible only in selected cases.

TOTAL		SEX		POLITICAL AFFILIATION			POLITICAL IDEOLOGY		
	TOTAL	MALE	FEMALE	DEM	REP	IND	CONS	MOD	LIBL
	100%	100%	100%	100%	100%	100%	100%	100%	100%
1. Abortion is wrong under any circumstances.	19%	19%	20%	17%	20%	20%	25%	14%	12%
2. Abortion is wrong, except to save the life of the mother.	7%	6%	9%	6%	8%	9%	10%	6%	4%
3. Abortion is wrong, except to save the life of the mother, and in the cases of rape or incest.	18%	18%	18%	18%	21%	16%	20%	18%	16%
4. Abortion is wrong, except to save the life of the mother; in the instances of rape or incest; and in the cases of infant deformity, disease or retardation.	11%	9%	13%	10%	12%	11%	11%	12%	10%
5. Abortion is wrong, except to save the life of the mother; in the instances of rape or incest; in the cases of infant deformity, disease or retardation; and where the child is unwanted and will not have a good quality of life.	11%	10%	11%	11%	12%	10%	11%	12%	10%
6. Abortion is permissible for any reason the woman chooses, until the fetus can survive outside the womb.	9%	10%	8%	9%	8%	10%	6%	9%	16%
7. Abortion is permissible for any reason except as a way to select the sex of the child.	4%	3%	5%	4%	4%	4%	3%	5%	5%
8. Abortion is permissible for any reason the woman chooses, at any time during the pregnancy, and no legal restrictions should be imposed, including no parental notification or no delay for informed consent.	7%	7%	8%	7%	7%	8%	6%	7%	11%
9. Abortion is permissible for any reason the woman chooses, at any time during the pregnancy; there should be no legal restrictions of any kind, and the government should pay for the procedure if the woman cannot afford the expense.	6%	6%	5%	7%	3%	5%	3%	7%	8%
10. Don't know.	8%	12%	5%	9%	6%	6%	5%	10%	7%

A third poll is in order since abortion advocates are fond of saying that most doctors favor a woman's right to abortion. A survey by the independent PPS Marketing Group in Fairfield, New Jersey, however, casts some doubt on that claim. They polled thirty-six thousand U.S. obstetricians by mail and 25 percent responded. In excess of 52 percent indicated that abortion should not be performed to terminate unplanned pregnancies; 55 percent said abortion should not be paid for by tax dollars. Joseph DeCook, speaking for the American Association of Pro-Life Obstetricians and Gynecologists (AAPLOG), which commissioned the survey, said, "More than 95 percent of abortions in America today are done as a solution for unwanted or unplanned pregnancies — exclusive of rape, incest, and possible legitimate medical considerations. He went on to say, "This poll indicates that the majority of obstetricians in this country oppose the practice of convenience abortion on demand as a solution for this serious problem."[73]

The Heirs of Hippocrates

Doctors Enter the Debate

Doctors are unavoidably part of the abortion debate. Our occupation demands it, and the public expects it. Though many of us don't deliver babies after our residency training, we all face the difficult ethical and technological dilemmas of the abortion debate. The ethical questions may be ages old, as we have seen in our examination of history, but new technologies complicate the debate. Genetics, in particular, has challenged our concept of life. Not only can we test the potential future health of a fetus, but we can also (at least to a limited degree) genetically engineer life. Needless to say, the concept of life is muddled when it is engineered by a M.D. or Ph.D.

Given the personal nature of our medical oath, the Hippocratic oath, I begin with a story about my first experience with this oath and my subsequent reflection upon it.

The Hippocratic Oath

On a Saturday afternoon in May of 1963, I stood to recite the Hippocratic Oath at the conclusion of our graduation ceremony. It was a very moving moment, and several classmates were weeping. The oath begins:

> *I swear by Apollo Physician and Asclepios and Hygeia and Panacea and all the gods and goddesses, making them my witnesses, that I will fulfill according to my ability and judgement this oath and this covenant.*[74]

I'm not sure why the faculty decided to retain the original wording of the oath, but they did. In any event, I mentally concluded, very quickly, that I was not on speaking terms with any of those mythical gods. Although my own spiritual life was very weak at the time, I substituted the name of Jesus in the oath. I didn't know it at the time, but that decision would prove to be prophetic.

I went on to recite:

I will not give to a woman an abortive remedy.[75]

The oath had been administered to medical graduates in European universities for centuries. Until recently, it was recited by almost every graduating medical class in America. However, many physicians have violated their solemn oath and continue to do so repeatedly.

Changing Medical Ethics

For centuries, medical ethics remained impervious to change. The ancient framework on which it was fashioned prevailed intact despite national turmoil and cultural upheavals. Today, that framework is crumbling in the face of social, moral, and judicial change.

Dr. Edmund Pelligrino, a noted medical ethicist from the Center for the Advanced Study of Ethics at Georgetown University Medical Center in Washington, D.C., has written a very lucid and perceptive article entitled, "The Metamorphosis of Medical Ethics: A Thirty Year Retrospective."[76] In the article, he states the most important root cause of the transformation has been the influence of moral philosophy, noting that as medical ethics increasingly has become a branch of that discipline, it has become more and more responsive to shifts in philosophical opinion and fashion.[77] However, since the mid-1960s, the code has been under attack, along with many traditionally accepted moral and cultural values.

Physicians today lack a comprehensive, firm foundation for medical ethics. The great moral and ethical traditions of the past are strange bedfellows to the equivocal state of contemporary moral philosophy. How is it possible to arrive at any truth which will satisfy, when the idea of truth is felt to be an unobtainable illusion? What is the effect on the field of clinical medicine in a society that condones abortion and euthanasia? How can physicians restructure the ethics of medical practice in an age where philosophy and ethics are problematic?

Difficult questions. But the answers are not ambiguous. Christian physicians need to frame their ethics in the context of the words of Jesus: "Therefore everyone who hears these words of mine and puts them into practice is like a wise man who built his house on the rock. The rain came down, the streams rose, and the winds blew and beat against that house; yet it did not fall, because it had its foundation on that rock. But everyone who hears these words of mine and does not put them into practice is like a foolish man who built his house on sand. The rain came down, the streams rose, and the winds blew and beat against that house, and it fell with a great crash" (Matthew 7:24-27).

Confusion In The Ranks

It is striking that the American Academy of Pediatrics, the national arbiter of sound pediatric practice whose stated purpose is to promote the optimum care and nurture of all children, has consistently maintained a Pro-Choice position. This, despite the fact that pediatrics is chiefly concerned with the continued growth and development of children. Thousands of pediatricians annually are trained in the sub-specialty of neonatology, the care of the newborn. Millions of dollars are spent each year in the care of prematurely born, sick infants. New fields of study have emerged within the discipline of pediatrics. These include perinatology, the study of events occurring near the time of birth, and fetology, the study of the fetus. Major emphasis in fetal medicine is centered in four areas: (1) the effects of maternal disease on the fetus, (2) the fetal effect of drugs administered to the mother, (3) the study of intrauterine fetal disease, and (4) the medical treatment of the fetus.[77] Pediatricians dedicated to the care of the fetus have to do some juggling of their own ethical values to rest comfortably in the capricious philosophy of the Pro-Choice advocates.

Moreover, a discipline dedicated to the growth and development of children needs to come to grips with its own definitions. Doctors Litt and Vaughan have defined growth and development as "the process by which the fertilized ovum becomes an adult person."[78] Growth refers to changes in body size; development, the differentiation of the human person. This process involves changes that inexorably and continuously define the individual as a unique human person. The progression by which the fertilized ovum becomes a human person is a question of degree, not of kind. All human persons are involved in growth and development, including the fetus. It is impossible to logically dedicate ourself to both the promotion and the destruction of the process.

The American Medical Association in 1994 published a *Code of Medical Ethics*.[79] This code, updated in 1997, maintains an uneasy neutrality in the abortion debate. Specifically it states that "the Principles of the Medical Ethics of the AMA do not prohibit a physician from performing an abortion in accordance with good medical practice and under circumstances that do not violate the law."[80] This, despite the fact that the AMA has in the recent past (1967) opposed induced abortion except when a threat to the life and health of the mother existed.

Historically, the AMA, in concert with a particularly strong feminist movement that was operative from the 1850s immediately prior to the Civil War through the turn of the 20th century, lobbied in support of criminal abortion statutes (1859, 1871).[81] Prominent feminists of that time held "an uncompromising view that abortion [was] 'child-murder.'"[82] The AMA concurred with that opinion and, with the feminists, supported legislation that would prohibit abortion and punish the offenders. Disingenuously, the United States Supreme Court in Roe.v.Wade endorsed the argued opinion that 19th century anti-abortion legislation was intended to protect pregnant women, not unborn fetuses.[83] This is directly counter to documented, written evidence that clearly and unequivocally shows that the founders of the feminist movement were concerned not only about the risks incurred by women, but also were uniformly critical of what they frequently referred to as "the horrible crime of ante-natal infanticide."[84] The AMA then shared these same concerns. What distinguished the feminist crusade from AMA efforts in this regard was that feminists addressed "the causes of abortion, not just the practice."[85] Thus, the AMA today, along with current feminists, has broken faith with its founders and is in opposition to its long-stated ideals.

We live in a time of changing values, where today's "truth" is at the mercy of personal and popular opinion. In Lewis Carroll's *Through the Looking Glass*, Alice complains to Humpty Dumpty that he has incorrectly used a word and confused its meaning. Humpty Dumpty scornfully answers, "When I use a word, it means just what I choose it to mean — neither more nor less." Alice speaks for many of us confused by standards and values that seem to be established on a foundation of sand when she replies, "The question is whether you can make words mean so many different things." Humpty Dumpty is not deterred. He would be at home in today's atmosphere of moral ambiguity; he ends the conversation by saying, "The question is, which is to be master — that's all."

Of course, real truth can never be mastered by the changing whims of opinion — it is established on God himself who declares through His prophet, "I, the Lord, speak the truth; I declare what is right" (Isaiah 45:19). The AMA, in the silence of its neutrality, has yielded to the currents of change fueled by the personal agendas of a few. Their silence is a loud discordant sound in the throes of the debate.

Science Speaks

As physicians, we need to ask ourselves, "What evidence does science offer us concerning the humanity of the unborn?" Despite the political grandstanding of the AMA, there is scientific evidence to address the question. As Geisler has said, "Modern science has placed a window in the womb."[86] The following is a summary of what science has to say about the beginning of human life.

• Genetic Evidence

Sir Thomas Browne, author of *Religio Medici* (1643), wrote that every man is older than he thinks, for our beginning is traced to the womb of our mother.[87] The study of human embryology supports this hypothesis. Human life begins as a fertilized egg (zygote) and is transformed through the process of growth and development into a man or woman. Some of this growth and development occurs in the uterus, much of it outside the womb. Truly, we all are 7-9 months older than we think.

The male sperm is not a human person. It can never be more than it is and apart from the female egg, it has no future. Likewise, the female egg will die unless there is union with the male sperm. The union of the two produces a zygote, imprinted with all the genetic information it will ever have. The male sperm and the female egg each have twenty-three chromosomes; the fertilized egg (zygote) has forty-six, the same as every adult human person. All the physical characteristics of the future adult are encoded in the zygote — hair and eye color, size, intelligence, talent, everything that distinguishes one human from another.

From that small beginning, the zygote will begin the process of cellular division and differentiation until the fourth through the eighth week of intrauterine life when a human form is distinguishable. By the end of the first trimester (age three months fetal life), the sex of the fetus can be distinguished. Growth and development distinguishes one stage from another, as a newborn infant is distinctly different than a teenager, who in turn is different from a mature adult. Every human being, whatever the stage of life, is in the process of differentiation and change, and every human person is encompassed within the context of this change.

• **Take a Look**

The most compelling evidence that the fetus is a human person is, that by as early as the fourth week of intrauterine life, it begins to look like one. The science of fetology (the study of the fetus) provides us with an amazing look at the tiny human person developing in its mother's womb. The following is a graphic summary of the growth and development of the pre-viable fetus up to the twentieth week of gestation (4 1/2 months).[88]

Intrauterine Age (In Weeks)	Physical Characteristics Noted
9	Heart structurally formed; head structurally formed with evidence of visible nose; chin, eye sockets and ear buds
12	Kidney functioning with urine excreted; swallowing and tongue movements; reacts to external stimuli (stroking lips cause fetus to respond by sucking; stroking closed eyelid cause blinking); intestines in abdomen
13	Fingernails
14	Head erect; growth of lower limbs; muscles fully defined
16	Ears stick out from head; forearms and lower legs crossed; fingers flexed; rapidly developing bony skeleton (all the bones in the body can be identified by x-ray)
18-20	Brown fat: site of heat production
20	Most of organs developed, though not fully mature

In addition, in this period of time before the fetus is able to survive outside the uterus, he is able to frown, grimace, swallow, squint, suck the thumb, move the tongue, and grasp with its little hands. Further, the fetus has its own unique fingerprints and blood type. Clearly, this is a human being in the process of development. In this case, seeing is believing. Dr. A. Liley, a prominent physician and an expert in the field of fetology, has said, "This is the same baby we are caring for before and after birth, who before birth can be ill and need diagnosis and treatment just like any other patient."[89] Same baby, same patient, same human person, you only need to look and see.

• <u>Growth and Development</u>

Finally, the most persuasive evidence is right before our eyes. Pediatricians, like parents, have the joyful opportunity to watch babies and children grow and develop. Almost every parent can tell you when their children first recognized them, when they sat unassisted, got their first tooth, walked, spoke in sentences, dressed themselves, tied their shoes, got their first menstrual period, or shaved.

Life is a series of changes. Even talents take time to mature. Singers will tell you that the human voice doesn't begin to reach its full potential until the late twenties. Baseball players are said to be in their prime by the early thirties. Babe Ruth, for example, hit sixty home runs in 1927 when he was 32 years old (you can look it up).

Growth, development and change characterize all of human life — from the zygote to the elderly. Even psychosocial maturation is dependent on the successful integration of many changes that go into defining the human person as unique and distinctly individual. Yet, personhood is not dependent on these changes. From conception to death, human life proceeds in an unceasing manner, without discontinuity or interruption. It changes, but does not yield its humanity. It is as human in its beginning, as at its end. Change does not define our humanity, it merely characterizes the stage of our life at a moment in time.

Difficult Medical Issues

Introduction

While we must always keep the sanctity of life and authority of God in the forefront of our defense of life, we must also acknowledge that human beings and human life issues are involved and that these issues bring with them an array of conflicting problems and emotions. Some of these issues are so highly charged and sensitive that they shape events and make easy solutions more problematic. In this section, we will briefly cover some of the more difficult medical issues relating to the debate.

• Definitions

In order to understand the discussion of these unique situations, more precise definitions of abortion are in order. Physicians recognize two distinct forms of abortion: *spontaneous* and *induced*. *Spontaneous abortion* is the termination of a pregnancy through natural causes and without the aid of mechanical or medical agents. These commonly are called miscarriages. *Induced abortion* is the intentional medical or surgical termination of a pregnancy before 20 weeks' gestation. An induced abortion is frequently called a *therapeutic abortion* if it is performed with the intention of preserving the pregnant woman's health. Formerly, an abortion performed for any other reason was called a *criminal abortion*. These were defined as abortions performed without *medical or legal justification*. Since Roe.v.Wade, physicians now refer to them as "elective pregnancy termination."

• Statistics

The best statistics relating to the incidence of therapeutic abortions are those obtained prior to Roe.v.Wade (1973) when all other reasons were considered criminal. Several studies published prior to 1956 reveal the incidence of abortion, performed to preserve the mother's health to be approximately 1 in every 250-350 deliveries.[90] Obviously, criminal abortions were performed outside of legal scrutiny, some by nonmedical personnel and under nonsterile conditions. In these cases, it is impossible to come up with any meaningful statistics regarding the number performed per year.

The mortality rate in criminal abortions performed prior to 1973 is assumed high, but actual figures are unobtainable. Case-fatality statistics published in 1972 for therapeutic abortions documented 4.1 deaths per 100,000 cases. We do know that large numbers of women have never died from legal or illegal abortions. Since abortions have been legalized, more precise mortality figures are available. In 1987, 0.4 deaths per 100,000 abortions were recorded, a 90% decrease from Roe.v.Wade.[91] The old cliché proves true: "practice makes perfect."

On the other hand, the changes in induced abortion rates since 1973 are astounding. Presently, 1.5 million pregnancies are prematurely terminated each year; approximately one-third of all pregnancies currently are aborted. Recent statistics reveal that between 3-5% of all women of child-bearing age have had an abortion, and that 3 of 4 are performed in unmarried women.[92] Today, abortion is one of the most common surgical procedures in the United States. What once was relatively uncommon and done only for very special circumstances has become a routine daily event.

Clearly, abortion now has become, for many, the preferred contraceptive method. It is well established that Japan and Hungary use it as a means of population control. This, despite the fact that abortion unnecessarily risks the life of every woman who subjects herself to one. In addition, the United States and many of the developed countries of the world ignore the immorality of the act and succumb to the expediency of personal convenience.

• **What Do Doctors Think?**

While most U.S. doctors believe that abortion should never be used as a contraceptive method, every medical school Department of Obstetrics teaches the "proper medical indications" for the termination of pregnancy. These generally fall into 2 major categories (fetal and maternal) and are listed in Table 2.

Table 2[93]	
Fetal Indication	**Maternal Indications**
Major Malformations • Anencephaly (congenital absence of brain spinal cord) • Bilateral cystic disease of kidneys (incompatible with life) Chromosomal Abnormalities • Down's Syndrome Inherited Metabolic Defects • Hemophilia Fetal Exposure to Teratogens (teratogen = an agent capable of causing fetal malformations) • Viruses (Rubella Syndrome)[1] • Drugs (thalidomide limb deformities) • Xray • Other Infections • Alcohol (Fetal Alcohol Syndrome)[2]	• Heart Disease (some forms) • Sever Hypertension (high blood pressure) • Blood Clotting Diseases (platelets abnormally consumed and clotting compromised) • AIDS • Severe Forms of Cancer (where mother's survival depends on treatment with x rays or drugs) • Advanced Kidney Disease with deteriorating function (particularly early in pregnancy)

1 Rubella Syndrome: Combination of newborn heart, eye and hearing defects secondary to maternal Rubella infection.

2 Fetal Alcohol Syndrome: A group of birth defects, retarded growth, compromised intelligence and heart abnormalities related to heavy maternal abuse of alcohol.

The problems cited in both "fetal and maternal indicators" are by no means all-inclusive, but rather used to indicate representative examples for purposes of better understanding and current medical thinking.

Medical malpractice textbooks of law have kept pace with the rapid advances of scientific technology, and specifically address the issue of the medical indications for abortion.[94] Lawyers are instructed as to which disorders mandate amniocentesis (the surgical withdrawal of a sample of amniotic fluid for testing from the amniotic sac of the pregnant woman) and trained to assess which tests on the collected fluid are appropriate. Further, they are taught to scrutinize medications prescribed during the pregnancy for the possibility of adverse fetal effect; to evaluate maternal infections for evidence of fetal damage; and to appraise the medical management of a variety of other complicated maternal health problems. It is clear that poor fetal outcomes are subject to the question as to whether an abortion ought to have been performed. Comprehensive guidelines are established by lawyers for other lawyers to use in assessing the proper use of abortion in "indicated cases." Thus, not only is our culture inclined to abortion for very trivial reasons, but legal pressure to consider abortion, as well as the real threat of a malpractice suit, further adds to the physician's burden. That they so often choose to do what is right, rather than give way to their fears, is a credit to the integrity of individual obstetricians and the medical profession in general.

• What Do Doctors Do?

One of the great advances of medical science in this century is the ability of doctors to "look" into the womb. In many cases, physicians now have mastered the technology not only to make pre-natal diagnoses, but to treat the fetus. Even more amazing are the sophisticated techniques that allow doctors to perform "in-utero" surgery and exchange transfusions in compromised, sick fetuses. Scientific methodology has progressed to the point where fetal cells shed into the amniotic fluid can be studied for chromosome identification. The presence or absence of certain substances known to be associated with fetal diseases or anomalies also can be studied. Indeed, failure to perform amniocentesis and make appropriate biochemical determinations prenatally constitutes a major deviation from acceptable standards of medical practice. Moreover, the procedure is safe, and the risk to the fetus is minimal.

One of the substances studied in amniotic fluid is α fetoprotein (AFP), which serves as a marker of fetal disease and is easily measured from small quantities of aspirate. It is synthesized by the liver, gastrointestinal tract, and the yoke sac of the fetus. AFP levels are highest between 14–18 weeks gestation. Doctors first assess gestational age by ultrasonography (a technique which utilizes ultrasonic waves to visualize body structure and organs). Once fetal age is determined, amniocentesis is performed and samples of amniotic fluid are analyzed.[95]

Increased AFP levels frequently are associated with anencephaly, meningomyelocele (a defect of the spinal cord where a malformed cord and associated nerve roots are outside of the body in a sac covered by a thin membrane), and omphalocele (a herniation of the abdominal contents into the base of the umbilical cord, contained outside the body in a thin sac). All of these serious and life-compromising diseases frequently can be prenatally diagnosed.[96] Many doctors currently believe that 80-90% of all anencephalic cases can be diagnosed before birth. We now know that most neural tube (precursors of the central nervous system) defects yield an increased AFP level and that elevations are sometimes noted in fetal death, congenital kidney disease, and intestinal blockage.

Prenatal diagnoses also can be made, using other techniques, on many genetic deformities, some forms of metabolic disorder, and a variety of endocrine (glandular) diseases. Sophisticated ultrasonographic procedures make it possible to diagnose fetal cardiovascular (heart and blood vessel) abnormalities, problems of the urinary tract, and a number of limb deformities, including dwarfism.

Of course, blessings often bring responsibilities, to say nothing of burdens. While these amazing techniques often make it possible for us to "peer into the womb," the burden comes with deciding what to do with the information obtained. There is always the danger that with increased knowledge, unreasonable expectations will surface, even the demand that the undesirable be aborted. In this brave new frontier of science, medical ethics and moral convictions are being stretched in ways never before conceived, and doctors are feeling the strain more than most.

Problem Areas

Granting that the fertilized egg is fully human leads to some serious moral-ethical dilemmas. It is a disservice to the seriousness of the issue to pretend that problems do not exist; indeed, it cheapens the debate. Below, we will examine some of these problem areas, which includes a discussion of what to do when the life of the mother is at risk or when rape occurs, and an exploration of the moral gray zone of new genetic technologies.

• The Life Of The Mother

Doctors almost unanimously have supported the view that therapeutic abortion to save the life of the pregnant woman is permissible. According to several polls, more than 90% of the general public concurs. Even the majority of people in the Pro-Life movement agree that this position is moral and acceptable.

Some ethicists have maintained that a fully developed human being (pregnant woman) has a higher value than one that has the full potential for humanity (fetus), but has not developed. A statement in support for this view can be expressed as follows: "What is, has more value, than what may be." This premise personally makes me very uncomfortable and is, I believe, incompatible with the teaching of Scripture. More in keeping with what the Bible says about the value and dignity of all life, regardless the stage of development, is the concept of "intention." In this view, long the position of the Roman Catholic Church, it is morally permissible to terminate the pregnancy if the intention is not to kill the baby, but to save the mother. Geisler, a Christian ethicist, agrees and further cites the right of "self-defense" when one's life is threatened, as the mother's is in these cases. Simply put, he contends that if the fetus poses a life threat to the pregnant woman, she has the Biblical and moral right to defend herself.[97] The Scriptures teach that an act of self-defense does not constitute blood guilt or sin (Exodus 22.2). The civil law would term this justifiable homicide. My only problem with this interpretation of Scripture is that the fetus is innocent and has no intention to harm. Nonetheless, this single exclusion to the right of induced abortion is supported by most, on the moral ground that the intention to preserve life is good, even if the method used is bad.

Having said this much, it is fair to state that the issue mostly is theoretical and hardly ever presents itself in real-life clinical situations. One could postulate several hypothetical examples — a pregnant woman with chronic kidney disease whose renal function is deteriorating early in the pregnancy; a woman with pelvic cancer, of one sort or another, who requires radical surgery and chemotherapy of the adjacent tissues. These examples and others, are within the realm of possibility, but how often do they occur? I discussed this issue with an Obstetrical colleague and friend who is highly respected in the Washington, D.C. metropolitan area and has been in practice for over 30 years. I asked him how many cases he had personally seen where the life of the mother was threatened necessitating abortion, and what percentage of abortions nationally fell into this category? His reply was brief and to the point: "0 and 0." It is reasonable to say, that while such cases *may* occur, thanks to the advances of modern medicine, they seldom, if ever, *do*.

The issue further is complicated in the matter of "partial-birth abortions." The technique was developed to end complicated, late-term pregnancies in which the mother's health was in jeopardy. Essentially, the procedure is performed in five steps: (1) the obstetrician uses ultrasonography to locate the baby's legs and then grasps one with a metal forceps, (2) the clamped leg is pulled into the birth canal, (3) grasping both legs manually, the baby's body is then forcibly delivered up to the head, (4) an opening is made in the base of the skull and quickly enlarged, and (5) a tube is inserted into the skull opening and suction applied until the entire brain is evacuated. The dead baby, with its collapsed skull, is easily removed.

On November 1, 1995, the House of Representatives voted 288 to 139 to ban this cruel procedure. Abortion rights activists argued that the House legislation was the first assault on the Constitutional right to abortion guaranteed by Roe.v.Wade. Senator Barbara A. Mikulski (D-MD) was quoted by the *Washington Post* on November 8, 1995 as complaining that the bill was a "radical and far-reaching" proposal to erode abortion rights "one step at a time."[98] Pro-life advocates countered that the abortion procedure was particularly cruel and inhumane. Under the provision of the bill, a physician performing the procedure was subject to being fined up to $250,000 or imprisoned for up to two years.

On December 7, 1995, the United States Senate approved similar legislation, voting 54 to 44 to ban late-term abortion. Senator Robert J. Dole (R-KS) and Robert C. Smith (R-NH) added the amendment that the procedure could only be employed to "save a woman's life" if it was threatened by "illness, injury, or physical disorder" and if no other medical procedure was appropriate.[99] The House legislation had permitted no such exemption.

Abortion advocates, in and out of government, focused their opposition to the legislation on the issue of woman's life and health. Privately, they conceded that their primary concern was the guarantee of abortion rights established by Roe.v.Wade. Proponents of the legislation, on the other hand, highlighted the bloody and violent aspects of the procedure, while openly acknowledging that their ultimate goal was a severe limitation, if not a ban, on all abortions.

Helen Dewar, reporting for the *Washington Post*, cited statistics released from the National Abortion Federation, an organization which represents medical personnel and facilities providing abortion services. They estimated that 450 of the 1,500,000 abortions performed annually in the United States (0.03 percent) utilized the late-term procedure.[100] Others insisted that the real incidence was much higher. Indeed, a leading abortion advocate and spokesperson recently admitted in March, 1997, that the actual figures were twice those reported. Officially, the American Medical Association (AMA) throughout the initial phase of the debate chose to remain neutral on the subject, although a medical study committee they appointed endorsed the ban on the procedure. Finally, in early 1997, under the pressure of severe and unrelenting criticism on the part of its physician membership, it backed down and denounced the procedure.

An article written by Jennifer Ferranti, published on December 11, 1995, in *Christianity Today*, quoted Dr. Martin Hasbell of Dayton, Ohio, who acknowledged performing end-term abortions. He stated that "about 80 percent of his cases were 'purely elective.'"[101] Dr. James McMahan (deceased October 28, 1995), a former Los Angeles obstetrician, admitted that, even in those cases where he cited mother's health as the reason for employing the procedure late in pregnancy, his criteria for making that determination were quite liberal. Indeed, "mother's health" often included issues such as depression, maternal youth, poor economic circumstances, and non-fatal deformities such as cleft palate. *Christianity Today* reported that Dr. McMahan performed these abortions up to the 40th week of pregnancy.[102] Babies aborted at this stage obviously feel pain to the same degree as a newborn infant and are fully alive until the last minute of the procedure. In actual fact, virtually none of the abortions citing "mother's health" had anything to do with the health and welfare of the pregnant woman.

I have asked many physicians on both sides of the abortion issue about the necessity of this procedure. All agreed that the method used was never necessary. Prominent physicians around the country concur that there is no medical condition which would ever justify the use of the procedure. In support of this view, the Physicians Ad Hoc Coalition for Truth, a group of over 300 medical specialists, issued a statement in September 1996 in which they categorically declared that "partial birth abortions were never medically necessary to protect mother's health or her future fertility." Former United States Surgeon General, C. Everett Koop, signed his name to the statement. Yet the language of the law has found a phrase that it cannot let go from its lexicon of usage. For example, the United States Senate bill allows for partial birth abortions "in matters of mother's health." President Clinton threatened to veto any legislation banning the procedure, cautioning that the proposed bill "fails to provide for consideration of the need to preserve the life and health of the mother, consistent with the Supreme Court decision in Roe.v.Wade." Senator Arlen Specter (R-PA) unsuccessfully tried to block passage of the Senate bill on the basis of "protecting mother's life and health."[103] A pro-choice obstetrical colleague of mine sarcastically commented that "mother's health" is a political buzzword, not a medical reality. Senator Carol Moseley-Braun (D-IL) had the audacity to suggest that "the government has no right to intervene in the relationship between a woman and her body, her doctor and her God."[104]

True to his word, President Bill Clinton, on April 10, 1996, vetoed bill HR 1833 that proposed a ban on partial-birth abortions. The House of Representatives, in turn, on September 19, 1996, voted on the question of overriding the President's veto. The House vote in favor of overriding the veto was 285-137, three votes more than the two-thirds majority required. However, the U.S. Senate, on September 26, 1996, failed to override the veto; 58 senators supported the ban, while 40 voted to sustain the President's veto, this being eight votes short of the two-thirds majority required to override. While Pro-Life sentiment was high in the U.S. Congress over the issue, an unwavering number of Democrats refused to yield to strong public pressure to ban the procedure, thus upholding the President's consistent support of a woman's right to abortion within the framework of Roe.

You can dress the word up in fancy clothes but partial-birth abortion, alias D and X abortion, alias end-term abortion, still spells murder and brutality. Anyone endorsing the procedure for political purposes should be ashamed. It is a tawdry way to buy votes. Any physician performing the procedure ought to be severely censured. Have we, as a society, forgotten to make a place for shame?

• Rape And Incest

In cases of rape and incest, a reasonable ethical question can be raised in support of induced abortion: "Is there a moral obligation to deliver a child who is conceived without consent, and frequently with violence?" It is of interest that many Christians try to ignore this very pertinent issue. Pro-Choice advocates are insistent that no women should ever be forced to have a baby against her will, regardless of the circumstances. In their view, the indignity and immorality of the rape and/or incest, obviate any rights of the fetus. Many Pro-Life people would agree. Even Norman Geisler, in an earlier edition of his book, *Christian Ethics*, wrote that conception by rape or incest was an evil "that must be nipped in the bud and not allowed to continue."[(105)] That he has completely reversed his position in the latest edition of this book only serves to underscore the difficulty that many Pro-Life Christians experience over this question. Simply put, does the rape of the mother justify the murder of the fetus?

The Old Testament unequivocally states that rape and incest are heinous crimes warranting death (see Deuteronomy 22:25 and Leviticus 20:11). While Jesus never specifically discussed either, he did say that he had come not to abolish the Law, but to fulfill it (Mark 5:17,18). Thus, some ethicists have argued that Christians are bound by the entire Old Testament moral law as it pertains to capital punishment. Since Israel operated under the legal guidelines of a punishment appropriate to the offense, it is telling that execution was commanded for these cases. Whether we agree with this position or not, rape and incest are grotesque evils. Women, often with a visible sense of revulsion, acknowledge how very difficult it would be to carry a baby for 9 months, whose presence daily would remind them of its beginnings. I believe, that except by the Grace of God, it would nearly be impossible.

Admittedly, rape and incest are abhorrent. But, is the fetus conceived by either act itself inherently evil? Doesn't the fetus have a right to be born irrespective of the way it was conceived? Does anyone seriously believe that abortion will erase the memory of the event or forestall future psychological implications? Sexually violated women need our prayers, encouragement, and support. In the spirit of the New Testament (James 2:14-19), this means more than, "I hope things work out for you. Having the baby is the right thing." Financial support, emotional and crisis-related counseling, plans for adoption (should the women choose this alternative), and even food and shelter may be required in getting them through the troubling times of the pregnancy and immediate post-partum period. Profession without practice and words without deeds make for an empty faith. Good intentions need to be turned into practical demonstrations of help. How often have we felt pity or found ourselves moved to tears, and then turned away without doing anything? The Gospel calls us to more. Violated women are our responsibility. If we mean what we say about life, this is one place to prove it.

• A Brave New World

In Vitro Fertilization (IVF)
IVF techniques have made it possible for couples, who otherwise have been unable to conceive, to have children. The babies born as a result of this methodology have been referred to as "test tube babies." The procedure is relatively simple: sperm and ovum are united in a laboratory Petri dish and the resultant fertilized egg (zygote) is implanted in the woman's uterus. The technology has brought hope to childless couples frustrated after years of

unsuccessfully trying to have children. However, IVF does raise some ethical problems. First, several fertilized embryos need to be implanted in the uterus in order to increase the chances of success. Many never do implant, thereby causing fetal wastage and death. Although the intention to conceive is a good and understandable one, the means used are morally objectionable. The inevitable deaths of living zygotes do not justify the 1 or 2 that successfully implant and survive.

An additional, more serious ethical problem may arise. Not infrequently, as many as 3-4 fertilized eggs or more implant, resulting in multiple, living fetuses capable of intrauterine development and subsequent birth. A procedure recently perfected in a New York City Medical Center has made it possible for couples to decide how many babies they want. The technique euphemistically is called "selective reduction of pregnancy." The name defines it. In essence, living fetuses are selectively removed to reduce the number of babies born. The surgical extirpation of unwanted babies in a multiple pregnancy has other applications. As an alternative to IVF, some hormones are known to stimulate multiple egg release from the ovary. After vaginal intercourse, several eggs may be fertilized and implant. Selective reduction of pregnancy can also be used in these cases to eliminate the number of unwanted potential children.

Proponents of IVF point out that natural embryo wastage occurs frequently and that no attempt is ever made to salvage those doomed to death. Obviously, natural wastage and the deaths resulting from IVF are not the same. The latter technique, in its present state of usage, not only anticipates multiple zygote deaths in order to achieve a successful pregnancy, it artificially plans for it. Natural loss is part of the biological process; deliberately sacrificing fertilized embryos is not and is morally indefensible. IVF is morally and ethically wrong in the same way that abortion is wrong. Here, good intentions are not enough.

Prenatal Diagnosis

As previously discussed, advances in medical technology have opened new vistas for obstetricians, perinatologists, and fetologists. Medical science has advanced to the point where many fetal diseases and/or deformities can be diagnosed before birth. This fact has been both a blessing and a curse to society. Often, it is not what the doctor knows, but how wisely he uses his knowledge. William Osler, the late brilliant Professor of Medicine at The Johns Hopkins University Hospital, had written, "It is a common error to think that the more a doctor sees the greater his experience and the more he knows."[106] The scientific progress in prenatal diagnosis has the potential for either great harm or great good. Like so many things, it all depends on how it is used.

A good application of science is the in-utero diagnosis and treatment of fetal Rh incompatibility disease. Samples of amniotic fluid serially can be sampled for worsening hemolysis of the baby's red blood cells. The presence of severe hemolysis before 34 weeks gestation is associated with a significant possibility of fetal death. The technique of intra-uterine blood transfusion has permitted survival of some of these babies. I recall how excited I was when the procedure was perfected in the latter part of the 1960s. At that time, I was doing virology research at the National Institutes of Health in Bethesda, Maryland. First, I felt a sense of wonder and elation; next, I remember thinking, "I wish that had been discovered when I was a pediatric Resident (in training)." Sadly, I recalled a severe case of profound hemolysis and death inutero. The memory of the decompensated and wasted fetus (hydrops fetalis) remains with me. Science has the capability for great good.

On the other hand, some have used these advances to justify killing sick or imperfect babies. Genetic syndromes are a case in point. As previously noted, amniotic fluid can be sampled and fetal cells studied for chromosome identification. Many genetic disorders can be diagnosed in-utero. The ability to make fetal diagnoses has also opened the door to aborting deformed, mentally defective, and physically compromised babies on the grounds that their lives would be impaired. Of course, many "impaired" people live useful, if not relatively normal lives, and few would consider them less than human. Most would certainly defend their right to life. Often, it is fear of the unknown that prompts some to want to abort a less than "perfect" fetus. Obviously, what is wrong in this type of thinking is that quality of life rather than sanctity of life is celebrated and valued. It debases all human life and judges its worth by the measures of function and utility. We are more important than either.

Another problem is the inescapable fact that prenatal diagnoses may be wrong. Two personal examples from my pediatric practice serve to illustrate this point:

> Denise, a 32-year-old woman with 3 children (Laura, Stephen, and Stephanie) ranging in age from 2 - 7 years became pregnant for the fourth time. Her previous pregnancies were completely uneventful, and her 3 children were healthy, active, and bright. She and her husband were healthy and well.
>
> Her pregnancy was proceeding normally until the sixth month when a "routine sonogram" was interpreted by her doctor as "compatible with dwarfism." She was sent to a metropolitan university medical center where she was examined and a repeat sonogram was ordered. The sonogram reconfirmed findings of limb shortening suggestive of dwarfism. Additionally, a cardiac defect was diagnosed. Denise was told that abortion was an option she should consider.
>
> She and her husband, Mark, both professed Christians, decided this was not an option and elected to have the baby. They and many people, including myself, began to pray for the baby. A baby boy was born at term after a spontaneous labor and a remarkably easy delivery. The child was completely normal, without evidence of dwarfism or heart abnormality. His birth weight was 8

pounds, length, 21 inches, and the Apgar score 9/10. The parents named him John.

Presently, at age 1 year, John is growing, gaining, and developing very well, without any evidence of defect or disease. A miracle or a mistake? Who cares. God was honored, the baby wanted, and the parents blessed. No one has blamed the doctors, but all who know the family have praised the Lord.

• • • • •

The second example concerns a 27-year-old woman named Laura, with a history of excellent health, who became pregnant for the first time. Her husband Bill was 29 years old and also in good health. Laura's first trimester was unremarkable except for mild, early morning nausea and her first three prenatal visits were uneventful.

At the 4th month of gestation, a sample of amniotic fluid was tested for α fetoprotein (AFP), which was reported as "high." Elevated AFP levels may be indicative of central nervous system defects. A repeat amniocentesis yielded the same results. A sonogram was "suggestive of a brain defect." The option of abortion was raised, but Laura and Bill rejected it on the basis of personal religious conviction. A baby girl was born on time — healthy, robust, and perfectly normal. Her parents named her Mary Elizabeth.

I have not presented these stories to embarrass the medical profession or to minimize the skills or sophistication of the doctors in my geographical area. To the contrary, I am frequently amazed at their accuracy of diagnosis. These 2 cases represent only 2 among many in which I personally have been involved. Very often, the prenatal diagnosis is correct. But occasionally, as described, it is wrong. Given the fact that human life is at stake, we, as physicians, should not wager so lightly with death.

The Human Genome Project

The Human Genome Project is an effort, undertaken by the National Center for Human Genome Research at the National Institutes of Health in Bethesda, Maryland, to locate the approximately 100,000 genes on the 23 pairs of chromosomes in each cell. To date, between 4,000-5,000 gene sites have been identified. The stated goal of the project is to locate each gene site by the year 2005 in spite of the fact that the entire gene script is believed to contain three billion bits of information.

Genes represent the code of life. They orchestrate our size, appearance, color, talents, intelligence, and even what diseases we may eventually get. As I am writing this, it has just been reported that doctors on the Human Genome

Project have isolated a cancer-related gene that is relatively common in the population and thought to be responsible for many different cancers, including those of the breast, stomach, lung, skin, and pancreas. [107]

Each of the several trillion cells in the human body (except red blood cells) contain the entire human genome. This information is encoded in each cell and packaged into 23 pairs of chromosomes. Each of the 46 human chromosomes contains the basic information which defines each human person.

Nearly 4000 genetic diseases which afflict humans have been identified. Scientists on the Human Genome Project are trying to learn more about each one of them, specifically which defective gene causes the disease and what protein is normally produced by each specific gene. Once this information is determined, the next step will involve attempting to fix or replace the gene or protein that has been abnormally altered. [108]

Thus, 2 independent lines of research may simultaneously be undertaken: (1) doctors may try to replace a missing or ineffective protein with the normal protein or supply what's lacking with a drug, and (2) gene therapy, the process by which normal genes replace defective ones. The potential implications are startling: to replace the defective gene in patients with Cystic Fibrosis, thus healing the lungs and gastrointestinal tract and removing the sentence of death that hangs over them; identifying the patient who carries the gene for hereditary colon cancer and beginning yearly surveillance for signs of malignancy, as well as initiating appropriate diet measures in the hope of preventing the disease; targeting the woman at high risk for breast cancer who carries the abnormal gene and stepping up regular monitoring to detect the earliest signs of a tumor — again, working towards the day when the defective gene could be replaced and all breast cancer eliminated from the population.

But potential pitfalls line the path of discovery. Social and ethical issues loom on the horizon. Before gene therapy is perfected, will the in-utero identification of a defective gene prompt the recommendation of abortion? Will some be tempted to tamper with each budding life, producing or eliminating genes according to their whim or prejudice? Will identifying prospective lethal genes trigger severe psychological distress, even suicide, in those not able to cope with the information about future risk? And who will benefit from all this science? Knowing how to effect a cure and implementing one are almost unrelated issues. How will testing, treatment, and counseling logistically be delivered to a world eager to share the benefits of each discovery? These are life issues that, one day, we will have to address. Both the public and the medical profession need to be prepared for them.

The Rest Of The Story

Roe v. Wade was a bad decision. Legal scholars still debate its constitutional merits, and many declare it legally problematic. [109] It is also fair to question whether any law can stand which fails to have the support of a majority of the people. Roe.v.Wade does not. It has divided, not united our country. Moreover, most of the public doesn't understand the applicability of the constitutional right to privacy and the woman's right to abortion. If, for no other reason than a legal one, Roe.v.Wade was a serious mistake that has adversely impacted our society and promises further mischief in the future.

But the extent of the problem is more than a legal one. As Elizabeth Mensch and Alan Freeman, both law professors, have pointed out, the decision was also a mistake because it was "sociologically inaccurate, and politically disastrous."[(110)] Since 1973, America has been a land divided. First, a storm of religious opposition was unleashed, which surprised most observers and even the Court by its intensity. The Christian community upheld the Biblical standard of the sanctity of life and left the Court to explain arguments of viability and privacy. In addition, the emerging debate exposed the moral divisions in our country. It became all too apparent that a secular humanism, that was atheistic at its core, was competing with the Judeo-Christian beliefs that had undergirded Western Civilization for 2000 years. The new secular morality of America was centered on self-rights and self-autonomy and rooted in a sense of self-sufficiency. The basic belief in the sovereignty of God slowly eroded, and people talked of new freedoms — sexual and reproductive, to name but two. Freedom, however, is either a blessing or a curse, depending on how it is used. When it conflicts with God's Word and with the rights of other individuals, it leads to moral laxity and social anarchy. Real freedom respects the freedom of others because it is birthed in justice, order, and the constraints imposed by living with others. Freedom, at the expense of others, represents license, which, in reality, is a form of bondage.

The abortion debate also polarized other segments of society. The feminist movement adopted Roe.v.Wade as their standard and demanded complete autonomy, asserting the rights of women over those of the fetus. As more militant, strident voices were heard over time, the more radical elements of the movement marginalized feminism. Interestingly, the American Medical Association, having adopted a Pro-Choice position under the cloak of self-proclaimed neutrality, found itself strangely aligned with disparate organizations such as the American Civil Liberties Union (ACLU), National Organization of Women (NOW), and Planned Parenthood of America. Politics make strange bedfellows.

Pro-Choice advocates unfairly stigmatized the Pro-Life position as extremist and trivialized the belief in the sanctity of life. While the Christian churches were initially divided over the abortion issue, in time alliances were forged between theologically and doctrinally distinct communions. Conservative Protestant evangelicals, charismatics of varying backgrounds, Pentecostals, and independent Christian churches joined forces with Roman Catholics in opposing what they perceived to be the evil of abortion. The fetus, the only one whose freedom was ever really at stake, finally had a strong and committed champion. Roe v. Wade indeed roused a "sleeping giant." While, formerly, we were shamefully divided, the abortion issue served as a catalyst of Christian unity. Here the words of Scripture were exposed to view: "And we know that in all things God works for the good of those who love Him, who have called according to his purpose" (Romans 8:28). God always manages to bring some good, even out of the worst of circumstances.

Roe v. Wade also was a disaster for American politics. The decision unleashed a flood of legislation by Pro-Life advocates in an attempt to erode the availability of abortion. In fact, the New York Times recently reported that a dozen abortion-related bills were submitted to Congress in 1995 alone.[111] Christian congressmen, in an attempt to curtail abortion rights, wrote legislative bills to repeal or modify abortion counseling to low-income women and adolescents; to curtail funding to obstetrical programs in U.S. medical schools providing training in abortion procedures; to cancel support for family planning programs that perform abortions with private money; to limit Federal Medicaid money for abortion; and to dismantle a variety of other programs which support abortion with government aid. Supporters of these legislative efforts conceded that their first goal was to "roll back" the gains abortion advocates realized during the Clinton administration. Detractors complained that the abortion debate was compromising other important societal issues. The extent of the political polarization was highlighted when President Clinton failed to move the U.S. Senate to vote on his nominee for the post of Surgeon General. Dr. Henry Foster's nomination never came to a vote because it was disclosed that he had performed many more abortions than previously acknowledged. He, thus, became another casualty of Roe.v.Wade.

Legislative efforts on other fronts proved successful for the Pro-Life movement. By 1995, 13 states had informed consent statutes that provide women considering abortion the right to be informed about the potential risks of the procedure.[112] Additionally, physicians were mandated by law to discuss alternatives to abortion and to educate women about the stage of fetal development of the baby inutero. Fourteen states also required by law that women be given a specified waiting period before the abortion procedure, during which information about the procedure, its risks and alternatives, be provided. The U.S. Supreme Court subsequently upheld the constitutionality of this legislation (Planned Parenthood v. Casey, 1992). During the years in which a Minnesota parental notification law was in effect (1981-1986), the teen abortion, pregnancy, and birth rate all dropped.[113] Emboldened by these statistics, the National Right to Life Committee promoted state by state legislative efforts in this area. The cost of time, effort, and money by sincere and dedicated people on both sides of the issue was staggering. As a result of all these legislative efforts directed towards abortion, truly ethical feminist concerns, such as job equality, family leave, health care, and day-care benefits (or allowances) have not received the attention they deserve.

Having said as much, it is reasonable to ponder whether the debate will ever end? In a book entitled The Politics of Virtue: Is Abortion Debatable? Elizabeth Mensch and Alan Freeman pose the question: "Is compromise possible?" They cautiously answer in the affirmative and propose possible ways in which the issue might be resolved.[114] D.J. Leyshon, in his scholarly legal review of abortion, outlines a hypothetical ideal Abortion Bill of Rights for his own country, South Africa. In it, he regards abortion permissible only in cases of where the mother's health is endangered (physically or mentally) and where serious risk exists that the baby, if born, "will suffer from grave and irreparable physical or mental defect." Abortions he categorizes as impermissible include: rape and/or incest, physical and mental handicaps not judged to be grave, unmarried and severely mentally retarded woman, and abortion on demand for specious reasons.[115] If his formulation were to be applied in this country, over 95% of currently aborted fetuses would be spared (approximately 1,425,000 babies per year). What Pro-life advocate would not leap at the chance to save so many, even if the legislation was less than perfect? Leyshon concludes by stating that peace ultimately will have to be made and that compromise needs to be reached by all parties in the debate. Christians will have to determine at what price "peace" is to be achieved and whether it is worth it.

While it is true that in political compromise, both sides must give up something important, compromise does not seem to me to be the way to approach this problem. Clearly, all choices do not have the same moral weight, but the moral standards of God can never be compromised, no more than we can compromise the Ten Commandments by deleting some of them. No matter how much one might desire it, "Thou shalt not kill" will always be an inviolable Commandment of God.

Constitutional law and Biblical morality are not the same thing. Constitutional law may be based on or influenced by Biblical teachings, but in any pluralistic society embracing democracy, the two will never be equal. Christians must never compromise moral principles, but they can work within their society to achieve the best laws they can get at any moment. In addition, the Christian churches and the Pro-Life movement need to expand their horizons: First, we must accept responsibility for every born child, while we continue to uphold unborn life. There are many practical ways in which this goal can be implemented. Pregnancy aid centers need to be financially supported to an even greater degree. In addition, financial support, including housing subsidies, should be extended to the woman in crisis. Additional support for the care of the newborn, including formula, clothing, and baby furniture, is a positive alternative to simply protesting the evils of abortion. Our voice need not be quieted while we work to alleviate the real needs of the mother and her baby. Christians also ought to work more diligently in the political and social arena to encourage adoption, rather than abortion. Indeed, President and Mrs. Clinton endorsed this approach, and received little response from the Pro-Life movement. Here is another potential way that Pro-Life and Pro-Choice advocates could unite in offering a positive alternative to abortion; second, we must see abortion as failure and loss, maintaining the high moral ground and reaffirming the sanctity of every life; and third, we need to be sensitive and responsive to a whole range of women's concerns, not only in Pro-Life issues, but also in the larger matters of rights and privileges within our society. Every American ought to be concerned about men who biologically father children, and then distance themselves from their care. Child support obligations are a first, but necessary, step in promoting responsibility in absent fathers. Furthermore, families and communities ought to see every newborn child as a gift and not a burden. In this regard, all of us ought to endorse generous family leave, flexible work schedules, and day-care allowances for those women who will re-enter the workplace. In a larger sense, this is what it ought to mean to be Pro-Life. Finally, we ought to be candid in acknowledging that some abortion issues are hard ones and do not lend themselves to simplistic responses.

At the same time, we need to be very aware of the antipathy that many segments of our society hold towards Christianity. Jesus, after all, did warn us to be "as shrewd as snakes and as innocent as doves" (Matthew 10:16). We are often reminded by Pro-Choice advocates of the Constitution's safeguard in the provision (Article I, Bill of Rights) separating the powers and authority of Church and State. The reminder is appropriate, but hardly necessary. Christians wholeheartedly support the concept of the separation of Church and State because it is a wise and prudent law protecting every citizen. Indeed, the doctrine is rooted in Reformation theology and we understand it to mean that the state cannot coerce anyone to adopt a particular religion, nor can it forbid the free expression of religion among its citizens. The First Amendment was intended to preserve religious freedom, insure the free exercise of it, and promote peace in a religiously pluralistic society. Unfortunately, its common application in our time has been to discourage any inclination towards religion and to prevent its public display. Many in the political and social arenas of our society are particularly hostile to Christianity, disparaging our beliefs and seeking to marginalize us by the use of innuendo and pejorative labels. Thus, every Christian with strong convictions founded on the authority of Scripture derisively is called a right-wing fundamentalist. For years, the Pro-Life movement contemptuously was referred to as a "Catholic thing." Today, as more and more Christians of every doctrinal and denominational stripe join forces in promoting the rights of the unborn, it is becoming difficult for the media to find a label broad enough to cover the movement. Nonetheless, we need to demonstrate our willingness to work within our society for the common good and to do it in a way that brings Grace to the debate. Clearly, only God can resolve this volatile issue and calm angry hearts.

After the victory at Gettysburg, President Lincoln said to one of his generals: "The fact is, General, in the stress and pinch of the campaign there, I went to my room and got down on my knees and prayed to God Almighty for victory at Gettysburg. I told Him that this was His country, and the war was His war, but that we really couldn't stand another Fredericksburg or Chancellorsville. And then and there I made a solemn vow with my Maker that if He would stand by you boys at Gettysburg I would stand by Him. And He did, and I will! And after this I felt that God Almighty had taken the whole thing into His hands."[116] In the final analysis, we do all that we can and then commit "the whole thing into His hands" — a good strategy for anytime.

Euthanasia: The Debate Intensifies

If you're going to care about the fall of a sparrow you can't pick and choose who's going to be a sparrow.

Madeleine L' Engle

INTRODUCTION

Euthanasia is the illegitimate sibling of abortion. The euthanasia movement has intensified in the past few years, perhaps because of advances in medical technology which prolong human life, even to a point beyond value and usefulness. Others would look, with horror, at patients in persistent vegetative states — prolonged comas — kept alive indefinitely. More than a few express fear at experiencing unbearable suffering or even at losing dignity in the death process. All of these concerns are reasonable and need to be honestly addressed. However, these issues are the product, not the cause, for the renewed enthusiasm in euthanasia.

Roe v. Wade was the watershed event that triggered the euthanasia movement. The slippery slope from abortion to euthanasia, correctly predicted by many, is not a cute catch phrase dreamed up by Pro-Life advocates; it is a sad reality of discernible fact. Roe v. Wade greased the slippery slope and abortion rights led inexorably to the demand for suicide rights. When the U.S. Supreme Court decided that the "right to privacy" entitled pregnant women to keep or abort their babies, the current euthanasia movement was born.

In 1993, Derek Humphrey, author and euthanasia activist, wrote a bestseller book entitled *Final Exit*, in which he outlined methods of suicide, in detail.[1] When recently asked why the movement had become such a hot issue, he replied that Roe v. Wade was the critical turning point. Thus, it is very

77

clear that abortion rights have had predictable and malicious consequences. If we study the language of abortion and euthanasia, we find startling similarities: a "right" to kill and a "right" to die, constitutional right to privacy, self-autonomy, and personal choice; the language is all self-directed. It is the language of I, me, and mine—a kingdom of self, not the kingdom of God. We are reminded of Ivan's statement in Dostoevsky's *The Brother Karamazov* that, in a world without God, "Everything is permitted."[2] The world of euthanasia, as much as that of abortion, is such a world.

HISTORICAL PERSPECTIVE

Some Ancient Antecedents

The etymology of euthanasia is derived from two Greek words: the prefix *eu* meaning "good", and *thantos*, "death." Thus, euthanasia literally means "good death". In the *American Heritage Dictionary*, *euthanasia* is defined as "the action of killing an individual for reasons considered to be merciful."[3]

Euthanasia, like abortion, has an old history, which is briefly worth noting. Historically, in the period spanning the late middle ages through the eighteenth-century, euthanasia was rarely practiced on the infirm and suffering old. In fact, in the ancient world and even as late as Renaissance Europe, the human life span was short, frequently ravaged by untreatable diseases and widespread plagues. It is, therefore, not surprising that the ancient Hippocratic medical code, which survived intact for over two thousand years with the help of the Christian Church, promised to sustain life—even in the midst of pain and suffering—not to end it. When physicians recite the Hippocratic oath they promise the following: "I will neither give a deadly drug to anybody if asked for it, nor will I make a suggestion to this effect."[4] And, more positively, it adds, "I will apply dietetic measures for the benefit of the sick according to my ability and judgment; I will keep them from harm and injustice." Euthanasia was not a common practice in the moral universe of Hippocrates and his latter-day followers.

But it should be noted that other attacks on life did exist in the ancient world, particularly in the interests of maintaining male lineage and, occasionally, population control. Up through the 3rd century A.D., the Greek and Romans practiced exposure of newborn babies, females more than males. Some exposed babies were claimed by others and raised to be slaves. The Greek proper name, *Kopreus*, "off the dung heap," adequately describes this early method of infanticide. Infanticide was, in fact, one of three methods of population control, including abortion, pre-coital contraception, and exposure.[5]

In the ancient world, euthanasia, as we now know it, was infrequently practiced on old people. But some ancient ethical codes, contrary to Hippocratic ethics, allowed for suicide in cases of undue suffering. Roman Stoicism, in particular, allowed those who could not suffer with dignity an "honorable" escape from life. Marcus Aurelius' *Meditations* and Cicero's ethical writings offered a philosophically-grounded defense of suicide, though such suicide was presented by them as self-afflicted, not socially or scientifically sanctioned by the ancient governments or medical communities.

Until the twentieth-century, the historic Christian church adopted the Hippocratic position on moral issues of life and death. For the church fathers, as for Hippocrates, life, even a life of pain and suffering, is valuable and worth preserving. The Christian church, not surprisingly, Christianized Hippocratic thinking, making it the mainstay of ethical teachings of life, much as Aristotle was Christianized in the history of the Church's early systematic theology. The effect of this Christianized Hippocratic tradition would be to preserve the true dignity of life for centuries in the Christian Church, until the advent of modern science and other forces that would challenge this ancient ethical tradition.

First Glimmers of Early Modern Science's Challenge to Life

Modern science has dramatically extended the human life span and, with it, the expectation for a life without suffering. The average life expectancy in the early modern scientific era (1550-1700), the age of Bacon, Newton and Boyle, was short by contemporary standards. At that time, approximately 10 percent of individuals reached the age of 50, as compared to our own average life span of 78 years. But with the progressive advancement of science and its concomitant extension of the human life span came the disabling health problems of old age and the temptation of euthanasia. Science, and its sister art, philosophy, now concerned themselves not only with prolonging life, but equally with ending it when suffering and "human dignity" were perceived to be at stake.

An example taken from an early modern British scientist and philosopher shows some of the groundwork that was laid for our modern problem of euthanasia. Francis Bacon, a literary humanist and scientist, as well as a self-avowed Christian, said the following about euthanasia in "The History of Life and Death": "In our times, the physicians make a kind of scruple and religion to stay with the patient after he is given up; whereas in my judgement, if they would not be wanting in their office, and indeed to humanity, they ought both to acquire the skill and to bestow the attention whereby the dying may pass more easily and quietly out of life."[6] Bacon's justification of euthanasia is perhaps part of his larger vision of the civilizing role of science in the advancement of learning. Bacon's proposal, however, was not taken seriously by seventeenth-century England; its significant reception would await the late-nineteenth and twentieth centuries.

Early Interest In Britain And The United States

In the late 19th century, a serious interest in euthanasia was beginning in England and the United States. It was a time of intellectual excitement, fueled by the fires of Darwinism, industrial modernization, and colonial expansion. Euthanasia emerged as a topic of debate as doctors, lawyers and social scientists explored the moral possibility of ending life when disease was incurable and painfully agonizing. Most physicians and medical journals adamantly opposed the idea.[7]

In 1870, Samuel D. Williams, a layperson from Birmingham, England, electrified the medical societies on both sides of the Atlantic when he gave a speech to a local philosophical society advocating the use of chloroform to end the lives of those with incurable disease suffering with intractable pain.[8] Williams' idea appealed to those intellectually inclined to accommodate the views of Darwin to all areas of study, both scientific and social. Indeed, Williams' proposal continued to stimulate discussion on euthanasia for a period of over 30 years as English intellectuals debated whether doctors had a moral right to end suffering life.

Harvard professor Charles Eliot Norton, a prominent American physician, read copies of Williams' speech and began, in 1905, to promote euthanasia in his own lectures. From 1895 to World War I, the atmosphere in the United States was charged, and talk of reform was everywhere present. Norton, a dignified and distinguished physician, albeit something of a free-thinker, found the concept of "mercy killing" fascinating. Underlying his interest was a strong moral conviction that the hopelessly suffering needed a champion, someone to promote their best interest, much as social scientists voiced strong concern for the poor and underprivileged.

Norton's stance, in turn, encouraged Ann Hill, a wealthy Ohio matron, whose mother was suffering from terminal cancer, to campaign for the legalization of euthanasia in her own home state. In 1906, a bill permitting euthanasia in patients when the disease was incurable and painfully intolerable was introduced and defeated by the Ohio state legislature. Ms. Hill's goal was thwarted, but the idea of mercy killing, once only whispered about, was in the open forum of serious discussion, had been exposed to public view and debate, and had even been endorsed by some medical journals.[9] Serious consideration and interest in the topic would subsequently wane for over three decades, only to resurface with increased vigor after World War II.

In Germany

For the next 30 years, the debates on euthanasia diminished in the United States and Britain. But storm clouds were gathering over Germany prefiguring an experiment in euthanasia that would begin in 1900 and culminate in the systematic murder of over 200,000 mentally ill or physically disabled people in a six year period between 1939-1945. These poor souls the Nazis callously labeled "life unworthy of life."

The story of Nazi "euthanasia" is particularly difficult for me to address because it raises the awful question of why the world's pre-eminent medical establishment of that time would collaborate with the Nazi architects of murder in gassing, shooting, poisoning, or starving to death 200,000 men, women, and children patients. The "how" is a grim mechanical story; the "why" exposes the dark and awful capacity human beings have within them for great cruelty. It is an ugly story that becomes even more unsettling when, as historians have documented, its beginnings can be traced to government cost-cutting concerns in a time of economic instability during the Weimar Republic.[10] In this time, during and after the First World War, psychiatrists began to experiment with chronic patients confined to mental asylums. During this dark period, a concept emerged that argued the weak, helplessly ill, and handicapped ought to die for the greater good of the nation. By 1935, strict economic analyses calculated to the reichsmark the annual cost savings to the nation by eliminating the 300,000 mental patients, epileptics, and chronically ill inmates in Germany's asylums. Despite Nazi efficiency, "only " 67 percent of that number were exterminated by the end of the Second World War.[11]

It will remain for historians to link the euthanasia program among German patients with the planned mass extermination of 6,000,000 Jews (out of the 9,600,000 who formerly lived in the countries that had come under Nazi domination), in addition to the over 10,000,000 Gypsies, Catholic priests, clergy and members of monastic orders, as well as German dissidents who died in Hitler's so-called final solution.[12] Many of the techniques learned in the euthanasia program conducted in Germany's asylums were, in fact, applied in the death camps at Belzec, Treblinka, and others. Gas chambers disguised as shower rooms were first used in German hospitals, and SS Dr. Fritz Mengele, in the name of medical research, performed barbaric and unspeakable operations on unfortunate, innocent concentration camp victims.[13] Ironically, all this inhumanity began with Germany's preoccupation with the economic burden of caring for chronically ill patients. The irony hits home when we consider that our own concern with euthanasia partly stems from the desire to get rid of the undesirable, particularly those who are costly and a burden to society. We should heed the words of Robert Proctor, holocaust scholar, who reminds us, "atrocity begins at home."[14]

In The Netherlands

The Netherlands is a thorn in the side of all Pro-Life advocates. It remains the only developed, modern country where euthanasia has been practiced in the breach, although it is technically illegal.

The story begins in the early 1970s with an elderly woman, paralyzed and incapacitated by a brain hemorrhage. Deaf and mute, she was living in a nursing home waiting to die. Her daughter, Geertruida Postma, a physician, intentionally administered a lethal dose of morphine after her mother repeatedly begged her to end her life. The woman died, and Dr. Postma was convicted of murder, since euthanasia was (and is) illegal in the Netherlands. The jury found the doctor guilty, but gave her a suspended sentence of one week in jail and one year of probation.[15]

The case had far-reaching implications in the country and for the euthanasia movement worldwide. During the ensuing decade, the Dutch high courts delivered a number of decisions regarding the legal permissibility of euthanasia and in 1984, the Royal Dutch Medical Association endorsed the court's decisions. As a result, physicians, for the first time, had the freedom to terminate life, without fear of prosecution, provided three conditions were met:

1. The patient requesting euthanasia was a competent adult, who repeatedly, over time, made clear his or her request to die.

2. The patient was in a state of "unbearable" pain or suffering, without hope of improvement.

3. Only a physician was permitted to terminate the life of the patient, and then, only after consultation with an independent second doctor who corroborated that the first two requirements successfully were satisfied.[16]

In 1993, the Netherlands established a law granting physicians immunity from prosecution providing they complied with the three conditions previously established by the Court. The law does not legalize euthanasia, but allows for it in the extreme cases described. Technically, doctors, who do not satisfy the requirements of the law, can be charged with homicide and prosecuted.[17]

Meaningful data on the Dutch experiment in "mercy killing" has been scant. In a Dutch health policy statement issued in 1992, following a scientific commission's study on the topic, it was estimated that 9,000 requests for euthanasia were submitted annually, with 3,000 being granted.[18] Further, the study determined that 1,000 cases of nonvoluntary (patient unrequested) euthanasia were performed annually (approximately one percent of all yearly deaths). Overall, approximately two percent of all deaths were by euthanasia, 0.3 percent by physician-assisted suicide and slightly less than 18 percent by passive euthanasia (withholding or removing medical treatment, allowing a patient to die). The majority of active euthanasia deaths were in terminal cancer patients.

According to the report, loss of dignity (57 percent) and pain (46 percent) were the primary reasons for death requests. Most importantly, and disturbing, was the finding that 54 percent of Dutch physicians had participated in euthanasia and that less than 20 percent of cases were reported to the proper governing authorities. Equally disturbing is the fact that only 25 percent of interviewed doctors believed that reporting requirements were necessary.[19] Consequently, many critics believe that there is serious underreporting of euthanasia in the Netherlands. This opinion is given credence in view of the fact that the study investigators determined that in 75 percent of cases, physicians completed the death certificate by listing "natural causes" as the reason for deaths proven to be actively terminated. Thus, there are concerns that closer to 10,000 euthanasia deaths may be performed annually in the Netherlands. While there is no definitive proof to support this contention, Ezekiel Emanuel, an American physician and medical ethicist, points out that in more than 40 percent of euthanasia deaths, drugs were used to shorten the patient's life in the absence of established court criteria. Moreover, in most cases, the dying patient was not even competent to give permission.[20] More disturbing is the fact that euthanasia was, not infrequently, offered to minors.[21] Daniel Callahan, a highly respected medical ethicist, has alluded to the potential for great mischief in the present Dutch policy. He writes: "The evidence suggests, that at best, the present practice in the Netherlands has laid the groundwork for a severe slippery slope. At worst — which I am convinced is already the case — the slide down that slope has begun."[22]

The more troubling aspects of the Dutch problem are patently obvious. Should anyone be surprised that the euthanasia program is out of control in the Netherlands? It was foolish to believe that it could ever be controlled or managed. Initial physician trepidation obviously gave way to easy familiarity and the less morally scrupulous became unrestrained in their judgments. The majority of Dutch physicians have once or currently still do participate in euthanasia. Most of those who do, lie about it and falsify death reports. Indeed, 75 percent of physicians in that country want to eliminate all reporting requirements. Many doctors are making independent decisions on patients who have neither requested nor given their consent to be killed. Thus, physicians in the Netherlands now find themselves juggling the dual roles of healer and killer; quite a departure from the Hippocratic dictum: "I will keep them [the sick] from harm and injustice."

The Recent Growth of Euthanasia in the U.S.

After World War II, the discovery of Hitler's death camps and the exposure of Dr. Mengele's surgical experiments on camp victims quieted euthanasia advocates all over the world. It would remain quiet until the 1970s and Dr. Postma's conviction by a Dutch court of murdering her ailing mother with a lethal injection of morphine.

It's not enough to recognize that euthanasia has had a resurgence in the last quarter century of U.S. history. We must also understand its various faces. This requires a definition of types. Basically, there are two kinds of euthanasia: active and passive.

> Active euthanasia refers to the act of intentionally taking a life, by whatever medical means, to prevent suffering.

> Passive euthanasia refers to withholding or withdrawing medical treatment in order to allow a person to die, thereby avoiding further suffering.

Active euthanasia can either be voluntary, involuntary, or nonvoluntary. What distinguishes *voluntary active euthanasia* from *physician-assisted suicide* is the person who directly causes the death. In the former case, a physician, or someone other than the patient, intentionally administers medicine or some other medical intervention at the patient's request and consent, in order to cause death. In the latter, a physician provides medicine or some chemical substance to a patient who intends to use them to commit suicide. *Involuntary active euthanasia* refers to the act of causing a patient's death when they are conscious and able to make a competent decision, but have not given their request or consent. *Nonvoluntary active euthanasia* is the act of causing someone's death who is incapable of requesting it (mentally incompetent, comatose, etc.). In both involuntary and nonvoluntary active euthanasia, the patients do not give their consent to the taking of their life.

Passive euthanasia, allowing patients to die by withholding or withdrawing treatment, can be distinguished from *indirect euthanasia* in that the latter administers narcotics or other drugs to the patient with the intention of relieving pain and suffering, only incidentally and indirectly causing death through respiratory depression. Both may be ethical and legal.

Definitions of the various kinds of euthanasia are distinguished by the intention of the physician and the consent of the patient. Active euthanasia and physician-assisted suicide purposely terminate the life of the patient and are illegal. Thus, they clearly are different from withholding life-sustaining treatment (passive euthanasia) or from administering a narcotic to relieve pain, such as morphine, that indirectly hastens death (indirect euthanasia).

In 1976, the parents of a New Jersey girl named Karen Ann Quinlan got approval from the State Supreme Court to disconnect their daughter's respirator. Quinlan had injured herself by mixing tranquilizers and alcohol and was in a prolonged coma. She was placed on a respirator when her doctors advised the parents that without assisted ventilation she would die. The parents were counseled by their parish priest that the use of a respirator represented "extraordinary measures" and that, morally, they were not obligated to use such methods to prolong life. Accordingly, they instructed the physicians caring for their daughter to turn off the machine. When the doctors refused, the case went to court, with the Quinlans pleading that passively allowing their daughter to die was morally defensible and in her best interests.

At the first trial, the judge ruled against the Quinlans. On appeal, the New Jersey Supreme Court held that there was a *constitutional right to privacy* (emphasis mine) which permitted the family of dying, incompetent patients to discontinue "artificial life support systems." Here, for the first time, the legal distinction between "ordinary" and "extraordinary" means of life support was invoked. Karen Quinlan's respirator was removed because of the Court assumption that it alone sustained her in her persistent coma; however, she survived nine additional years in coma after the respirator was disconnected.[23]

In 1989, Janet Adkins, a 54-year-old Oregon woman, developed Alzheimer's disease. After an experimental treatment for the disease failed, she contacted

Dr. Jack Kevorkian, a retired Michigan pathologist, who had developed a suicide machine. Since Michigan, at that time, had no law against medically assisted death, Mrs. Adkins traveled there to meet him. She would become the first of Kevorkian's assisted suicides.[24] By 1992, the Michigan legislature would pass a law making medically assisted euthanasia a criminal offense. One year later, Kevorkian announced that he had assisted a Michigan man, Thomas Hyde, in dying. The doctor promptly was charged with violating the new law and prosecuted. In 1994, the case went to trial in Oakland County, Michigan, the jurisdictional site of the offense. Kevorkian admitted to the charges of supplying the means for Hyde ending his life, but said he did so to end his suffering, rather than to cause his death. He was acquitted.[25] Kevorkian has since earned the sobriquet, "Dr. Death." Kevorkian asserts that the basis for his concern is "the right not to have to suffer." At the core of his concern, obviously, is "the right to choose."[26] Sound familiar?

Indeed, Roe v. Wade is at the heart of the euthanasia debate. Peter Bernardi, in a 1994 study, reported that a nationwide database search revealed that 34 separate "termination-of-treatment" cases, heard before court jurisdictions all over the United States, cited Roe v. Wade. The language of euthanasia obviously is the language of abortion. Strikingly, in Kevorkian's home state, the Circuit Court of Michigan reviewed Michigan v. Kevorkian and ruled that the language in the original ruling banning medically assisted death was "unconstitutionally overbroad" in that it interfered with a person's "right" to commit a "rational suicide."[27] What Callahan has written for the Netherlands equally applies to the United States – "the slide down that [slippery] slope has begun."

At least one U.S. court case has highlighted the many sensitive issues raised by this topic. In 1983, a 25-year-old Missouri native, Nancy Cruzan, was involved in a serious car accident. Whether she survived is a matter of debate. Cruzan was sustained in a persistent vegetative state for 7 years. A death diagnosis was uncertain, even among the physicians attending her. Everyone agreed that she would never recover.

Following the tragic accident, the physicians responsible for her case implanted a feeding tube in the stomach and provided for her hydration by intravenous feedings. This was done with the consent of her husband. Ms. Cruzan did not recover from her coma and was transferred to a state rehabilitation hospital.

When it became clear to those caring for her that there was little hope that the patient would escape severe brain damage and irreversible coma, her parents requested that the Missouri trial court authorize the withdrawal of feeding tubes and IV hydration so that their daughter could die passively and peacefully. The trial court accepted their arguments, but the Missouri Supreme Court, on an appeal years later, disagreed and reversed the lower court ruling. The higher Court based its decision on (1) an unqualified state interest in the preservation of life, (2) the anticipated wishes of Nancy Cruzan, and (3) the difference between artificial feeding and other forms of medical care. The second and third items obviously were important, but secondary to the state's interest in protecting and preserving life.

In December 1989, the U.S. Supreme Court heard the case on appeal and six months later upheld the Missouri Supreme Court's decision, arguing that an incompetent person was unable to give her consent to refuse "life-saving" treatment. Since the Court had no conclusive evidence about Ms. Cruzan's prior wishes, the appeal to allow her to die was denied. The Court further agreed with the Missouri Courts that the patient was not dead and could live many years in her vegetative state. Chief Justice Rehnquist, writing for the majority, acknowledged that while many state courts had held that "a right to refuse treatment" was encompassed by the constitutional right to privacy clause, the U.S. Supreme Court had never done so and would not in the Cruzan case.

Further evidence about Ms. Cruzan's wishes subsequently was submitted to the Missouri court and withdrawal of feeding and intravenous tubes finally was authorized. Nancy Cruzan died in December 1990.[28] This tragic case raises many serious questions, among these are considerations of extraordinary care, medical definitions of death, the problems raised by sophisticated medical technology, and the lack of a consensus opinion among physicians and ethicists as to what constitutes a natural way of allowing a patient to die. These issues will be covered later in some detail.

It would be naive to conclude that all of this activity had no impact on public opinion. A survey conducted in 1992 by the Harvard School of Public Health in collaboration with the *Boston Globe*, polled 1004 people. The results revealed shifts in public opinion regarding euthanasia. For example, 75 percent of people polled believed that withdrawing life support systems from the terminally ill should legally be sanctioned; 64 percent supported lethal injection to hasten the dying process. In addition, approximately 20 percent of respondents said they would ask their physician to actively terminate their life or to assist them in committing suicide. Being a burden to family (47 percent) was the primary motivation in seeking euthanasia, with pain and suffering a distant second (20 percent). Slightly more than 10 percent would ask someone else to help them die (family, friends, etc.), yet only 14 percent would participate in the process on behalf of someone else.[29]

Thus, it is evident that the American public has considerable interest in euthanasia and its legalization. This was verified in the results of three referendums proposed in 1991 and 1992. The voters in Washington state in 1991, by a margin of 54 percent to 46 percent, defeated Initiative 119, which would have legalized euthanasia and assisted suicide.[30] In 1992, California voters defeated Proposition 161 by the same margin.[31] The referendum proposed would have permitted physicians to prescribe or administer lethal treatment to terminally ill patients. That same year, a similar proposal narrowly passed in the state of Oregon. The narrow margin of victory in either direction exposes the deep ambivalence the public has over the issue of "mercy killing."

Analysis of the survey cited above underscores this fact: the majority people obviously are fearful of existing in a persistent vegetative state and of being a burden to their families; most want safeguards against that eventuality. On the other hand, few would personally ask their physicians to kill them or to help them kill themselves. In addition, few seem to relish the idea of anyone other than a doctor being directly involved in the process. The poll results are divided because Americans are wrestling with their apprehensions about euthanasia and are very unsettled.

MORALS IN THE DEBATE: WHOSE MORALS?

Active Euthanasia: Advocacy

When, if ever, is it morally permissible to kill a sick and suffering patient? The basic appeal of euthanasia advocates is mercy. Even more basic is the assertion of self-autonomy and the right of self-determination. Self-autonomy affirms that our body is our own to do with as we will; the right of self-determination contends that we have the right to determine when we have lived long enough and to end life when we find the journey intolerable. The ancillary issues of dignity, pain and suffering, financial burden, and dependency stem from these two bold assertions. Are they right? Surely, mercy matters a great deal, but can it ever override the universal prohibition of murder?

Arguing for active euthanasia on the basis of self-autonomy would appear to be stretching that right as far as it can go. What could possibly be left except for the predetermination of our final destination — providing our belief system allows for one? Moreover, euthanasia advocates contend that morally there is no distinction between killing and letting someone die. If that is true, one could even adopt the position that actively taking the life of a suffering patient is more merciful than allowing nature to take its course, since it hastens the death and shortens the pain.

The Right To Die With Dignity

Proponents of euthanasia argue that everyone has the right to die a dignified death, reasonably free of pain and suffering. They contend that allowing someone to die slowly and painfully is cruel and unnecessary. In this view, an agonizing death is merciless, even dehumanizing.

Some have even appropriated the ethical principle of intention. Many opponents of euthanasia have justified giving terminally sick patients with unremitting pain higher doses of analgesics than usually recommended in an attempt to control pain, even if, in the process, death should inadvertently ensue. Here, since the intention was to control pain and not to harm, no guilt is incurred. Invoking the same standard to themselves, some euthanasia advocates have claimed that the purpose of injecting a lethal drug to a suffering and dying patients is to relieve their agony and thereby justified. In addition, they dismiss arguments that declare assisted suicide is fundamentally inconsistent with a physician's role as healer, insisting instead that dying patients who are suffering with unbearable pain are more concerned that their agony will not be relieved.

Many supporters of euthanasia cite public opinion polls that demonstrate strong public support for assisted suicide in terminally ill patients. In their view, legislation permitting physician-assisted suicide ought to be adopted to bring society's laws in line with its moral and ethical values.

Physicians remain strongly conflicted. Some favor legalizing physician-assisted suicide in select cases; many do not. In the meantime, science continues to expand the limits of medical skill which allow us to keep people alive longer. Unfortunately, improving health and delaying death are noble goals that are not always controllable.

Mercy, Mercy

The quality of mercy is deeply embedded in our national psyche and is the driving force behind all our social welfare programs. Physicians are exhorted to a lifetime commitment of healing the sick and relieving their suffering. At the core of this virtue is the heart of God. David sings of the Lord, "Praise the Lord, O my soul who... crowns you with love and compassion" (Psalm 103:4). God is a merciful God whose compassion is perfectly revealed in Jesus. William Blake, the Romantic poet (1757-1827), wrote of Christ:

> For Mercy has a human heart,
> Pity, a human face,
> And Love, the human form divine,
> And Peace, the human dress.

"The Divine Image"

The Gospels attest to the compassion of Jesus: when he saw the crowds who had gathered to hear him, "he had compassion on them, because they were harassed and helpless, like sheep without a shepherd" (Matthew 9:36). Clearly, his ministry of healing was marked by the quality of mercy. Indeed, Paul calls God "the Father of compassion and the God of all comfort who comforts us in all our troubles, so that we can comfort those in any trouble with the comfort we ourselves received from God" (2 Corinthians 1:3,4). As God is a God of consolation and encouragement, He likewise equips and exhort us to comfort others in extremity.

Thus, that compassionate part of God's nature is within each human being made in His likeness. Only the most hardened are unmoved by pain and suffering. Consequently, the appeal to mercy by those who endorse euthanasia rights strikes a responsive cord in every sensitive person. Generally, the appeal is made along several familiar lines: the relief of prolonged sufferings, the recognition of the extreme financial and emotional burden families may experience in caring for the terminally ill, and the cost to society as medical successes prolong life at the expense of comfort and well-being.

Euthanasia advocates touch several sensitive nerves in the debate. Why would any compassionate person want to prolong suffering? Doesn't mercy dictate that we help suffering people to achieve a good death? How can any caring person not be moved by the unrelieved burden on families who attend a terminally ill loved one in great pain? How much can we afford? Isn't a peaceful death the more humane and moral way to die? More than the sagacity of Solomon is needed to answer these very appropriate questions; only the wisdom of God will do.

A Christian Rebuttal

Central to the debate is the fundamental question: who's in charge? Christians contend that only God is sovereign and has the right to take life. Job recognized that "in his hand is the life of every creature" (Job 12:10). Self-autonomy and self-determination claims to the contrary, but the Fifth Commandment has always read, "You shall not murder" (Exodus 20:13). Moses recognized God as the only authority over life and death: "See now that I myself am He! There is no god beside me. I put to death and I bring to life…" (Deuteronomy 32:39). Job knew that God was the keeper and the taker of life: "Naked I came from my mother's womb, and naked I will depart. The Lord gave and the Lord has taken away; may the name of the Lord be praised" (Job 1:21). The sovereign hand of God is at work in every human being and He has declared that He will not share His authority with another: "I am the Lord; that is my name! I will not give my glory to another…" (Isaiah 42:8). Inherent in the scriptural understanding of the glory of God is his divinity (Habakkuk 2:14), holiness (Psalm 29:1), and sovereignty. We have neither the authority nor the moral right to kill. We live under His authority and desires; He reigns. That's what it means to be God.

Pain and Suffering

It is interesting that while physicians are being asked to kill suffering patients, the concept of suffering is nowhere addressed in any current, standard medical or psychiatric text. Pain is, and we frequently link the two together as if they were the same, yet they are not. Doctors understand pain, although we are uncomfortable with it. But suffering is too metaphysical, so we join the two in an attempt to hide what we don't understand within the context of what we do. Pain usually is described medically by its intensity and location and obviously involves the character of the sensation experienced, i.e., sharp, dull, boring, or burning. Suffering, on the other hand, touches the soul and frequently is associated with anguish and fear. Job said, "I will speak out in the anguish of my spirit. I will complain in the bitterness of my soul" (Job 7:11). How do we measure that?

We also recognize pain (in pleasure) unrelated to suffering. Childbirth is one example; exercise is another. We welcome the pain with the anticipation of a greater good, understanding and accepting that one accompanies the other.

A larger issue is whether we legitimately have a moral obligation to relieve all pain and suffering. Scripture usually links the two together and suggests that we do. The ministry and example of Jesus implies that. At least we are obligated to try. On the other hand, all of us intuitively know that there is suffering we cannot touch — perhaps because God would not have us do so. In this sense, it may even be beneficial, and humans are required to endure it and more importantly, to accept it. At best, we can help another bear it, but we cannot bear it for them. Examples include discipline and grief.

All of us then, at one time or another, must confront the mystery of suffering. The secular world would have us believe that suffering is a great evil to be avoided at all costs. This is not the Christian view because it certainly is not scriptural. The Bible teaches:

• **Suffering is a part of life.**

In a fallen world, suffering is unavoidable. Nothing will release us from the possibility of it — neither wealth, social status, holy living, or success. Several scriptures attest to this Biblical truth.

(Job 5:7) "Man is born to trouble as surely as sparks fly upward." The scripture declares that Job was "blameless and upright, fearing God, and shunning evil" (Job 1:1). Yet, he suffered grievously.

(John 16:33) Jesus said, "In this world you will have trouble. But take heart! I have overcome the world." In Christ, we have the final victory over suffering.

(Romans 8:18) "I consider that our present sufferings are not worth comparing with the glory that will be revealed in us." The clear meaning is twofold: some suffering is bound to come into every life and we have to accept its unavoidability; and, despite that fact that we all must suffer, those who are in Christ, are assured a future eternal benefit. Nietzsche, a late nineteenth-century German philosopher, was wrong when he said, "It is not so much the suffering as the senselessness of it that is unendurable." To the contrary, though we may not always understand why suffering occurs, it makes perfect sense in God's universe.

• **Suffering is a consequence of sin.**

We must be careful how we handle this truth. The Israelite in the time of Jesus believed that sickness was a direct consequence of personal sin. According to Old Testament Jewish theology, the more serious the illness, the more serious the sin. For this reason, Job's friends scrutinized his life to discover the source of his moral imperfection. However, Job teaches us that suffering is a great mystery befalling good and bad alike. Job never came to understand the reason for his personal suffering, but he did learn to trust God while he endured it. At the last, he was even content despite his lack of understanding.

But, some might object, the clear teaching of Scripture is that suffering is a consequence of sin. This is true in the sense that "all have sinned and fall short of the glory of God" (Romans 3:23). We are all sinners living in a fallen world, and pain and suffering are a part of this world. Clearly, sin has its consequences, in this life and the next. The Apostle Paul writes to the church in Rome, "There will be trouble and distress for every human being who does evil" (2:9); and again, "the wages of sin is death" (6:25). Yet in our anguish, we hear God's consoling offer of deliverance, "but the gift of God in Christ Jesus is eternal life" (6:25).

Yes, trouble and sorrow come into every life, not always with a discernable reason, but always with the promise of relief.

• Suffering builds character.

Often, we prefer to be excused from the building program. But, just as the pain of exercise builds muscles, the pain of suffering, from whatever source and of whatever intensity, can be used by God to build something better in us. Since God allows it, we must believe that there is a principle of love at work in our suffering. For the Christian, our faith instructs us that "our light and momentary troubles are achieving for us an eternal glory that far outweighs them all" (2 Corinthians 4:17,18). By comparison, what we will realize in eternity is far greater than what we are asked to endure on earth. Moreover, Paul assures us of earthly benefits for those who endure suffering in Christ: "We rejoice in our sufferings, because we know that suffering produces perseverance; perseverance, character; and character, hope. And hope does not disappoint us, because God has poured out his love into our hearts by the Holy Spirit, whom he has given us" (Romans 5:3-5). This is not a morbid view of life, accepting suffering for its own sake, but rather, the triumphant cry that comes with knowing that God, in the midst of the pain, is working out something good in all those who trust him and who have yielded their lives to him.

For this reason, the avoidance of suffering may not always be in our best interests. While we are not required to seek it out, or even like it, we are asked to learn from it, and what we learn will determine its real value. God wants to produce a harvest of peace and righteousness in every life, but it only comes when we are ready to submit everything to him. Perhaps the most sublime words ever spoken were those of Job, who, when he had lost all, was able to say, "Though he slay me, yet will I trust him" (Job 13:15). Trusting through tears and hurt and feelings of betrayal may not make sense to skeptics and cynics, but often in our sorrow, God chooses to visit us.

• The paradox of pain.

Sometimes, things are not what they seem to be. What seems pleasurable may turn out to be lethal, while unpleasant things may prove to be very beneficial. Pain is like that. In a modern classic on suffering, *Where is God When it*

Hurts? Philip Yancey refers to pain as the "gift nobody wants."[32] He describes spending some time with Dr. Paul Brand, an eminent and highly honored physician, who runs a leprosarium in Carville, Louisiana. Leprosy is a chronic, infectious disease easily transmitted from one person to another, yet with a diminished capacity to cause disease. Often, these fundamental concepts are confused. A person may acquire an infection, yet never develop the disease associated with it.

The disease was much feared and highly misunderstood in Biblical times. Indeed, it seems a variety of skin ailments fell under the broad category of leprosy.[33] The Babylonians were the first to appreciate its transmissibility and establish practical measures to expel lepers from the community.[34] By the time of Jesus, leprosy was a dreaded disease, and those who had it were religious and social outcasts.

The condition, in its more severe form, causes the patient to experience the absence of sensation in the hands and feet. A terrible part of the disease is the insensitivity to pain. Children cut themselves with razor blades and experience no pain; mothers burn themselves while cooking yet don't remove their hand from the fire. These people have been known to have surgery without anesthesia. Think of a life without pain! But would that be so wonderful?

Pain can be a blessing. What parent cannot identify with an earache that keeps a child awake at night? It is the pain that prompts the parent to bring the child to the doctor where an ear infection is diagnosed and treated. Without the pain as a warning signal, how many children would develop the complications of brain abscess or meningitis? Likewise, we warn a child that the stove is hot and the stove proves it, prompting pain and withdrawal of the hand that has been burned. What a blessing! The leper, not feeling the pain, horribly burns and permanently damages his hand. The ability to feel pain in advance of the heart attack, as a warning of early tooth decay, or as the signal of a damaged muscle or joint while exercising are blessings given to us by God. No wonder Dr. Brand remarked to Philip Yancey, "Thank God for pain! I don't think he [God] could have done a better job. It's beautiful."[35]

This principle of learning from pain often is carried over to spiritual matters. Sometimes, the tragedies, pain, and suffering of life can nudge us along the path of conversion. Approximately 29 years ago, I developed viral encephalitis (infection and inflammation of the brain) as a consequence of a flu-like illness that progressed over several weeks. One morning, I suddenly experienced blinding headaches, dizziness, and visual hallucinations. The symptoms persisted over a three week period. During this time, I was bedridden, unable to walk, and barely able to eat. What followed was a three-year convalescence of recurrent headaches, muscle twitching, profound fatigue and depression. While I continued to work throughout this period, each day exacted a terrible toll on my body. At times, I wanted to die. Sometime during this time of pain and suffering, I began to take a spiritual inventory of my life. Although I always attended Sunday church services, my heart had been far from God. I rarely prayed and felt quite capable of managing my own affairs.

Suddenly, in my early 30s, I was confronted with something in my own body that I was totally unable to manage. For the first time, I experienced my own vulnerability. This seminal event would prompt a seven-year odyssey culminating in my spiritual conversion and return to God. My pain, while I was experiencing it, was a terrible curse. I felt so lonely and often wondered, "Why me?" But it was my pain that moved me back to God.

C.S. Lewis, in his book, *The Problem of Pain*, accurately addresses the paradox of what that pain and suffering meant to me. He wrote, "the human spirit will not even begin to try to surrender self-will as long as all seems to be well with it… . But pain insists upon being attended to. God whispers to us in our pleasures, speaks in our conscience, but shouts in our pains: it is His megaphone to rouse a deaf world."[36] I had been deaf to the voice of God for years, but I heard my pain. In retrospect, I never want to experience anything like that again, but I wouldn't have missed it for anything. For me, it really was the best and the worst of times.

Yancey asks the question, "Where is God when it hurts?" The answer is, "Right there with us in the pain and suffering." The mystery of our faith is that God became one of us in the person of Jesus, coming not as a conqueror, but "as one who suffers." Perhaps, the prophet Isaiah describes it best:

> He was oppressed and afflicted,
> yet he did not open his mouth;
> he was led like a lamb to the slaughter,
> and as a sheep before her shearers is silent,
> so he did not open his mouth…
>
> Yet it was the Lord's will to crush him and cause him to suffer,
> and though the Lord makes his life a guilt offering,
> he will see his offspring and prolong his days,
> and the will of the Lord will prosper in his hand.
> After the suffering of his soul,
> he will see the light of life and be satisfied;
> by his knowledge my righteous servant will justify many,
> and he will bear their iniquities.

Isaiah 53: 7; 10,11

The apostle Paul tells us that Jesus willingly and humbly accepted suffering in submission to the Father's will and that, because of his obedience, the Father exalted him to the highest place (Philippians 2:9-12). The author of Hebrews writes of Jesus: "Although he was a son, he learned obedience from what he suffered and, once made perfect, he became the source of eternal salvation for all who obey him…"(Hebrews 5:8,9). Jesus suffered death so that He might become a source of life for every believer. Clearly, we have a God who knows suffering first hand.

In one of the great mysteries of the Christian faith, the Bible clearly tells us that although we also share in the sufferings of Christ, "If we endure, we will also reign with him" (2 Timothy 2:12). Faithfully bearing up and persevering in suffering will have its ultimate reward when Jesus returns. With this thought in mind, Paul writes to the Philippian church: "I want to know Christ and the power of his resurrection and the fellowship of sharing in his sufferings, becoming like him in his death, and so, somehow, to attain to the resurrection from the dead" (3:10,11). God is courageous enough to practice what he preaches. He has experienced pain and suffering for us and, in the midst of our pain, is with us, ministering to us, bringing good out of evil, and preparing us for Himself.

How do these principles apply to euthanasia? Proponents of euthanasia argue that "mercy killing" is the solution, particularly with those who have incurable illness and are experiencing unbearable pain. It is true that we should not passively tolerate pain and suffering. But clearly we do not have the moral right to end our, or someone else's, life. So what do we do? The hard but most ethical solution is to control the pain. The Washington State Medical Association has prepared a manual on pain control in which they state that "adequate (medical) interventions exist to control pain in 90 to 99 percent of patients."[37] Many treatment modalities are available to physicians for effective pain management. One of the best is the judicious use of opiates, particularly morphine. In reality, most cases of uncontrollable pain are related to improper use of analgesics.

In addition, many mechanical devices are available to deliver a continuous infusion of pain-controlling medicines. One of these, a pump, allows for patients to self-activate doses for "breakthrough pain." Another is a patch impregnated with an opiate which releases controlled amounts of medication, absorbed through he skin for uninterrupted relief. Slow-release morphine tablets also permit less frequent dosing and very effective pain management.[38]

Despite the ability of physicians to manage pain effectively, many patients continue to suffer needlessly. Increased efforts to educate patients and doctors in acute pain management is needed. Even the terminally ill in intractable pain can find relief, but killing the patient is a totally unsatisfactory, unnecessary, and repugnant method of pain control. Rather than eliminating the patient, we ought to concentrate on the achievable goal of alleviating the pain.

What Is Life Worth?

If we are to answer the question of the value and dignity of suffering, we need to extend our rebuttal to an even more fundamental question: what is life worth? Sadly enough, our opponents frequently leave the moral plane of reasoning and reduce the entire debate to the issue of whether or not the cost of an individual life is worth sustaining.

In *What Kind of Life: The Limits of Medical Progress*, Daniel Callahan addresses the psychological and financial burdens of medical success.[39] He points out that scientific technological advances have made it possible for physicians to extend and improve the quality of human life, which, in turn, has resulted in the public's expectation that a longer and healthier life is every citizen's basic right. Concomitant with these facts is the reality that our population is aging. The problem is how to support this growing and needy population.

Medical science holds forth the promise of much benefit, but, in fact, has delivered modestly, with ever-increasing costs. Some people have a false hope in science, believing that there is nothing that more and better technology can't accomplish. Yet, as medical costs continue to soar, we now find ourselves with the burden of rationing care. Thus, Callahan raises the question whether better health is the major determinant of happiness and contentment. He urges a national debate "to talk openly, meaningfully and sensibly in the public arena about health as part of our way of life."[40]

Further, he urges a societal perspective, rather than our individual-centered approach to health care. That is, he argues for a system of managed health care. In his proposed health care system, a minimum level of care would be guaranteed to all, while placing firm limits on individual demands. Thus, he posits a health care system which exists with a healthy tension between setting firm limits (rationing) and a decent level of care for all. In his system, the focus would be on primacy of caring, with limits on the expectation of curing.[41]

Jerome Kassirer, in an editorial in the *New England Journal of Medicine*, has another perspective. While acknowledging that managed care has provided some benefits for medicine, he argues that a market-driven health care system compromises every physician and represents a serious conflict of interests. Doctors are trained to provide a variety of services, recommend appropriate treatments, and improve the physical and emotional quality of their patient's lives. Managed care, however, rewards limited utilization, volume of patients seen, and the sparing use of specialists. On this basis, Kassirer rejects market values as a framework for health care, arguing that a wealthy country like the United States, "spending enormous sums on tobacco, alcohol, and cosmetics should be able to meet the basic health needs of its citizens." He concludes by expressing the complaint heard most often from practicing physicians: "we were never trained to restrict care; we pledged, instead, to provide it."[42]

Both positions have obvious merit and potential drawbacks. Health care has consumed an increasingly disproportionate amount of our gross domestic expenditure: 11.1 percent versus 7.2 percent (mean of all developed nations of the world).[43] In this regard, we lead every single nation. Can we afford to continue this way or must we rethink, as Callahan suggests, our values and our way of life? On the other hand, we might ask whether cost should ever be the overriding factor in the doctor-patient relationship. Market economy carries its own morality and has the potential to cheapen our value of life. Advocates for euthanasia argue that mercy killing would ease the financial burden on an overtaxed system.

Perhaps, we ought to take a moment to consider that we enjoy a health care system second to none. People come here from all over the world to train and be treated. There is no evidence of an exodus in the opposite direction. If the proponents of cost containment have their way, Americans will have to reorder their priorities and drastically scale down their health expectations. Managed care does effectively lower health care costs, so it is a concept that we cannot afford to discard completely. But do we really want to completely revamp an eminently successful system, savage our research programs, and settle down into acceptable medical mediocrity?

If our answer to this question is no, as I suspect it is for most reasonable people, we need to ask ourselves some tough questions. What price tag are we willing to place on human life? Are we willing to settle for the concept that we should protect, preserve, and nurture life only if we can afford it? That is morally indefensible, incompatible with the scriptures that hold that human life is of inestimable worth, and antithetical to the Christian view that no material value can be placed on life made in the image of God.

Perhaps we, each of us, ought once again to examine the standards by which God values human life. Throughout history, God has intervened in the affairs of men. The great creedal truths of the Christian faith attest to our belief that this is so. These truths establish how much God values us. His standards ought to be the ones to which we aspire. Today, many think of man's value in terms of wealth, prestige, and power, with superior merit ascribed to the concepts of self-determination, self-autonomy, ease, and convenience. If we measure with faulty scales, our measure is flawed. God, on the other hand, measures us in terms of Himself and His love for us. By this standard, no cost is too much in sustaining a human life.

The Terminally Ill

The terminally ill patient poses the most difficult challenge to those who oppose euthanasia. Advocates of euthanasia state, "If a patient is going to die soon anyway, why not help him pass away without pain and suffering?" We have already talked about the value of Christian suffering. But the very question of terminal illness poses additional difficulties that need to be addressed.

With the development of better treatment modalities and the sophistication of life-extending remedies, the line between life and death has become blurred. While many people still die suddenly through stroke, heart attack, and overwhelming infection, many other diseases are slow to kill. Even a fatal untreated cancer, from onset to death, takes three or more years. Of course, appropriate treatment prolongs both the quantity and quality of life. Thus, the problem for the physician and the family is to predict the time of death accurately. Moreover, correctly estimating the likely time of the terminal event is becoming increasingly more problematic. Diabetics, stroke victims, cancer patients, and individuals with chronic renal and liver disease are all living longer and more productive lives. In view of these facts, advanced directives by the patient advising doctors and family about life termination wishes will be harder to honor. Physicians will not "pull the plug" on terminal patients unless death is imminent. Determining that moment is fraught with difficulty. It is hard enough to distinguish between a living person and a dead one since doctors differ as to the precise definition of death. That statement alone would be morbidly humorous, were it not for the fact that medical technology can keep someone "biologically alive" for years. So, for those who favor euthanasia, the basis for determining the moment to terminate life is eroding and makes, in many cases, personal wishes moot.

What are we to make of a terminally ill patient's express wish to die? Dr. James H. Brown and his associates studied this group in 1986 and published their results in the *American Journal of Psychiatry*. They concluded: "The striking feature of (our) results is that all of the patients who had either desired premature death or contemplated suicide were judged to be suffering from clinical depressive illness; that is, none of those patients who did not have clinical depression had thoughts of suicide or wished that death would come early."[44] Depression is the real driving force of the death wish in the terminally ill. The real tragedy is that we, physicians included, don't pay enough attention to this fact. These patients are not less responsive to medication than other depressed individuals. It is our collective inability to deal with death that causes us to ignore this aspect of the illness.

Terminally ill patients need counseling, appropriate medication, and compassionate care. If they are provided with that, suicide and death thoughts will disappear, or at least lessen. On the other hand, if we isolate them and treat them as outcasts, much like the lepers of antiquity, we will feed their feelings of burden and hopelessness, thus encouraging their death wish. As Burke Balch points out, terminal patients need to process their feelings of impending death and to settle unresolved issues in their life. It is not good to circumvent this process.[45] Rather, we should aid it by compassionately caring for the dying, providing the best treatment available, and relieving the emotional burdens attendant with their situation. These are the appropriate responses to terminally ill patients who express a desire to die.

Finally, from the Christian ethical perspective, it is not merciful to kill the suffering patient with incurable and terminal illness. It inflicts the agony attendant with death, both to the sufferer and the family. Moreover, even if the dying patient were relieved of some suffering, killing is an evil act and contrary to the Commandment of God (Exodus 20:13). Relieving burden, in our utilitarian society, frequently means eliminating inconveniences. God does not confuse the distinction between these things, even if we sometimes do. The desired end may not be the best one, or even a good one, for that matter. The deeper meaning of life is not to be found in the manner of our death. As usual, the Bible has the best word on the topic:

Man's days are determined; you have decreed the
number of his months and have set limits he cannot
exceed.

Job 13:5

Passive Euthanasia

*Active euthanasia refers to the act of intentionally killing a suffering person; passive
euthanasia essentially means allowing someone to die.*

Active euthanasia is never permissible, whereas, sometimes passive
euthanasia is morally permissible, sometimes it is not. It depends on the circumstances surrounding the act. When natural means of life support are
withheld from the dying patient the act is called *unnatural passive euthanasia*;
when unnatural means are withdrawn, the term used is *natural passive
euthanasia*.

Unnatural Passive Euthanasia

Normal L. Geisler, a noted Christian ethicist, defines unnatural passive
euthanasia as allowing someone who is irreversibly ill to die by deliberately
withholding natural things ordinarily used to sustain life, including food,
water, and air.[46] The problem arises when we try to decide what to do with
things that are not usually considered extraordinary, but are not, on the other
hand, household items. These "gray zone" treatment modalities include intravenous feedings, oxygen masks, antibiotics, antipyretics or fever-controlling
medicines, and analgesics or pain-controlling medicines. It seems to me that it
is reasonable to provide fluids by mouth or intravenously. Failure to do so is
cruel and would eventually result in vomiting and diarrhea, fever, a rapid heart
beat, disorientation, and shock. Obviously, a dehydrated patient suffers unnecessary discomfort. Feeding a patient food, on the other hand, is mandatory if
the patient is able to eat by mouth, but unnatural if feeding tubes surgically
placed in the stomach or intravenous tubes with feeding solutions are used. If
the patient cannot eat by mouth in a terminal event and is unconscious, this
type of feeding prolongs death rather than life. Nasogastric feeding tubes
(through the nose and down into the stomach), on the other hand, should be
used if the patient is conscious but cannot swallow. Oxygen should always be
supplied, since depriving oxygen causes great suffering and the use of it is not
extraordinary. Suffocation is a cruel death. Antipyretics and analgesics neither
prolong life nor hasten death, they simply are a kind deed which relieves fever
and discomfort. Every attempt should be to keep patients free of both. Finally,
the use of antibiotics in the terminally ill and dying is more problematic. In
some cases, they may needlessly prolong an inevitable death, without confer-
ring any appreciable benefit. In other, they may make the passing more comfortable and even tolerable.

A case illustrating unnatural passive euthanasia may be helpful in understanding this classification.

> A newborn male infant was born in a hospital I attend. I was not involved in his care and only heard about him days later. The boy was diagnosed at birth with Down's Syndrome. Shortly after birth, he was found to have intestinal atresia (congenital malformation of the intestinal tract resulting in blockage). The surgeon who was consulted, after discussing the matter with the parents, elected to ignore the infant and let him die. Fluids were withheld, the intestinal tract was not surgically repaired, and the baby starved to death — suffering as well from severe dehydration, vomiting, abdominal distention, and very high fevers. The approach to the care of this baby was morally indefensible. Down's Syndrome is not a fatal disease; it is a genetic disorder compatible with long life. Intestinal atiesia is a surgically correctable defect. This newborn was not a candidate for natural euthanasia, let alone the unnatural variety practiced here. Accepted ethical criteria for withholding treatment demands irreversible sickness. Obviously, this baby was not wanted. A judgment of "not fit to live" was passed on him, and he was cruelly murdered.

Natural Passive Euthanasia

It is not always wrong to allow someone to die, provided that the patient has a irreversible disease, is in the death process, and only unnatural methods of treatment are withheld. The term unnatural refers to the more sophisticated treatment modalities such as respirators or other life-sustaining machines. The use of these devices only prolongs death, but does not bring life. Withholding extraordinary measures of life-support leads to a patient's death, but only indirectly. It again must be stressed that withdrawing life-sustaining treatments is permissible only for the terminally and irreversibly ill. Curable diseases should be cured.

On the other hand, keeping a comatose patient with an incurable disease alive on a life support system is not only unnecessary, but also unethical and unscriptural. The Bible reminds us that there is a time for all things, including a time to die (Ecclesiastes 3:2). The psalmist tells us that the length of our days is numbered (Psalm 90:10), and scripture attests to that fact that life and death are in God's hands (Genesis 2:16-17).

Some ethicists contend that there is morally no difference between actively terminating someone's life and allowing them to die. Even those who believe this have varying opinions about the permissibility of either. There are those who state that both are ethically allowable depending on the circumstances;

others see a clear distinction between the two and condemn active euthanasia while allowing passive euthanasia, providing the previously stated guidelines are observed. Daniel Callahan, a bioethicist, takes a different perspective, seeing little distinction between killing and allowing to die, yet finding the one immoral and the other permissible. He contends that patients are equally dead whether we commit the act or fail to do things that allow them to die. Thus, commission or omission aside, "it is our decision that is responsible for their death."[47]

For all of that, Callahan believes that the distinction between the two has moral validity on three points: (1) metaphysical, (2) moral, and (3) medical. Simply summarized, Callahan asserts that, metaphysically, we cannot stop the death process, since, as he puts it, "Death always wins in the long run." Second, Callahan claims that, while the end result of causing or allowing death is the same, the agency of death is different. If, for example, I kill someone by an injection, I am the agent of death. On the other hand, if I allow someone to die, the disease caused the death and I am removed from moral culpability. Callahan, further, develops his point by explaining that when a doctor removes a patient from the respirator and death ensues, the disease kills the patient, not the physician. Conversely, pulling a tube out or turning off the respirator when there is no good reason to do so, brings moral culpability. Third, Callahan would have us protect the historical role of the physician as healer rather than killer. In this construct, disease kills and physicians heal. He rightly claims that doctors should apply their considerable knowledge to curing and comforting. To do otherwise provides fundamental ambiguity about the doctor's role and the opportunity for serious misuse of the power implicit in his skills.[48] Further, he makes the excellent point that excessive treatment can be as detrimental to the patient's welfare as inadequate therapy. He reminds doctors that they are not obligated to keep someone alive at any cost. Then he remarks that death is not the greatest enemy of all and that doctors are not ultimately responsible "for what disease and mortality do to people."[49] This small section, in an excellent book, is a tour de force and ought to be required reading for every medical student.

Geisler, from a similar perspective, strongly asserts that allowing someone terminally ill to die naturally by not intervening heroically is not contrary to God's law. He cites several reasons, which can be briefly summarized as follows. God alone is sovereign and establishes the length of our days. We may prolong biological life, but we can neither add nor subtract from what God has ordained. Withholding heroic treatment from a terminally ill patient with an incurable sickness does not violate the concept of the sanctity of life, but rather, allows a humane and dignified death within its proper time-frame. Passive natural euthanasia avoids the sin of scandal and attendant guilt while preserving the proper role of the physician. Moreover, the dignity of the natural death process is comforting to family and friends. Allowing death acknowledges the inevitable, while extending death through extraordinary means prolongs death, not life.[50]

Several additional points need to be addressed to round out the discussion of the natural passive euthanasia. Pain medication should be used to relieve the discomfort sometimes associated with the terminal event. While giving a death bolus is never justified, physicians may have to use doses far in excess of those normally recommended. Concerns about addiction are moot. Some doctors refrain from prescribing an adequate dose to relieve pain for fear the patient will become addicted. Balch cites evidence in the medical literature that shows "that only 0.04% of terminal patients treated with morphine become addicted."[51] Side effects of opiates can be effectively managed, and people can actually come to tolerate large doses of medication. In the dying patient, the goal is to control pain and alleviate suffering. That goal can and ought to be realized. If the person dies while morphine is being given to relieve pain, there is no moral culpability. The intention to relieve pain is good; the evil effect of death is the result of a good action taken. There is no excuse for allowing the dying to needlessly suffer. If the treatment used to relieve pain hastens death, it is a justified application of medical skills to a bad problem. Ethicists call this the **principle of double effect.**

The following case illustrates the principle of Natural Passive Euthanasia. The patient was terminally and incurably ill, was provided intravenous fluids, fed, had his fever and pain controlled by appropriate medication, and was not put on heroic life-extending treatments. He died in the natural course of events, reasonably comfortable, and in the company of his family and loved ones. This example of natural passive euthanasia in my experience may help understanding the distinction between allowing to die and actively killing the patient.

> Early in my pediatric resident training, I assumed the care of Bradley, a 12 1/2 year-old Native American boy from a local Indian reservation. He had been newly diagnosed with acute lymphoblastic leukemia and was started on appropriate chemotherapy. A medical staff pediatric hematologist (blood disease expert) was the physician of record and oversaw the care of the patient. Bradley had a wonderful response to therapy and went into a two-year remission, free of symptoms and clinical evidence of disease. Two years after diagnosis, however, he relapsed. Additional medication was given and Bradley entered into a rocky remission of sorts. At the end of six months, the disease overwhelmed him, and he entered the University Hospital in critical condition. Within days, his condition worsened, and it was apparent to all that he would soon die.
>
> Bradley called for me and I visited him in the early evening, knowing it was the last time I would ever see him alive. He was on intravenous fluids, oxygen by mask for comfort, and liberal doses of analgesics to relieve pain. A

decision had been reached by the hematologist and the parents that no extraordinary measures would be employed and that we would try to make the death process as comfortable as possible.

As I entered his hospital the evening of his death, Bradley brightened. He said, "Dr. Frank, I'm so glad you're here. You'll get me better again, won't you?" I replied, "Bradley, I'm glad I'm here with you. You know I'm doing everything I can to help you." Bradley studied my face and turned away, knowing the truth. I sat with him and his family, watching as he peacefully died. Then, I went out and cried. William Osler, a distinguished physician of the late 1800s, once wrote, "A rare and precious gift is the art of detachment." I suppose he was right, but he never met Bradley.

In this case, the disease was irreversible and terminal. No cure was known at the time. Extraordinary measures to prolong death would have been cruel, accomplishing nothing of merit. The decision to allow Bradley to die was a good one. He accepted it and died surrounded by family and friends. He held my hand while he slipped away, and I think we both felt better for it. Given the circumstances, I would do the same again, but I pray that I never have the occasion to test my conviction.

Making The Right Decision

Making the morally right decision about natural passive euthanasia is, at best, difficult and often fraught with doubts and fears. In my experience, it is easier to talk about medical ethics than to practice ethically.

Medical technology has created a new realm of problems and possibilities, and science can be a mixed blessing. On the one hand, we have treatments that extend a patient's life; on the other, these same therapeutic advances can unnecessarily prolong life. Also, the potential for bad and good raises two additional moral dilemmas: (1) the very important decision of when to put someone on life-extending treatment, and (2) the equally important and probably harder decision as to when to disconnect life support.

It is very important that the patient's wishes be honored. This will be possible, of course, only if the person is conscious and competent to render a decision. If not, a living will, if available, should be consulted and the written wishes respected. If no living will exists, family members or those responsible for the patient's care, in consultation with the physicians managing the case, should arrive collectively at a decision in keeping with the best medical knowledge available.

In the best of all worlds, the pastor of the patient also will be involved in the decision and prayer will form the framework of the solution. Occasionally, it is possible to be so involved in the business of the process that we can easily forget the essential of prayer. Someone has called this the tyranny of the urgent. Again, the scriptures instruct us as we seek God in the trouble:

> "They cried unto the Lord in their trouble, and He
> saved them from their distress. He sent forth His
> Word and healed them…" (Psalm 107:19,20).

As Christians, we acknowledge that God is sovereign. All our days have been determined by Him. It may be that, in this situation, our allotted days are coming to an end or God may yet decide to heal. We pray because He tells us to ask (James 4:2), we persist in prayer because he encourages it (Luke 11:5-10), and at the end, having asked and asked again, we submit all to His will, confident that we will "receive mercy and find grace to help us in our time of need" (Hebrews 4:16). We appreciate science and use it gratefully as a gift from God, but our trust is in the Lord.

Biblical Standards

God, Our Creator

God made man and woman. As our creator he has authority over us and determines our lifespan. There is a time to die, and we can do little about it. He does hold us responsible for all human life, ours and others. "Whoever sheds the blood of man, by man shall his blood be shed; for in the image of God has God made man" (Genesis 9:6). Thus, centuries before Moses and the Ten Commandments, God condemned murder.

Approximately 1500 years before Christ, Moses was given the Law at Mount Sinai. The fifth commandment clearly states, "You shall not murder" (Exodus 20:13). The Hebrew form of the verb used usually referred to a premeditated and deliberate act.[52] Jesus would later expand on the teaching of the text and present a neat gradation of anger with corresponding punishment (Matthew 5:21-26). The meaning of this teaching is clear: Murder is reprehensible and forever wrong. Not only is the act condemned, but also the very thoughts leading to the act are under God's scrutiny and judgment. Thus, careless, malicious talk, gossip, and uncontrollable anger that stir the person to action often betray the behavior of a murderer at heart. Finally, the apostle Paul teaches, "Do not take revenge, my friends, but leave room for God's wrath, for it is written: 'It is mine to avenge; I will repay', says the Lord" (Romans 12:19). God gives life and is capable of dealing with transgressors against his law.

Just as God alone is capable of giving life, he reserves the right of taking it away. A Biblical justification for killing can only be made in cases of self-defense (Exodus 22:2), capital punishment (Genesis 9:6), and a just war (Romans 13:1-5). Many Christians would disagree with the Biblical affirmation of the second and third items. In both of these cases, however, the scripture speaks to justice administered by legitimate government, which has the moral obligation to protect the defenseless and promote the general welfare. This does not imply blind obedience to an evil government, for the lower laws of civil authorities must never supersede the higher laws of God. When they do, we have the responsibility to obey God and deny man. In any case, Biblical justification for killing is for the protection of those victimized, never for the perpetrators of evil. Whatever our opinions about these special cases, we can all agree that only God, and those whom he authorizes, have the right to take a life. No one else has the right to kill or to permit another to kill them. Nobody, legitimately, should be given that kind of power, and no individual should relinquish that power to another. To do so is to invite misuse with far-reaching social and legal consequences.

The Fifth Commandment: Murder, Suicide, and Scandal[53]

For the same reason that murder is condemned, suicide is prohibited. Killing one's self is a rejection of God's sovereignty and betrays a lack of confidence in both his love for us and his ability to deliver us in our time of need. Further, it denies him access to the solution of our problems. The scriptures make it clear that suicide is abhorrent to God. The Biblical basis for this claim is as follows:

First, since God is the sovereign Master of life, everyone is responsible before Him for their life.

> You are worthy, our Lord and God, to receive glory
> and honor and power, for you created all things, and
> by your will they were created and have their being.
> (Revelation 4:11)

Second, our proper response is to receive life gratefully and preserve it for His honor. The correct Biblical understanding is that we are to maintain good stewardship over our lives. We are not the owners, free to dispose of it as we choose. King David, writing of himself, rejoices:

> (I) asked you for life and you gave it to (me)…
>
> Psalm 21:4

Further, the Talmud also regards suicide with abhorrence and denounces it as a heinous sin. Rabbi Rashi interprets Genesis 9:5,6 as holding men and women strictly accountable before God if they kill themselves. He elaborates, "A person may not do injury to himself. Where self-harm ends in suicide, all teachers agree it is forbidden."[54]

Third, suicide is a sin against God, neighbor, and self. God expressly forbids it (Exodus 20:13), and scripture exhorts us to love God with all our being (Deuteronomy 6:4,5 and Mark 12:30). Thus, suicide is contrary to loving God.

Suicide also offends love of neighbor (Leviticus 19:18 and Mark 12:31) because it severs forever all ties with family, friends, and society in general, depriving them of our presence, help, giftedness, and friendship. Further, suicide is gravely contrary to love of self (Mark 12:31). There is placed within each person, by God, the natural inclination to preserve and perpetuate our life. We are to love ourselves at least as much as we love others. Most suicides would never dream of murdering someone else, yet yield to despair and kill themselves. We have no right to kill others or ourselves, nor to yield that right to anyone else.

Fourth, suicide is a scandal to others. Scandal is an act or circumstance, grossly offensive in nature, that brings disgrace to oneself, offends the social community, and tempts or leads another person to do something evil. In this sense, the person giving scandal becomes his brother's tempter. Suicide is self-murder; it takes on the gravity of scandal when others are tempted to do the same. Further, our suicide may be the cause of someone losing faith. Thus, it takes the form of a bad witness. Jesus said, "… if anyone causes one of these little ones who believe in me to sin, it would be better for him to have a large millstone hung around his neck and to be drowned in the depths of the sea. Woe to the world because of things that cause people to sin! Such things must come, but woe to that man through whom they come" (Matthew 18:6,7). The Catechism of the Catholic Church, commenting on this passage writes, "Scandal is grave when given by those who by nature or office are obliged to teach and educate others."[55] The person who gives scandal offends the Gospel. The apostle Paul wrote "We endure anything rather than put an obstacle in the way of the Gospel of Christ" (1 Corinthians 9:12).

Respect for ourselves and others, to say nothing of God, ought to be reason enough to view suicide as a grave sin. Active euthanasia, passive unnatural euthanasia, and medically-assisted suicide are contrary to God's law and morally offensive. They scandalize society, compromise the participants, and offend the honor of God. There is no Biblical justification for any of them.

Greater Love Hath No Man

The greatest evidence of love that one person can give to another is that they sacrificially give up their life for them. When Jesus said to his disciples, "Greater love has no man than this, that he lay down his life for his friends" (John 15:13), he was speaking of his approaching death offered as an act of love for them and for us. Sacrificing yourself for someone you love is hard; giving yourself for an enemy is another matter. Yet the scriptures tell us that Jesus laid down his life for us while we were yet enemies (Romans 5:8). We were undeserving of him, fit objects for his indignation, yet he died for us.

There have been many examples of those who have willingly died to save another. One of my favorite examples, often told among the many stories of selfless heroism in World War II, concerns Father Maximillian Kobe, a Polish Catholic priest who took the place of another destined to die in a German concentration camp.[56] His action was one of sacrificial love. Such deeds highlight and help define God's love, which is selfless and sacrificial; they are the most sublime examples of the scriptural injunction: "Each of you should look not only to your own interests, but also to the interests of others" (Philippians 2:4).

Thus, the teaching of scripture instructs us that suicide is a heinous sin, unless we give ourselves up to save someone else. In that case, an evil act becomes a glorious gift and imitates the Lord who did it for us.

God's Sovereignty[57]

God's sovereignty is implicitly tied up with the Biblical concept of him as judge. In turn, what the scripture means by justice is included in the notion of judgment and righteousness. God's righteousness means that He is a just and honest judge whose justice is not dispassionate. He loves and favors what is right and true. He hates inequity and loves righteousness. God is wholly identified with goodness and desires us to live as He wants us to and in relation to Him.

Another aspect of God's justice, consistent with the view of Him as judge, is his authority. When we say that God is the judge of this world, we mean that He has supreme ruling authority. The Bible clearly states, "Know that the Lord is God. It is he who made us, and we are his; we are his people, the sheep of his pasture" (Psalm 100:3). God made us and owns us; we are not our own. As our owner, He has complete authority over us, with the right to reward us if we obey, and punish us if we don't.

In Biblical times, judgment was considered an attribute of a good king, whose duty and responsibility was to discern the facts and judge accordingly. God's discernment is true since He knows all things and the truth is never hidden from Him. In a clearly messianic passage which anticipates Jesus, the prophet Jeremiah says, " 'The days are coming', declares the Lord, 'when I will raise up to David a righteous Branch, a king who will reign wisely and do what is just and right in the land' " (23:5). God not only knows what is right, He sees and knows all things so that our very thoughts are not hidden from Him. The psalmist writes, "The Lord knows the thoughts of men…" (94:11). Nothing can escape His scrutiny. He judges what he knows and we must bow before His omniscience. Further, the Bible teaches that not only is God the sovereign judge of the world, but that Jesus is His agent: "The Father judges no one, but has entrusted judgement to the Son…" (John 5:22,23).

For these reasons, all of humankind is under the Lord's sovereign rule. Our life, as well as the life of any other person, is not ours to do with as we please. Anything contrary to His Word contradicts His proper rule over us and is, in itself, a grave sin.

HOW DO WE JUDGE THE JUDGMENT OF THE COURT?

Having set forth Biblical standards for judging the complex moral issues of euthanasia, we are now in a better position to evaluate the legal and ethical judgments of our high courts. We shall focus especially on those cases that have fanned public interest and that have proved divisive for the medical community.

To begin, let us reiterate that it is unlawful for a physician, or anyone else, to intentionally cause the death of a patient or to force them to take their own life. The patient has rights and within the context and prohibitions of what we previously have discussed, these should be respected. In fact, it is presently unlawful for a physician to assist a patient in committing suicide; over 30 states have specific statutes prohibiting this activity.[58] In reality, the law is more often ignored than honored.

Nonetheless, as we saw in our review of key euthanasia litigation, the courts have sometimes ruled in favor of Biblical standards and sometimes not. Let's return to two of the critical cases that have been at the center of debate for the public and medical community, the cases of Cruzen and Quinlan, and examine for the first time, the celebrated case of Baby Doe.

The Nancy Cruzan case was different from the Karen Ann Quinlan case in one important essential. Not only was the patient unconscious as well as incompetent, but her gastrostomy tube feeding was the source of the controversy. In Miss Cruzan's case, the tube had been inserted shortly after her accident, with the consent of her husband. Following her estrangement from her husband, her parents requested its removal since their daughter had been on a respirator for a long time and had no hope of recovery. The parents specifically petitioned the Court for the removal of the gastrostomy tube, not the cessation of the respirator. Regrettably, the issue whether gastrostomy tubes are heroically invasive was never fully addressed by the U.S. Supreme Court in this case. Rather, the Court's ruling was more focused on what was known about the patient's wishes regarding life support measures in cases of terminal illness, and less about her rights. Indeed, the right of liberty and privacy appropriately was not recognized by the Court as applicable. Actually, it seemed more intent on protecting the state's unqualified interest in preserving life, and this right was upheld. Unfortunately, the Court never addressed the more essential question of what constitutes a natural way to allow death.[59] In this regard, little definition was provided in the Cruzan ruling, as the more fundamental issues pertaining to euthanasia were not resolved.

In contrast, the Karen Ann Quinlan case established the legal precedent that patients in a persistent, vegetative state need not be kept "biologically" alive through the use of heroic life-support systems. Moreover, it made a legal distinction for the first time between "ordinary" and "extraordinary" methods of life support. The ruling is in keeping with the Christian ethical view of passive natural euthanasia, and has helped to bring clarity into the debate about what constitutes life.

In 1982, a newborn with Down's Syndrome and esophageal atresia, Baby Doe, was allowed to die of starvation in Indiana. Two pediatricians called in consultation recommended that corrective surgery of the esophagus be performed. The obstetrician of record, and two others consulted by him, disagreed and recommended only analgesics for pain. With the latter approach, death would be anticipated within a week. The family agreed with the obstetricians.

The hospital, concerned about the legal implications of this decision, asked for an emergency ruling by the local court. The court concurred that withholding treatment was permissible, basing their decision in great part on the parents' decision. The judge wisely made provision for a panel to rule as to whether or not there should be an appeal to a higher court. It was decided not to appeal the ruling. After five days of life, the baby starved to death.[60]

Approximately two weeks after the baby's death, the Reagan administration issued a directive informing hospitals receiving federal funding that failure to feed and care for handicapped infants was a form of discrimination and was specifically prohibited by law. Over a period of two years, the ruling would be modified four times. All four of the modified directives were struck down in the courts or revised because of public protest.

The American Academy of Pediatrics, the American Medical Association, the American College of Obstetricians and Gynecologists and the American Academy of Family Physicians were strong and vocal critics of the Reagan administration, arguing that medical decisions were the right and privilege of parents, with the support of the medical personnel managing the care of the patient. In 1986, the Supreme Court agreed, stating that anti-discrimination laws had not been violated in the Baby Doe case, and in effect, approving several lower court decisions allowing "informed" parents to choose non-treatment over intervention. Despite this ruling, many physicians and ethicists alike were concerned that sufficient safeguards were not in place to prevent similar government intervention at some future date. Final regulations written by the Department of Health and Human Services have done little to allay fears — this, despite the fact that three specific exceptions, in which medical treatment was not required, were attached to the regulations. These exceptions are: (1) when "the infant is chronically and irreversibly comatose, (2) when treatment would merely prolong dying rather than preserving life, (3) when treatment would be futile for infant survival and inhumane."[61]

John C. Moskop and Rita L. Saldanha, biomedical ethicists, recently expressed concern that the Baby Doe rule might have far-reaching, deleterious effects on the overall care of sick newborns. First, they stated that while some babies might be spared harm because of more aggressive intervention, they worried that other seriously handicapped infants might have their lives unjustifiably prolonged. They questioned the wisdom of aggressively treating conditions that are severely compromised and incapacitating. Second, they speculated that the federal regulations might restrict physicians and parents from making decisions in the best interests of the baby — namely the pressure to prolong compromised life actually might do more harm than good. Finally, they voiced their concerns about dwindling health care resources becoming exhausted as increasing numbers of handicapped infants leave intensive care nurseries with severe disabilities. Finally, Moskop and Saldanha ask a very pertinent question that needs to be taken very seriously: "Does current policy 'save' these infants from medical neglect in the neonatal period only to neglect their continuing substantial needs?"[62]

The Baby Doe case highlights the many moral and ethical dilemmas physicians encounter in the problem of passive euthanasia. The decision not to treat Baby Doe was a tragic one. By what criteria is a baby with Down's Syndrome judged to be "not worthy of life?" The baby had a genetic disorder with a surgically curable problem. No one, not even the parents, has the right to dismiss a life so casually. It is moral relativism gone amok that decides that such babies are expendable. Proponents of euthanasia claim that allowing a "defective baby" to die is a act of mercy and spares the family untold suffering. They cite the financial burden of raising a handicapped child and the psychological toll on the family. In 1983, the US Supreme Court agreed with this line of reasoning and upheld the right of the parents to allow Baby Doe to starve to death. In many respects, it marked the beginning down the slippery slope that Schaeffer and Koop had predicted four years before.

The Reagan administration acted in the best interests of the baby nobody wanted. While the effort was laudable, the action taken was somewhat clumsy and sorely annoyed a divided medical community. Nonetheless, the administration was able to grab the high moral ground away from euthanasia advocates on the basis of protecting the civil rights of the handicapped and vulnerable newborn. Unfortunately, under closer scrutiny, the administration lost credibility. It had been responsible for cutting federal aid for many programs that protected the rights of those very same handicapped. In this regard, their actions regarding Baby Doe can be construed as blatant hypocrisy.

Pediatricians, as a group, were also severely divided for several reasons. First, they were exasperated at the prospect of government meddling in patient care, a matter generally perceived to be the proper concern for doctors and their patients. Even strong Pro-Life doctors were concerned about this issue. Second, many pediatricians were troubled that their proper role of child advocacy was being challenged. The strong stand by the American Academy of Pediatrics in response to the Reagan administration was felt by many to send mixed messages to a confused public. In reality, many pediatricians were supportive of treating Baby Doe and others like her. On the other hand, they were angry at being told they had to do so. Most pediatricians I know genuinely love children. They do not relish being viewed solely as skillful technicians. Neonatologists, in particular, agonize over the small, premature babies they resuscitate and keep alive by the sophisticated technology available in state-of-the-art pediatric neonatal intensive care units. Deciding when it is no longer morally responsible to artificially maintain a very small preemie has become one of medicine's most troubling predicaments. What is the ethical and proper response to a baby born too early and too small to live unassisted? How far ought doctors to go in trying to correct the many insults attendant with premature life? Infants born at 25-26 weeks gestation possibly will suffer severe, chronic respiratory and neurological problems if they survive the newborn period. Some countries refuse to resuscitate babies this young. The dilemma is a real one, and neonatologists suffer the choices.

In general, doctors don't like to make quality of life choices or practice by the dictates of the marketplace. But, pediatricians have always had trouble advocating that everyone, no matter the clinical situation, be resuscitated. Nowhere is this conflict more evident than in the nursery. At present, the law requires that only in those hopelessly compromised can treatment be withheld, when "treatment would be virtually futile" in terms of infant survival.

The rule, in my opinion, is a good one, but not without its ethical problems. Moskop and Saldanha are right when they express concern that saving the handicapped morally dictates that resources be made available to help these babies grow up and achieve their fullest potential. Of course, they are wrong in stating that the value of these babies is dependent on whatever health status they subsequently will achieve. While we desire that all children reach their maximum capacity of development, their value does not depend on it. The value was long ago determined by God.

IS THERE A DOCTOR IN THE HOUSE?

Like the law courts and Christian churches, the medical profession has wrestled with the euthanasia issue. Physicians have been particularly vulnerable in this debate because they frequently have to define life and death—no easy task—and, in certain circumstances, they have to take into account the special problems of certain kinds of euthanasia, particularly involving end-stage AIDS, living wills, and postmortem pregnancy.

Generally speaking, the historic position of medicine, greatly strengthened by the influence of Christianity, has been a steadfast opposition to euthanasia. This position is maintained in the 1994 and 1996-97 editions of the AMA's Code of Medical Ethics.[63] While sympathy is expressed for those terminally ill and suffering who may come to the conclusion that death is preferable to life, the code nonetheless states that "permitting physicians to engage in euthanasia would ultimately cause more harm than good."[64]

Even more striking is the next sentence in the AMA's Code, which categorically states:

> Euthanasia is fundamentally incompatible with the physician's role as healer, would be difficult or impossible to control, and would pose serious societal risks.[65]

The Code then elaborates on the proper rule of the doctor in managing the care of the incurable and terminally ill. In effect, several key points are enumerated, namely: (1) the patient's needs in the final moments of life must be aggressively met; (2) incurable patients must never be abandoned; (3) dying patients ought to be emotionally supported, cared for in a compassionate and comforting manner, and receive adequate analgesics to relieve their pain. All of this must then be delivered and communicated in a way that presents and respects the patients' rights and role in participating in their own care.[66]

The AMA *Code* makes an equally strong statement about physician-assisted suicide, reiterating with the very same words the strong prohibition against doctors participating in the euthanasia process. A more qualifying statement is made about treatment decisions for seriously ill newborns. The *Code* urges that primarily whatever treatment is offered would be given from the "child's perspective" on the anticipated quality of life to be realized. It urges that several factors be considered before treatment is initiated, namely: (1) a reasonable chance of success; (2) attendant risks associated with treatment and nontreatment; (3) the anticipated possibility that treatment, if successful, would extend life; (4) associated pain and discomfort with the treatment planned; and (5) the anticipated quality of life with or without treatment.[67]

The statement is reasonable and fairly balanced. The fifth point and what follows, however, opens the door for potential, serious abuse.

> Care must be taken to evaluate the newborn's expected *quality of life* from the child's perspective. Life-sustaining treatment may be withheld or withdrawn from a newborn when the pain and suffering expected to be endured by the child *will overwhelm any potential for joy* during his or her life. When an infant suffers extreme neurological damage, and is consequently not capable of experiencing either suffering or joy *a decision may be made to withhold or withdraw* life sustaining treatment (emphasis mine).[68]

Most people would understand the reluctance to resuscitate seriously brain-damaged newborns who left on their own would expire. The more qualifying statements of the *Code* regarding pain and suffering and "potential for joy" are more problematic and allow for decisions birthed from a perspective of moral relativism, which believes that there are no God-given truths and that man alone determines what is right. This view, of course, rejects God's sovereignty over life, is against the Biblical concept of the Sanctity of Life, and is based on the humanistic philosophy that rejects God-given values and accepts the values of situational ethics.

Contrary to this belief system, moral values ought not to be the children of human experience. Morality and ethical behavior properly have their basis in scripture. Since secular humanism rejects this premise, the barriers that protect human life get eroded, and self-determined quality of life issues are promoted in their stead. Thus, the value of human life is cheapened. Ultimately, the most serious consequence is that in devaluing the incurably sick and seriously handicapped, we begin to devalue all of human life. It is, indeed, a quick slide from one position to the other. And to think, it all too frequently begins with a plea for mercy.

What Do Doctors Think?

Despite the AMA's largely conservative position on euthanasia in its <u>Code of Medical Ethics</u>, it would be misleading to suggest that the medical community speaks with unanimity on this issue. In the matter of euthanasia, as in abortion, the medical community is divided. Physicians debate the ethics of mercy-killing and physician-assisted suicide, while reflecting on the extent to which they have an obligation to prolong life. Uneasy with the present definitions of death, many physicians also acknowledge being uncomfortable with the hopelessly ill and dying. As sophisticated technology expands the boundaries of life, its margins of definition become blurred, and death becomes a more uncertain enemy. When physicians strive to find the intellectual and moral vitality to confront these life and death issues, they are forced to face their own feelings about death and the meaning of life. In the meantime, our society hesitantly continues to move towards a tacit acceptance of euthanasia, often, dragging doctors along with them.

Doctors Speak Out

Daniel W. Amundsen perceptively writes that while physicians classically have embraced a tradition that uncompromisingly respects life, there is no corresponding strain in classical medicine to actively prolong life. As Christianity emerged in antiquity and subsequently flourished, the prohibition against abortion, suicide, and euthanasia became stronger. On the other hand, the prolongation of life, without antecedent roots in classical medicine, neither became a virtue nor a duty.[69]

Marcia Angell, physician and editor of the *New England Journal of Medicine*, in 1988 discerned that a national consensus had emerged favoring euthanasia under certain circumstances. She wrote a balanced and reasoned perspective on the topic listing the usual arguments for and against it. Particularly revealing is her perception of physician concerns at that time. She succinctly stated that many physicians believed that euthanasia was appropriate in certain circumstances and that it should be legalized, but that they should not be the ones to perform it. She cited a University of Colorado poll conducted by the Denver Center for Health Ethics and Policy that same year which showed that three fifths of polled physicians favored euthanasia legalization, while one-half "would not perform it themselves."[70]

An editorial in the *New England Journal of Medicine* in 1990 severely took the medical profession to task for its "repeated and firm rejection of any participation by physicians in assisted suicide."[71] The editorial labeled this stance as a "paternalistic and cruel insistence on life at any cost" and an example of "professional scrupulosity." Further, it made the startling claim that the rigidity of the medical profession invited abuses "exemplified by the Kevorkian-Adkins case." Physicians were chided for holding onto an eternal perspective on life which was characterized as a "single-minded devotion [of life] to its maximal duration." Finally, the editorial concluded by asserting that "the issues deserve a thorough and thoughtful analysis and should not be obscured by inflexible rules that often have little relevance to the people we serve."

It is shocking that these views were written seven years ago. That they were expressed in an editorial of one of the nation's leading medical journals is even more shocking. The angry, strident tone set in an eloquent, well-written article captures the sense of urgency perceived by its writers. It is a measure of the desperation then felt by euthanasia proponents that the Christian (never expressly named) world view was so callously trashed. The ripple effects of Baby Doe and Dr. Kevorkian had numbed physicians until they accepted this pro-euthanasia diatribe with nary a complaint.

In a 1994 article, written with an obvious attempt to be more conciliatory, Francis G. Miller and several associates made a plea to legalize physician-assisted suicide "with adequate safeguards to protect vulnerable patients, preserve the professional integrity of physicians, and ensure accountability to the public."[72] In their paradigm, the overall responsibility for regulating these deaths would reside in "regional palliative-care communities."[73] In a representative scenario, the physician managing the care of the terminally ill patient, who desires suicide assistance, would request a consultation with a state-certified, independent palliative care consultant, who, in turn, would review the case. Following that, the consultant would report to the palliative-care committee and a decision would be made. In difficult or disputed cases, the committee would be available to review again those cases rejected by the consultant.

Dr. Miller and his colleagues envisage the role of palliative-care consultant being filled by physicians "with experience in treating dying patients, who were knowledgeable about and committed to comfort care, skilled in the assessment of the decision-making capacity of patients suffering from terminal or incurable conditions, and well educated about the ethics of end-of-life decision making." Of course, new training programs would have to be funded and developed and certification procedures established.[74]

Further, Dr. Miller et.al. propose regional palliative-care committees made up of professional and lay members, who in addition to their adjudicative duties, would educate clinicians in pain management, ethical standards of informed consent, and the procedural details of life terminations. They also anticipate a variety of other educational duties implicit in the legality, biology, and mechanics of physician-assisted death.

Keep in mind that none of these specialists currently exist except in the minds of their creators. The start-up costs alone of such a program, duplicated thousands of times over throughout the United States, would be astronomical. Also, think of all these "death specialists" let loose on an unwary public — doctors trained to kill in the most scientific manner, upscale models of Dr. Kevorkian, and all financed by the states and Federal government. To paraphrase

Walt Kelly's Pogo, "When I don't have anything to worry about, I begin to worry about that."

Physicians Surveyed on Euthanasia

Dr. Ezekiel Emanuel, oncologist and medical ethicist, in his comprehensive study of euthanasia, summarizes several physician surveys in the United States taken between 1990-94. These reveal that anywhere between 13 and 44 percent of American physicians admit to being asked to commit euthanasia and physician-assisted suicide and that between 1 and 20 percent have complied with the request. In addition, approximately 30 percent of physicians indicated that they would be willing to perform euthanasia were it legalized. Unfortunately, Emanuel reports, "most of these surveys have serious methodologic flaws that make the data suspect and their interpretation problematic."[75]

In 1994, *Internal Medicine News* and *Cardiology News* reported on a survey of physicians, nurses, and social workers from three New York medical centers. Of the 546 survey respondents, 199 were physicians, 276 were nurses, and 71 were social workers. The survey cited in the magazine *Physician* noted that among the three health care professionals, nurses were the least likely to favor physician-assisted suicide while social workers were the most likely, and physicians fell in the intermediate group. Interestingly, the survey also revealed that those respondents who were most informed about pain management were least likely to favor physician-assisted death.[76]

Also in 1994, Jonathan S. Cohen and a number of associates surveyed 1355 randomly selected physicians in the state of Washington to assess their attitudes about legalizing physician-assisted suicide and euthanasia. They used highly recognizable euphemisms for both terms in order to "avoid ambiguity in the survey." Of those surveyed, 938 (69 percent) responded. 48 percent agreed that euthanasia was never justified, 42 percent disagreed. 54 percent thought euthanasia should be legalized, but only 33 percent felt they could perform the procedures. In reference to physician-assisted suicide, 39 percent agreed that it was never justified, 50 percent disagreed; 50 percent felt that procedure should be legalized, but only 40 percent would be willing to participate in doing it. Interestingly, of the group surveyed, hematologists and oncologists (among the specialists most experienced in caring for incurably ill and dying patients) were most opposed to euthanasia and assisted suicide; psychiatrists most in favor.[77]

The authors concede the wariness of physicians in embarking on a national plan of legalization without ample safeguards. While only 10 percent of surveyed doctors were neutral on the question, general ambiguity was perceived among most physicians. The authors did report that "a substantial number of physicians believe that currently available treatments may be inadequate to eliminate pain and suffering for terminally ill patients and were dissatisfied with their legal options."[78]

Subsequent polls have mirrored the widening polarization of American society. Between 1994-96, support for euthanasia among both physicians and the public seemed to be gaining momentum. For example, in 1994-95, Jerald G. Bachman and a number of associates surveyed (by questionnaire) three random samples of Michigan physicians and lay people. The physicians were all in specialties frequently associated with the care of the terminally ill. 1119 of 1518 physicians surveyed and 998 of 1307 lay adults responded. 56 percent of physicians and 66 percent of the public favored legislation of physician-assisted suicide as opposed to a ban. Conversely, only 37 percent of physicians and 26 percent of the public preferred a complete suppression of the practice.[79]

Dr. Melinda Lee and associates, reporting from the Oregon Health Services University in Portland, conducted a mail survey in 1995 of Oregon physicians who were "eligible to prescribe a lethal dose of medication" should the Oregon Death with Dignity Act passed in November 1994 be enacted.[80] 2761 of 3944 eligible physicians surveyed responded. 60 percent favored the legalization of physician-assisted suicide (in some cases)[81]; 46 percent were willing to participate in the practice[82]; 21 percent of the respondents admitted to receiving requests for assisted suicide[83]; and 7 percent admitted to complying with such requests.[84] Nonetheless, many physicians expressed some concerns about possible complications ensuing in the death procedure methods and 50 percent of respondents were not confident they could accurately predict which patients had six months or less to live.[85]

Even more startling is a 1995 report by Dr. David A. Asch, an internist affiliated with the University of Pennsylvania Medical School, who surveyed intensive care nurses.[86] Dr. Asch's poll represents a nationwide survey of clinical nurses directly involved in the care of the terminally ill. He reports that 852 nurses (17 percent) acknowledged that they had been asked by dying patients or their family members to assist in their death[87]; *16 percent of those asked complied with the request* and an additional *7 percent withheld physician ordered treatment* (underline mine).[88] Dr. Asch reports that high-dose opiates were most commonly used in hastening death. Some of these patients (8 percent) were killed without physician order, authorization, or knowledge.[89]

It would appear that, in our confused and conflicted society, we provide more rights and protection for the criminal than for the dying and very vulnerable patient. As such, we are poised for one more challenge to our Supreme Court. In the foreseeable future, the United States will likely look to another court decision to resolve a moral problem. Some recent court rulings already have short-circuited public debate on euthanasia and forced unsound and morally indefensible positions on an unwary public. We seem to be embarked on a path that will once again force us to relive the errors of Roe.v.Wade. Apparently, we have difficulty learning from our mistakes. This time, the potential impact on our society promises to be even more devastating. More frightening is the fact in these troubled times, physicians face many fears and uncertainties of their own. Some of these will be covered in the next section.

The Fear Of Not Knowing

Feeling Vulnerable About Pain and Death

Pain is both the enemy and the friend of the doctor. I described earlier in this chapter how pain was God's gift to man, a necessary warning signal and the watchman of disease. Paradoxically, pain has also been the adversary of doctors. Historically, there is little mention of pain in ancient textbooks of medicine, primarily because there were so few safe pain-relievers available (emphasis mine). Opium was one of the best and was frequently used, even by the ancients, for pain relief. The problem was that extracts of the drug were crude, impure, and uneven in the concentration of narcotic available. Sometimes, even a small amount was more than enough to kill the patient, whereas in other cases, a lot had little or no effect. Thus, physicians had little confidence in these drugs and usually didn't use them.[90]

Until the mid-19th century, surgery was especially horrifying. Pain pointed to the trouble, was associated with the surgical procedure, and screamed its presence in the convalescence. Pain was the friend and enemy that needed to be controlled. Doctors often credit God with being the first anesthetist: "So the Lord God caused the man to fall into a deep sleep; and while he was sleeping, he took one of man's ribs and closed up the place with flesh" (Genesis 2:21). But man would have to unlock his secrets. Crude attempts to control pain include opium, Indian hemp, mandrake, henbane, hemlock, alcohol, mescal, and hashish.[91]

A major landmark in medicine was the use of general anesthesia in 1846. Dr. W.T.G. Morton put a young patient to sleep for a minor surgical procedure. When the man woke up, the surgery completed, medical history had been made. It was the first step in the long story of man's triumph over pain.

Having conquered pain at least in part, the last great enemy of the physician remained — death. Here doctors found themselves outmatched, laboring against the inevitable. As doctors struggled against what they knew would eventually come to every patient, they also battled against their own feelings of impotency and inadequacy. Doctors are trained to know and to do, and not knowing makes us very apprehensive.

This is especially true about the definition of death itself. Doctors are uncertain how to precisely define death. The development of sophisticated life-sustaining machines forced the medical profession to reevaluate their definition of death. Classically, death was described within the context of the permanent cessation of the flow of vital body fluids. The obvious need in modern science for more precise criteria led doctors to a functional definition that demanded the irreversible cessation of spontaneous respiration and circulation.[92] The modern field of organ transplantation, however, made this definition obsolete and required further refinement of criteria and tests of death that would allow harvesting of organs before deterioration. For these reasons, the medical profession began to develop its current concepts of brain death. Beginning in 1968, and extending over a period of 13 years, the definitions were refined until, in 1981, the President's Commission selected a whole-brain criterion of death. To declare brain death, doctors must now verify the precise cause of brain damage and the patient's use of any potentially anesthetizing or paralyzing drugs must be ruled out. In addition, the establishment of brain death requires the absence for 12 hours of all reflex movement above the neck and the cessation of spontaneous breathing, despite the inhalation of oxygen for 10 minutes with the ventilator discontinued. If more immediate organ harvesting is required, the observation period of the dead person may be shortened to six hours provided additional tests confirming brain death are added.

Critics of the current criteria argue that it is not applicable to patients in irreversible coma who have suffered irreparable damage to the cerebral cortex, and, therefore, is only partially successful in accurately defining death. They, in turn, promote the higher-brain concept of brain death which relies on the anticipated capacity for mental activity with self-awareness. By this definition, patients who have no prospect of regaining consciousness could be candidates for organ harvesting.[93] Peter Singer has already suggested using organs from living brain-damaged babies to ensure freshness.[94] Indeed, in some countries, immoral people have made a fortune in illicitly harvesting organs from patients not yet dead.

Because of this potential for abuse, doctors have labored to come up with a death definition that balances saving lives and transplanting healthy tissue. Many favor the whole-brain criterion of death for several reasons: agreement has never been reached about the precise location in the cerebral cortex where consciousness and cognition reside, thereby rendering precise decisions about death problematic[95]; in most cases, simple tests of whole-brain death can be conducted at the bedside; and switching to a higher-brain definition might encourage unscrupulous organ harvesting. This potential for abuse alone is sufficient to maintain present standards.

Physician Attitudes Towards The Incurably Ill (Case Study)

In confronting the unknown, however, more than knowledge and technical skill is needed. These will make a successful practitioner, but only the grace of humility will give permanence to the profession. Medicine is both science and art. Science has to do with curing; something we are well trained to do, within, of course, the limitations of our knowledge. Art, on the other hand, has to do with caring, frequently in the absence of our ability to cure. Humility is required to understand the difference and to appreciate our responsibility to our patients, in their living and dying. Indeed, doctors have just as much responsibility to help patients deal with the dying process, as they have the privilege to participate in the care of the living. Thus, physicians must learn to overcome their own fear of death, acknowledge its inevitability, and train themselves to assist the patient in the process.

Instead, all too often, doctors distance themselves from their incurably ill and dying patients. Visits become less friendly and warm, a sense of detachment develops, and the encounters with the patient become briefer and less personal.

I learned this lesson the hard way in medical school when I treated a middle-aged man named George who had crippling disabilities and unremitting pain. His situation taught me that physicians must meet the pain and suffering of patients with Christ-like love rather than callous inattention to the human person and infatuation with quick technological fixes.

During my third year in medical school, in the Fall of 1961, I was assigned to an internal medicine rotation at the Veteran's Hospital of Syracuse, New York. As part of the rotation, I made rounds with the house staff and attending physicians, was assigned patients to follow, and generally made myself available to whatever was happening on my assigned ward.

After rounding for over two weeks I noticed that we often ignored, or at best spent very little time, with George who was confined to bed and suffering from advanced arthritis of the spine. The condition is called Ankylosing Spondylitis or eponymically, Marie-Strümpell Disease. The disease is three times more frequent in men than women, usually begins between 20–40, and involves recurrent back pain, occasionally progressing to total incapacitation secondary to fulminant arthritic spinal disease and deformities. The prognosis in the more severe and progressive form of the disease is bleak and successful treatment problematic.

One afternoon while walking briskly down the hospital corridor enroute to attend a patient, I was stopped by a call from the man with advanced spinal disease. When I entered the room, he immediately asked me why all of us were neglecting him? Before I could respond, he went on to say, "Look, I know what I have. And I know you're doing everything you can to help me. I also know there is very little hope that I will ever be able to walk again. I'm not asking for miracles. What I need is kindness and for you to treat me like a human being. Stop treating me like a leper!" When he finished blurting this out he was sobbing and I was having trouble controlling myself. We chatted for awhile and I left, not before promising to visit him each day.

I learned a lot from George during the remaining six weeks of my rotation, and most of it had nothing to do with Marie-Strümpell Disease. To me he would no longer be just "the patient in Room 22 with spinal arthritis." He taught me about the vulnerability of not knowing and the fear attendant

with feeling helpless in the face of incurable disease. These
are lessons I'm still learning.

The image of the family doctor sitting at the bedside of the very ill or
dying child does more than evoke nostalgia. It speaks to a quality disappear-
ing in contemporary medicine - the ability to compassionately make a place
in our lives for dealing with what we do not understand, are helpless in curing, and fearful about confronting. That, perhaps more than anything else, best
defines the art of medicine and the call of the physician.

SPECIAL PROBLEMS

Euthanasia, like abortion, has its special problems. When, if ever, can a person
draw up a "living will," specifying eventual treatment or cessation of treatment
in cases of serious and terminal illness? When, if ever, do doctors have a right
to refuse treatment? When, if ever, does a patient's desire for treatment supersede the physician's decision to withhold it? And, finally, regarding two special
cases in the late-twentieth century: (1) when should doctors conduct deliveries in postmortem pregnancies? and (2) when, if ever, should doctors alleviate
the suffering of end-case AIDS patients through euthanasia?

Living Wills

The success of medical technology has been a mixed blessing. We enjoy in this
country the most advanced methods to diagnose and treat our sick.
Sophisticated machines both point to the source of our ailments and labor to
keep us alive. An inventory of our recent achievement is a proud chronicle of
the combined efforts of dedicated and talented physicians and scientists:
antibiotics, vaccines, dialysis units, microsurgery, organ transplantation, respirators, and a broad array of pharmacologic agents all attest to the success of
twentieth-century medicine. During my years in medical school, pediatric
residency training, and virology research at the National Institutes of Health
(1959-69), virology (the study of viruses) entered into the glory years of discovery that saw vaccines developed to polio, measles, and german measles. In
just a few years, the iron lungs to treat polio victims would be put in storage,
pediatric residents would admit that they had never seen a case of measles, and
birth-defect babies related to in-utero german measles infection would be just
an uneasy memory. Presently, polio has been eradicated from the world, and
some of my young associates in practice think of measles as a disease of antiquity. During these years of marvelous discovery, it sometimes seemed there
was no limit to what medicine could accomplish. Within a few years, life-
expectancy statistics would confirm that Americans were living longer as the
medical profession labored to improve health and forestall death.

In time though, people began to fear a downside to the blessings. Medical
technology could indeed prolong lives but sometimes to a point beyond all

sense. In the early 1970s, the "death-with-dignity" movement was born. The public began to express the fear that the human person was in danger of being ignored as science geared up to replace diseased organs and to hook up patients to life-prolonging machines. A conviction soon developed that patients ought to have some control over their lives, even to the point of rejecting life or extending medical care, if they so desired. These perceptions kindled a nostalgia for the old-time doctor who knew his patients and suffered with them through their illnesses. A three-part reform agenda was enunciated by the "death-with-dignity" movement, according to the following broad principles: (1) patients were entitled to a greater degree of self-determination in deciding their fate; (2) a system was needed to care and comfort the sick and dying, directed to nursing management and pain control, as opposed to aggressive medical care oriented to prolonging the inevitability of death; and (3) special efforts would be made at training doctors to focus on the patient as an individual, to restrain the urge to do more when more was unnecessary, and to better understand and accept the dying process and death. Out of these reforms, "living wills" and the hospice movement were born.[96]

In the past decade, over forty states have enacted "living will" or "natural death" legislation that would facilitate and empower people to draw up advanced directives, specifying their desires for starting and stopping life-prolonging treatment. Despite intense efforts at public education, less than 15 percent of Americans have signed "living wills." Most observers conclude that this law has had little impact on the manner in which most of us die.[97] On the other hand, a whole new set of moral dilemmas has been created in its stead.

A Doctor's Right To Refuse Treatment?

It is morally wrong to refuse treatment that would save our life. No one has the right to do so; indeed, it is a form of suicide and violates God's laws. Not only do patients not have the right to refuse life-saving treatment, nor to direct physicians to stop it, but doctors also have no moral obligation to follow such directives. To the contrary, the medical profession is, and rightly ought to be dedicated to saving lives and preserving health. Ordinary medical treatment directed to the curably sick is the moral obligation of every physician. In the same vein, it is the responsibility of every ill patient to seek out and accept medical treatment aimed at repairing health and safeguarding life.

On the other hand, there is no ethical responsibility to artificially prolong death in the incurably and terminally ill. While, admittedly, confusion exists as to the moral obligation to accept some life-extending treatments such as chemotherapy or organ transplants, there is no ambiguity in patients who are curably sick. Here, it is morally necessary to accept life. The expressed will of the patient need be honored only if it falls within the guidelines of these parameters. No directive, legal or otherwise, can ever bind another to an immoral act.

A Patient's Right To Choose Life?

In this age of self-autonomy and self-determination, a potential evil has surfaced — the perceived right of caretakers to decide, apart from patient directives, when life is not worth living. Some physicians and ethicists are now arguing that a patient's desire to live may be disregarded if current medical standards are violated. For example, Dr. Marion Danis and her associates recently reported in a study on nursing homes, that patient advance directives were ignored by nurses 25 percent of the time. In approximately 20 percent of these cases, sick patients were denied treatment they previously had requested.[98] Apparently, doctors are equally arrogant in their abuse of power. In 1971, Dr. Louis L. Brunetti and his associates published a physician survey conducted approximately 20 years after the enactment of "living-wills" legislation. The poll revealed that approximately 30 percent of doctors believed that a physician's judgment superseded the patient's preference regarding the employment of cardio-pulmonary resuscitation (CPR) in the terminally ill.[99] This astonishing fact underscores the pretentious haughtiness exhibited by some members of the medical profession who believe that their opinions about life and death matters are of greater relevance than those of the patient.

In a similar study, the Society of Critical Care Medicine issued a report in 1990 asserting that physicians have the right not to institute treatment desired by a patient if they consider it "burdensome" or believe that loss of function accrued would be disproportionate to the benefit derived.[100] In other words, doctors increasingly consider themselves the final arbiter as to which life is worth living. Now that is a scary thought.

Doesn't it seem logical that with more and more people claiming to have the right to choose death for themselves and others, that patients ought to be able to choose life as well? Apparently not, according to some doctors, who believe they have the right to deny treatment to those whose quality of life they deem too poor to deserve it.

Postmortem Pregnancy

Modern technology has a way of creating problems where none formerly existed. A case in point is the rare, but real, situation of keeping the body of comatose pregnant women biologically functioning for the sole purpose of preserving the fetus until viability outside the uterus is possible. Eleven cases had been reported in the United States through 1993 and these are cited in a very comprehensive review of the subject by Professor Julien S. Murphy.[101]

These few patients touch on the issues of abortion and euthanasia and highlight the many complex moral and ethical issues implicit in both. Interestingly, in an era of complex technology, these cases illustrate the ambiguity surrounding the very meaning and definition of pregnancy. Four comatose women have been sustained through their pregnancies; three delivered live babies.[102] One pregnant woman was maintained for 27 weeks before spontaneously entering into labor and subsequently delivering vaginally a three pound nine ounce infant. None of these patients required life support, and by medical definition were alive.

On the other hand, maintaining brain-dead women on life-support systems to sustain the in-utero fetus is a very different matter. Murphy refers to these women as "ventilated pregnant cadavers." She argues that pregnancy requires life and personhood, neither of these being characteristic of dead bodies. Moreover, she advances the feminist view of pregnancy which demands two essential requirements: first, the capacity for consciousness, and second, the free choice to become and sustain pregnancy. From these basic premises, Murphy reasons that keeping brain-dead pregnant women biologically functioning on life-support systems is immoral and unethical since it violates a woman's right of reproductive freedom and the autonomy to make choices about the pregnancy. Further, she claims that it breaches the virtual cadaver's "right to privacy" guaranteed by the Constitution.

Murphy has compiled a list of seven brain-dead pregnant women maintained on life-support systems for the purpose of biologically sustaining the babies in-utero.[103] Four of the seven women had live babies removed, at least two at the point of fetal maturity. This is all the more remarkable considering the difficulty of sustaining pregnancy in a mechanically ventilated comatose woman. The obvious problems of fetal nutrition, oxygenation, infection control, temperature maintenance, and nursing care to a dead "patient" are almost, but obviously not, insurmountable.

The cases are of interest to me medically, but obviously have far-reaching implications in the abortion and euthanasia debate. The entire premise upon which feminists have structured their insistence on a pregnant woman's inherent right to reproductive freedom is centered on the right of choice. Conscious people are capable of making choices, but comatose people are not. Persistent and irreversible coma precludes even regaining the capacity for consciousness and informed choice. Thus, it is essential that human consciousness be maintained as part of the working definition of pregnancy. If it is removed, the elaborate house of cards built on self-determination, personal autonomy, and freedom of choice will come tumbling down. Having started with this premise, feminists must maintain it to the end. To strengthen their position and defend it against further attacks, the dead woman must be defined as a non-person. Curiously, they find themselves in the position of arguing that the rights of the cadaver still outweigh those of the fetus. This dilemma is resolved by asserting a pregnant woman's right to a speedy death, claiming that this right supersedes any of the fetus. A major concern among feminists is that by eliminating some of the core, foundational requirements of what it means to be pregnant, the right-to-privacy contention supporting reproductive freedom will be eroded and possibly even lost.

Conversely, while this issue has received scant attention in philosophical and ethical journals, and virtually none in the general community, a Pro-Life rebuttal is evident and readily mounted. First, surely the right of the fetus, a human, live person, supersedes that of the dead woman, regardless of the status of her personhood. The fetus in the comatose pregnant woman is not sick, has the capacity to grow and develop, has the realistic expectation of extra-uterine survival, and is entitled to life support — as is any curably sick patient. Euthanasia is illegal in any person with the reasonable anticipation of survival. In addition, just as any mentally sound person would choose life over death, we can logically assume that the fetus, were the choice posed to it at some future date, would also choose life. Second, in each case cited by Murphy, the mother had already made her choice to sustain the pregnancy and eventually have the baby. Certainly, it is reasonable to assume that some bonding had already taken place between the woman and the fetus, and that, consciously, the mother had already accepted the baby as hers and implicitly had given her consent to maintain its life. Thus, even by feminist definition and logic, sustaining the pregnancy to maintain the fetus is the continuation of an act of love already begun. Third, there is the legitimate concern and interest on the part of the extended family who desire that the fetus survive in the hope that good will come out of tragedy, and life emerge from death.

The state has a Constitutional right and obligation to protect all human life. In this case, removing the life-support system from the pregnant woman is both abortion and euthanasia to the unwary victim, the fetus. Although some state that prolonging biological function in an irreversibly comatose individual is a futile exercise and without redeemable benefit, the objection is nullified in this case because there is a fetus involved with the realistic possibility of survival. If the right to privacy guarantees women certain legal rights and has Constitutional validity, then the fetus ought to have the right not to be molested or have its life taken. As a matter of fact, how can a dead body have a Constitutional right to privacy? How will it ever know if that right is violated? Certainly, dead bodies have the basic right to be treated respectfully and with dignity. Doing so emphasizes our respect for the person that once inhabited that body. But, in reality, laws mandating the careful and reverent handling of corpses are enacted for the community the deceased leaves behind and the larger community bearing witness to the loss. Moreover, organs are legitimately transplanted with consent and the community is thus enhanced with the prospect of renewed life. In these cases, implicit consent has already been given by the mother in deciding to maintain her pregnancy, and the dead woman, in essence, is donating her body to her consciously accepted and affirmed baby. Thus, humanity is not diminished, but rather enhanced by sustaining the baby. Even technology is dignified in this noble and very laudable effort. At its very heart, the act is selfless, directed toward the good of another, and uplifting to the human spirit. Pregnancy is thus ennobled and the precious relationship between the pregnant woman and her baby valued to its reasonable conclusion.

End-Stage AIDS

In conclusion, it is fitting to discuss a disease that has caused great suffering in the second half of the twentieth century and promises to grow even larger in the next century: AIDS. More specifically, end-stage AIDS has provoked a lively controversy about suffering and euthanasia.

Dr. John Stansell recently spoke about end-stage AIDS at a Human Retrovirus Conference in Washington, D.C. He said, in essence, that when everything possible has been done to ease the pain and suffering in terminally ill AIDS patients, it is appropriate for physicians to assist them in dying. He made his appeal based on several points: (1) AIDS patients do not die a "natural death,"; (2) their pain is not easily controlled; and (3) some AIDS patients yearn for death. He added the usual cautions: the suffering must be unrelenting and doctors must have exhausted all other means in comforting the patient. Dr. Stansell even shared with the conferees his favorite death potion: a mixture of sustained-release morphine and secobarbital taken with two glasses of cabernet wine over a 15 minute period. This combination, in his words, will bring "relief from suffering and easy transition to death in approximately 60 to 90 minutes."[104] He appropriately called pain and depression the "two great unappreciated and untreated complications of late-stage AIDS." He ended by citing the overriding importance of a caring, comforting physician who has established a good relationship with his dying patient.

Dr. Stansell obviously has a very difficult and, I'm sure, an often frustrating job, and apparently, it is one he takes very seriously. From his comments, it is obvious that he understands that the art of what he does is as important as the science, and his stated goal of relieving unrelenting suffering is a good one. It is in his final solution that we disagree. It is good to relieve suffering; it is not good to kill people. This truth is simple, but not simplistic. There is little disagreement, on my part, about the duty of a doctor to ameliorate pain, only about how far that duty should take us. In the final analysis, if all that we can do fails, the patient must be on his own to endure it. Our highest moral duty is not to relieve suffering, but to do what is right according to God's holy standards.

Secondly, it is very hard to define "unnecessary suffering." To claim that all suffering is unnecessary is to claim that it is always without merit. Indeed, as we covered earlier in this chapter, suffering may be redemptive. It is possible that God has allowed it to accomplish some greater good about which we know little or nothing. Is pain control, then, the highest goal we should aspire to or are there other values that ought to motivate us? I knew a young man who recently died with end-stage AIDS. In many respects, his leaving was more meritorious than his living. He had led a dissolute life of debauchery, unrestrained drug abuse, and chronic alcoholism. He had rarely worked, frequently was in trouble with the law, and was estranged from his family. Most of his adult life had been spent in jails and drug rehabilitation centers. It is honest to say that he was careless in his choices and reckless in his living. Family and friends found him often to be surly and his temper was explosive.

AIDS, literally and figuratively, brought him to his knees. Through his pain, God captured his attention. Before his death, the young man repented of his lifestyle and its excesses. In addition, he reconciled with his family, entrusted his life to the Lord, and died in the arms of his mother. Surely, his pain and suffering were redemptive. Suicide would have short-circuited his journey to God, and the evil of the act would have compounded the tragedy of his life.

Dr. Stansell, it seems, is an expert in providing analgesic relief to his patients. He succinctly outlined a very up-to-date approach to pain control. The problem, as he stated it, is that "some AIDS patients yearn for death." In great part, the yearning may be born out of depression and the futility of the situation. It is the frustration that everyone experiences, admittedly to a much lesser degree, when our life seems out of control and the unwanted end we feared is upon us. Doctors cannot completely relieve this problem. Indeed, aside from counseling and antidepressants, it is beyond us, for there are deeper things of the human spirit that even modern medicine cannot touch. No patient has the right to kill himself or to ask someone else to be an accomplice to murder. It is too much to do or ask.

Finally, it is a mistake to assume that the only way we can comfort sick and dying patients is to kill them. The Christian faith instructs us to "comfort those in any trouble with the comfort we ourselves have received from God" (2 Corinthians 1:4). Our God, in the person of the Holy Spirit, is called the Comforter. Often, we are called to be His vehicles of consolation and encouragement. Dr. Stansell is providing comfort and compassionate care to his dying patients. In the long run, that will mean more to them then serving as the instrument of their demise.

SUMMING UP

Euthanasia, like abortion, has triggered great controversy in our nation. Roe.v.Wade, in 1973, created the climate for our conflict. Today, once again, a lack of judicial restraint threatens to broaden the gap that divides us. The framers of the landmark abortion decision sought to create a constitutional right to abortion where, legitimately, none existed. Now the courts are repeating the errors of Roe in proposing a constitutional basis for the right to die.

The Supreme Court has recognized the right of terminally ill patients to refuse undesired medical treatment. Legislation in some states already has been enacted legalizing physician-assisted suicide, and these measures, although hotly debated, are gaining public and physician support. In March 1996, the U.S. Court of Appeals for the Ninth Circuit in San Francisco, short-circuiting the need for further public debate, prematurely recognized a constitutional right to determine the time and manner of one's death. The basis for this right astonishingly was discovered in the due process clause of the U. S. Constitution by Judge Stephen Reinhardt, writing for the majority. Except for the special case of the fetus, our law seems to have all sorts of safeguards about most matters pertaining to life. Apparently decisions about death are not so privileged.

The error of the San Francisco court was compounded in April 1996 by the U. S. Court of Appeals for the Second Circuit in New York state. Although the New York Court disagreed with the fundamental basis for Judge Reinhardt's arguments supporting euthanasia, it added to the San Francisco court's error by essentially blurring all legal distinctions between the incurably dying patient on life-support refusing treatment and the terminally ill patient off life support desiring death. In many respects, for the advocates of life, the New York court decision was the more frightening. In both cases, the courts pre-emptively chose to decide the proper time and way to die for all suffering and dying Americans, thus fueling the fires of an already mounting national debate on euthanasia. As in Roe, decisions about life and death are becoming the sole property of the courts who have appointed themselves the moral as well as the legal guardians of the people. Tragically, the values and beliefs of our judiciary are as conflicted as those of society. That this is so should come as no surprise to most of us since the weight of the Court's opinions regarding life and death are based on the twin secular notions of self-determination and self-autonomy — the right to decide, apart from God, how we will live and die. In this, we have chosen to define, as we go along, our own concepts of life and the value of man. How different this is from the revealed will and purposes of God.

To God, life is precious and sacred. Human beings are not things to be used, but individuals worthy of dignity and our greatest respect. The value of each person is not to be found in their health, strength, accomplishments, abilities, prestige, wealth, power, or skin color. Rather, our dignity resides in our Creator who has shared His life with us. Our life is a journey that must be preserved, protected, and respected until the very end when all our days are used up. Our honor is God-derived and preserved by Him. For this reason, we may not despise ourselves or others. We are obligated and commanded to regard our life as good and to maintain it with honor to the glory of His Name and for our own good.

Reclaiming The Land

INTRODUCTION

> *We have been the recipients of the choicest bounties of heaven. We have been preserved, these many years, in peace and prosperity. We have grown in numbers, wealth and power, as no other nation has ever grown. But we have forgotten God. We have forgotten the gracious hand which preserved us in peace, and multiplied and enriched and strengthened us; and we have vainly imagined, in the deceitfulness of our hearts, that all these blessings were produced by some superior wisdom and virtue of our own. Intoxicated with unbroken successes, we have become too self-sufficient to feel the necessity of redeeming and preserving grace, too proud to pray to the God that made us! It behooves us, then to humble ourselves before the offended Power, to confess our national sins, and to pray for clemency and forgiveness.*

Abraham Lincoln
April 30, 1863
National Day of Fasting, Humiliation and Prayer[1]

Today, no less than at the time Lincoln wrote, our nation again is divided and we are engaged in another civil war. It is amazing that his words are so relevant 134 years later. At the heart of the conflict, once again, is a fundamental difference in values and ideas, however this time, geographic boundaries do not divide us. Our nation was founded on the twin beliefs that God was sovereign and the Bible was His Word. As late as 1892, the Supreme Court of the

United States was able to write in Church of the Holy Trinity v. United States:

> Our laws and our institutions must necessarily be
> based upon and embody the teachings of the
> Redeemer of mankind. It is impossible that it should
> be otherwise; and in this sense and to this extent our
> civilization and our institutions are emphatically
> Christian… this is a religious people. This is histori-
> cally true. From the discovery of this continent to the
> present hour, there is a single voice making this affir-
> mation… we find everywhere a clear recognition of
> the same truth… these, and many other matters which
> might be noticed, add a volume of unofficial declara-
> tions to the mass of organic utterances that this is a
> Christian nation.[2]

When I attended high school in the 1950s, each homeroom began the day with the teacher reading a psalm and the class, in unison, praying the Lord's Prayer and pledging allegiance to the flag. From our founding until the middle of the 20th century, our nation officially recognized Thanksgiving, Christmas, and Easter as national holidays and openly celebrated their spiritual meaning. State legislatures prohibited public blasphemy, enacted "Blue Laws" against commercial traffic on the Sabbath, and our nation collectively acknowledged that we were founded under God and that, in Him, we put our trust. Movies and magazines maintained a stricter moral standard and entertainment, in general, was more wholesome and family oriented.

Many, including myself, believe that America is not now, nor has it ever been, a Christian nation. However, the Christian faith has, until this century, been a significant and legitimate part of our national life. Today, despite the fact that large numbers of Americans remain personally committed to their faith and believe in traditional, Biblical values, our public identity has largely become secular. Our country has underrated God and deified man. We have chosen to put our trust in science and education, rather than in the Lord, and have exalted human reason and confidently asserted our independence from God. We have elected to believe that, unaided by Grace and God's Holy Spirit, we can only improve and that self-fulfillment and unlimited progress are our destiny. We have replaced God's eternal Law with the silly notion that morality is whatever we deem it to be. We have raised an old god with a new face and worshipped at the altar of sensual pleasure and self-gratification. And, in the process, we have triumphantly declared that God is dead and claimed the rights of self-determination and self-autonomy. Our country is very sick and the prognosis for recovery is guarded. We have come to a crossroad in the debate about the direction we should take as a nation. Will we, once again, turn to God and live, or will we, like so many other great civilizations, retreat into the pages of history, a defeated and disillusioned people?

The Bible says that "where there is no vision, the people perish" (Proverbs 29:18 - KJV). America needs a fresh Godly vision of what it can become. Faced with the burden of writing a Constitution and forming a nation, Benjamin Franklin once urged the members of the Constitutional Convention to turn to God for guidance. Excerpts of his speech are taken from Catherine Drinker Bowen's wonderful classic, *Miracle at Philadelphia*:

> "In this situation of this Assembly, groping as it were in the dark to find political truth, and scarce able to distinguish it when presented to us, how has it happened Sir, that we have not hitherto once thought of humbly applying to the Father of lights to illuminate our understandings?... I have lived, Sir, a long time, and the longer I live, the more convincing proofs I see of this truth — that God governs in the affairs of men.... I firmly believe this, and I also believe that without his concurring aid we shall succeed in this political building no better than the builders of Babel. We shall be divided by our little partial local interests; our projects will be confounded and we ourselves shall become a reproach and bye word down to future ages. And what is worse, mankind may hereafter from this unfortunate instance despair of establishing governments by human wisdom and leave it to chance, war, and conquest.
>
> "I therefore beg leave to move that henceforth prayers imploring the assistance of heaven and its blessings on our deliberations be held in this assembly every morning before we proceed to business, and that one or more of the clergy of this city be requested to officiate in that service."[3]

Our nation was formed under God as a unique republic established with the principle of self-government and existing with the consent of the governed. Our new country, birthed in freedom, has now endured for over 200 years and has become a haven for the lost, down-trodden, and disadvantaged. While some consider this a weakness, we have made it a strength. Our Constitution, a miracle in the writing, has become a model for the nations. We are not a Christian nation, but one founded by men and women whose hearts and minds were captured by God. We are not a theocracy, but a democracy established with the unwavering conviction that God's grace was upon this country. Our way has been met with success and our people have prospered because in the planning and building we acknowledged God and invoked His blessings. The psalmist captured an eternal truth when he wrote, "Blessed is the nation whose God is the Lord" (Psalm 33:12). It is time to recapture the vision of what once made us great. It is not an exaggeration to suggest that the time is long past due.

What can Christians do to reclaim the land for life? My answer does not specifically advocate Pro-Life activism regarding abortion and euthanasia, something that Christian churches and right-to- life groups offer extensive counseling about; rather, it offers more general advice about how to unite ourselves and present our case to the secular world. Too often, Christians pursue their activist causes without first prayerfully considering how God would have us wage war against evil—in this case, abortion and euthanasia. In so doing, our model plan for battle frequently imitates the world's, substituting anger and violence for the values of the Gospel. Instead, we will consider here what Christian thinkers have called a "theology of disagreement," and upon this Biblical foundation for Christian dissent we will discuss the Bible's proposals for how we should conduct ourselves as we wage war against evil. Our problem, as I see it, is not that we lack plans for how to legally and politically oppose abortion, but rather that we communicate ungodly attitudes in our Christian warfare that result in a negative witness for our cause.

A THEOLOGY OF DISAGREEMENT

By This You Shall Know Them

A Christian has the dual responsibility of being salt to a society that has lost its flavor and at the same time representing Christ to those with whom he disagrees. Salt was used as a preservative in the ancient world; it was also utilized as a flavor enhancer. Salt, properly applied, can bring bland food to life. In addition, salt was associated with purity.[4] For example, the Lord commanded Moses to sprinkle the holy incense with salt before it was offered as a pure and sacred fragrance to Him (Exodus 30:31-37).

The Apostle Paul picked up on this theme when he wrote, "Let your conversation be always full of grace, **seasoned with salt**, so that you may know how to answer everyone" (Colossians 4:6). Metaphorically, then, the Christian is a preserver of truth in his society. He flavors his community, aware that a heavy hand ruins his flavor, just as oversalting ruins food. He is reminded that as pure white salt stands out in contrast to the food it flavors, so too, the Christian's life ought to stand out as a model of purity. In addition, as salt properly applied blends in with the food yet retains its distinctive flavor, Christians ought to be in society without being of it. Jesus said the same of His disciples in praying to His Father (John 17:15,16): "My prayer is not that you take them out of the world, but that you protect them from the evil one. They are not of the world, even as I am not of it." Believers always need to carry with them the awareness that their allegiance is to a higher Kingdom.

Finally, just as salt becomes a holy thing when used for holy purposes, the apostle Peter exhorts every Christian to be holy, just as God is holy (1 Peter 1:15, 16). Biblically, to be holy is to be set apart to God. The concept implies being set apart from sin and moral impurity. Just so, the Christian life ought to reach for God's standard of moral behavior and stand out in contrast to the unbeliever. For these reasons, Jesus said to His followers, "You are the salt of the earth. But if the salt loses its saltiness, how can it be made salty again? It is no longer good for anything, except to be thrown out and trampled by men" (Matthew 5:13). If a Christian is not living properly, his professions of faith and moral pronouncements will have no effect on his world. Unless salt remains salt, it simply has no value.

On the other hand, a salt cellar left on the table and unused, adds nothing to the flavor of the food. Salt has to come in contact with the food to make a difference. Continuing the metaphor, the Christian has to touch his society, not just live in close proximity to it. The challenge is in flavoring our world without losing our identifying mark as disciples of Christ. Jesus said on the night of his betrayal, "By this all men will know that you are my disciples, if you love one another" (John 13:35). Love is the distinguishing mark of the follower of Jesus. Francis A. Schaeffer, in his essay entitled "The Mark of the Christian," wrote: "It is possible to be a Christian without showing the mark, but if we expect non-Christians to know that we are Christians, we must show the mark."[5] *Christianity Today*, in its recent reprint of this essay, said that, in this seminal work, Schaeffer effectively articulated a "theology of disagreement."[6] While he wrote the piece to remind Christians how to conduct themselves properly in disagreeing with each other, he emphasized that all people are our neighbors, and ought to be loved on that basis alone.

In the parable of the Good Samaritan (Luke 10:30-37), Jesus reminds us that love accepts no limiting boundaries. Since every person is made in the Divine Image of his Creator (Genesis 1:27), everyone is worthy of respect and love. Secularists who deny this truth invariably devalue themselves and others. Jesus taught that all people ought to be loved as much as we love ourselves (Matthew 22:39) and linked this commandment to the greatest of all the commandments, to love God with all of our being (22:37,38). The Apostle John adds that "anyone who does not love his brother whom he has seen, cannot love God whom he has not seen" (1 John 4:20). The only tangible proof we have that we love God is to love the people He loves.

Redeemed or unredeemed, enlightened or ignorant of the truth, every human person deserves our love and respect. For this reason, belligerence and angry hostility have no place in the Christian's behavior. No believer can effectively represent the Lord when he consistently presents an unloving face to the secular world. Schaeffer wrote, "There is only one kind of person who can fight the Lord's battles in anywhere near a proper way, and that is the person who by nature is unbelligerent."[7]

John D. Woodbridge, in the same issue of *Christianity Today*, wrote an article entitled "Culture War Casualties." He argued that the rhetoric of warfare has compromised the church and blunted its effectiveness in our present national conflict over values. Further, he asserted that angry and pejorative words not only distort our opponent's position, they damage the credibility of our own.[8]

Words that sarcastically and hostilely label and confine often remove the attacked person or group from honest and effective dialogue with us. For example, if I call an abortion doctor a murderer, he is unlikely to wish to discuss the issue with me. However, it is possible to label an action or behavior without slandering the person responsible for it. I may honestly say that abortion is murder, without calling the physician who performs one a murderer. Dialogue permits honesty without yielding to character assassination. In fact, an abortionist may deny that abortion is homicide because he doesn't believe the fetus is human, or because he believes that the woman's freedom to choose overrides the fundamental rights of the baby in utero. In our view, this position may be misguided, illogical, or ignorant. But calling someone a "murderer" or "stupid" or a "baby-killer" marginalizes him and removes him from all further discourse. Abortionists have occasionally changed their minds and even, in some cases, become ardently Pro-Life. Bernard Nathanson is a prime example. Formerly, a strong advocate of abortion rights and an abortionist himself, Dr. Nathanson currently is a staunch Pro-Life supporter. Jane Roe's name (a pseudonym) is linked with the landmark 1973 U.S. Supreme Court decision that made abortion a legal right for all women. Several years before that decision, she had an abortion and was convicted of a criminal offense by a Texas court. In 1970, she filed suit to petition the Texas Criminal Appeals Court to overturn the law prohibiting abortion. The Texas Court denied her appeal. But three years later, the U.S. Supreme Court held that the Texas law was unconstitutional, and further ruled that she had a constitutional right to an abortion since the unborn child was not a person. In 1995, Jane Roe declared to a national audience that she had become a Christian and had changed her mind about abortion. Since then, she has emerged as a Pro-Life activist, speaking regularly at public rallies about the evils of the surgical procedure permanently linked to her name.

Angry rhetoric lowers the moral tone of the debate. Woodbridge rightly asserted that we have no right to demonize anyone, even if our cause is a just one.[9] Indeed, we are commanded by our Lord to adhere to a higher standard of love, rather than hatred for our enemies. He even told us to pray for them, not to yell at them (Matthew 5:43-48). However, this should not mean that we ignore the reality of sin or withdraw ourselves from the conflict. The challenge is always to present Biblical truth in a loving, kind, and respectful way to a society that denies its validity and denigrates its Author.

It is silly to make believe that there isn't a problem. Even worse, it would be tragic to compromise the truth in order to placate those hostile to it. Godly balance is needed. Forgoing the rhetoric of conflict and battle will not end the controversy. On the other hand, choosing our words wisely so that they might flavor our conversation will further our cause. The Lord never intended that we rub salt in our opponent's wounds. By the same token, he also never intended that we remove the salt from the table. Learning how to apply it in a Godly way honors the instruction of Scripture without compromising the desired result — the furthering of God's Kingdom on earth.

Overcome Evil With Good

Christianity is no stranger to conflict. Our religion is evangelical and confrontative. Jesus promised his followers that they would be persecuted because of him, even hated (Matthew 10:21-42). On the surface, this appears to be a contradiction. Jesus prophetically is referred to by the prophet as the "Prince of Peace" (Isaiah 9:6), angels announce his birth with the promise of peace (Luke 2:14), and Jesus tells us he bestows peace, as no one else can (John 14:27). Yet the inevitable result of His coming is conflict — between Him and Satan, between believers and unbelievers, between those who accept the truth and those who fight it. Indeed, conflict may even intrude into the believer's family (Matthew 10:34-37).

The apostle Paul, acknowledging the inevitability of the battle urges his young companion Timothy to "fight the good fight of faith" (1 Timothy 6:12). The history of Christianity is replete with the testimony of those who fought for their faith. Justin Martyr and Tertullian vigorously fought against the heresies of Marcion who held that the God of the Old Testament was evil and not the father of Jesus; he also denied the humanity of the Lord.[10] Athanasius contended against Arianism which argued that Christ was a created being. In defending the Nicene Creed and helping to define the doctrine of the Trinity, he is regarded as a champion of the Faith. His critics found him harsh and uncompromising.[11] Augustine fought against Pelagius, who denied man's innate sinfulness and minimized Supernatural Grace. Martin Luther fought against the Pope, the Emperor Charles V, his own Augustinian order, and many leading theologians of his time. He took his stand on the Holy Scriptures and insisted that sinners were justified not by deeds, but by faith alone. His life was one of controversy and conflict. Calvin, John Knox, Pope John Paul II, and Billy Graham also are known as fighters for the Faith. It is reasonable to say that it is impossible to be a true soldier of Jesus Christ and not fight.

The question is not whether we are prepared to fight and proclaim the Gospel to a world that often doesn't want to hear it, but how we will conduct ourselves in the fray. History provides many examples, both how to and how not to do it. Clearly, the Crusades and the Inquisition are sorry pages in our faith's history. Bloodshed and violence are not acceptable methods of fighting the "good fight." On the other hand, the early martyrs, the abolitionists committed to non-violence in the time of the Civil War, Dietrich Bonhoeffer's courageous stand against Nazism, Helder Camara's defense of the South American poor through non-violent means, and Martin Luther King Jr.'s non-violent stance of passive-resistance against the evils of racism are shining examples of those who conquered through faith and moral persuasion. The psalmist could have been speaking of them when he wrote:

> With your help I can advance against a troop;
> with my God I can scale a wall.

ENT

He is a shield for all who take refuge in him.
For who is God besides the Lord?
And who is the Rock except our God?
It is God who arms me with strength and makes my
way perfect.

I pursued my enemies and overtook them;
I did not turn back till they were destroyed.
I crushed them so that they could not rise; they fell
beneath my feet. You armed me with strength for
battle; you made my adversaries bow at my feet.
You made my enemies turn their backs in flight,
and I destroyed my foes.

Psalm 18:30-32; 37-40

Here, the metaphor of war is used to describe spiritual battle, won through the all-sufficient power of the Holy Spirit. All of the examples listed above were unyielding in their defense of the Truth. In this, they followed the prophets who would not yield to idolatry and evil, preferring instead suffering and even death for the cause of Christ and His Gospel. The author of Hebrews prophetically anticipated their martyrdom in saying, "the world was not worthy of them" (11:38). What they, and all the heroes of the Faith listed in Hebrews 11, had in common was that they overcame evil with good. Here, they followed the instructions of Jesus and the Holy Scriptures:

If it is possible, as far as it depends on you, live at peace with everyone. Do not take revenge, my friends, but leave room for God's wrath, for it is written: "It is mine to avenge; I will repay," says the Lord. On the contrary: 'If your enemy is hungry, feed him; if he is thirsty, give him something to drink. In doing this, you will heap burning coals on his head.' Do not be overcome by evil, but overcome evil with good.

Romans 12:18-21

Discrediting The Gospel

Those who don't learn to fight evil God's way discredit the Gospel of His Son. Every time a believer, or one who represents himself as a believer, resorts to violence and hateful rhetoric in attacking the enemies of the Faith, he is guilty of the sin of murder and scandal. The Gospel instructs us to respect everyone and to treat all people with dignity. When we don't, our behavior not only harms the person we are attacking, but also may tempt another to sin. That kind of behavior becomes scandalous when we incite another to do the same. Moreover, it cheapens any future witness we hope to bring.

Jesus reserved his harshest criticism for the teachers of the law and the Pharisees. By contrast, He was kind and very gentle to sinners. The Gospels attest to this in His encounter with the Samaritan woman at the well (John 4:1-26), the woman caught in adultery (John 8:1-11), the man born blind who begged at the Temple gates (9:1-41), the sinful woman who washed His feet with her tears and dried them with her hair (Luke 7:36-50), and His treatment of Judas, whom He knew had betrayed him (John 13:21-30). These are only a few examples of His compassionate treatment of people caught in the web of sin, whose lives offended the community and the Commandments.

On the other hand, Jesus never compromised the truth or lowered God's standards of righteousness. He also never altered his message to placate those hostile to the Gospel. In many cases, He even ended his encounter with sinners by exhorting them to amend their lives. He didn't condone evil; he vigorously confronted it with truth and goodness. It is instructive to remember that Jesus was unyielding towards religious hypocrisy (Matthew 23:23,24), spiritual pride (vv 1-12), and the outward practice of religion without the accompanying inward conversion of the spirit (vv 25,26). The Bible clearly teaches that those who neglect or squander the spiritual provision given to them will be impoverished. The uncompromising truth is that those entrusted with the Gospel and with shepherding the flock of Jesus have a grave responsibility to rightly handle the Word of Truth and pass on uncontaminated that which was entrusted to them.

On July 5, 1995, the leadership of the County Medical Society to which I belong, wrote an open letter to Pro-Life activists which was published in our local newspaper. In it, they condemned the violence directed by anti-abortion groups towards area physicians and their families. Some of the tactics employed included threatening letters, stalking of physicians, and the promise of violence or death to those who persisted in aborting babies. The Pro-Life cause was right, but their methods were malicious and antithetical to the Gospel of Jesus Christ. Every time this happens, the Scriptures are discredited and the cause of life damaged.

Going The Extra Mile

What, then, is a more Biblical attitude towards those with whom we disagree? Jesus taught, "If someone forces you to go one mile, go with him two miles (Matthew 5:42). The Roman soldiers, under law, could press anyone but a Roman citizen into carrying their equipment for one mile. Simon of Cyrene was thus pressed into carrying Jesus' cross. In a larger sense, Jesus instructs us, that rather than giving way to bitterness and resentment when we are reviled and sorely used, our intent always ought to be to return evil with good. According to the Gospel, the Christian is commanded to never seek retaliation for any affront. Our intent should never be to harm. Rather in love, respecting the other person's dignity and worth, we bring correction, or even rebuke, always with the goal of winning over our adversary and promoting the Kingdom of God. This is indeed a high standard and only achievable by the grace of God. But when we apply this teaching of our Lord to our lives, we imply that God is able to bring victory in His way and in His time. The early Christian martyrs appeared to be thoroughly humiliated and defeated. Yet, the testimony of their death and their manner of meeting it stirred countless thousands to embrace Christianity. How does history judge them and their persecutors? And who really won the battle?

A WAR OF IDEAS

> Mine eyes have seen the glory of the coming of the Lord; He is trampling out the vintage where the grapes of wrath are stored; He hath loosed the fateful lightning of His terrible swift sword; His truth is marching on.

Battle Hymn of the Republic
1862

In American history, there is a long tradition of identifying God's eternal justice with Christian warfare. Indeed, the Christian hymnals hold many songs that make reference to warfare and being a soldier in the army of the Lord. Two that come to mind, in addition to the "Battle Hymn of the Republic" are "Onward Christian Soldiers" and "Soldiers of the Cross." Bible references invoking the analogy of the battle and war abound. The point emphasizes that the language of warfare and conflict has long been a part of Christianity. Conflict is the reality of the tension that all committed Christians live as sojourners in this world. Indeed, the Books of the Prophets crackle with the language of battle. How could they not?

In our society, many choose to ignore God as some outdated concept. While many politicians still give Him lip-service, our culture moves ahead as if He didn't exist. Of course we're in a war. We just have to be sure we know who the enemy is and which side we're on. In the first century, the world was conquered by the Gospel, not by spears. Today, as Paul reminds us, the weapons we fight with are spiritual, having the power to demolish every force directed against the Lord and our Faith (2 Corinthians 10:3-5). In his letter to the Ephesians, Paul writes that "our struggle is not against flesh and blood, but against the powers of this dark world and against the spiritual forces of evil in the heavenly realms" (Ephesians 6:12).

Who Will Join The Battle?

We are, indeed, in a war. Two sides are locked in battle and the soul of America hangs in the balance. Both are sincere and determined, and neither will yield.

Their views are incompatible and the result, at present, is uncertain. This is not rhetorical excess. It is truth. Dr. James Dobson, in the June 19, 1995, issue of *Christianity Today*, responded to John Woodbridge's criticism of the rhetoric of warfare.[12] He rightly points out that Christians can not afford to cop out of the fray. To deny the truth of what we see all around us requires that we deny our calling to follow Christ. Jesus never provoked anyone for the sake of vain argumentation. On the other hand, he never ran from the truth and never surrendered to the lie. Jesus faced the culture of His time and passed moral judgment on it. He also recognized that Satan was the real enemy of the truth, even calling him a liar and the father of lies (John 8:44). The source of the problem in our society is spiritual, not intellectual. Truth is foreign to Satan and to all those under his influence.

Jesus looked at the people of his culture and declared, "The harvest is plentiful, but the workers are few. Ask the Lord of the harvest, therefore, to send out workers into his harvest field" (Luke 10:2). The people of his day were also captive to ignorance and lies. They were lost and caught in the conflicts of their day. Yet Jesus didn't see them as the enemy. He didn't condemn Mary Magdalene or label her a whore, nor did He approve of her behavior. Instead, by His love and acceptance He captured her heart, later showing her great favor by first revealing Himself to her after His resurrection. At first, Paul was an enemy of the early church, even participating in the murder of Stephen. Yet, Jesus saw the potential in him and eventually made him a champion of the faith. The good thief on the cross was justly condemned for his sins. Jesus did not condemn him. Rather, responding to his plea for mercy, He forgave him and welcomed him into paradise. Indeed, rather than enemies, Jesus saw each of these people as potential members of his Kingdom. He never lost sight of the fact that His struggle was a spiritual one and that His real enemies were not flesh and blood. This adequately describes our situation today. This is no time to drop out of the battle. Jesus knew what He was talking about when He said, "I am sending you out like sheep among wolves. Therefore, be as shrewd as snakes and as innocent as doves" (Matthew 10:16). *Eerdmans Bible Commentary* explains that "the defenselessness of sheep in the midst of wolves means that their position must be supported by both wisdom (the subtlety of the serpent) and innocence (which would mean that, as they were doing God's will they would have his protection)."[13] Let us not deny the conflict or the danger, but rather elect to follow the Good Shepherd wherever He leads. What else can sheep reasonably do?

A Call To Fight Falsehoods

If we are at war, what is our battle plan? Today, in the battles over euthanasia and abortion, the Christian Church runs the risk of falling into two traps. Both are excessive responses to a legitimate crisis and both are inappropriate. One is to allow zeal to give way to pejorative rhetoric and/or violence. Although this tactic is practiced by a distinct minority, it is intolerable and anti-Christian. It discredits the Gospel and cheapens our witness. The second, to remain silent, plays into the hands of the abortionists who desire nothing more than to stifle the Christian voice.

In ancient Israel, a Jewish woman named Esther was married to the Persian king Xerxes. Haman, his advisor, hated the Jewish presence in the land and particularly loathed Mordecai, a court official and Esther's uncle. Haman devised a plot to destroy the Jews. Mordecai went to Esther appealing for her help, urging her to go to the King and plead with him for her people. Esther demurred. Mordecai then relayed the following message to her: "Do not think that because you are in the king's house you alone of all the Jews will escape. For if you remain silent at this time, relief and deliverance for the Jews will arise from another place, but you and your father's family will perish. And who knows but that you have come to royal position for such a time as this?" (Esther 4:12-14).

God is sovereign. If we keep silent in this hour of crisis, He is more than able to raise someone else up for the relief and deliverance of America. Remaining silent in our seemingly unthreatened world, may seem prudent, and for the moment it may even be the safer route. But it betrays God and shirks our responsibility. Moreover, God does not honor those, who in the fateful hour of decision, decide to remain uninvolved. Christian theologians and leaders have told us as much. J. Gresham Machan (1881-1937), a Christian theologian and apologist, has written: "Peace is indeed yours, the peace of God which passeth all understanding. But that peace is given you, not that you may be onlookers or neutrals in love's battle, but good soldiers of Jesus Christ."[14] Is it exaggerating to suggest that soldiers who are AWOL are cooperating with the enemy?

Society's Anti-Christian Bias

Unfortunately, much as the Christian community may desire to speak, we are often silenced by society. John W. Whitehead believes that the message of the Gospel is being "stifled and censored" in America.[15] He cites many examples in the public domain to support his contention and quotes Professor Harvey Cox who has written: "Secularism is not only indifferent to alternative religious systems, but as a religious ideology is opposed to any other religious system. It is therefore a closed system."[16] Indeed it is a closed system that has captured the minds of many academic elite, as well as a considerable number in the political and judicial arenas. It tolerates no dissension.

For example, Supreme Court Justice Stevens has written: "Unless the religious view that a fetus is a 'person' is adopted… there is a fundamental and well-recognized difference between a fetus and a human being; indeed, if there is not such a difference, the permissibility of terminating the life of a fetus could scarcely be left to the will of the state legislatures…"[17] Note that Justice Stevens in less than one sentence cavalierly dismisses the Biblical concept of the Sanctity of Life and makes a sweeping assertion that most people, except for the religious, recognize that the fetus is not a human being, but one in process of being.

Clearly, smear tactics and ridicule are the principal weapons secularists employ in attempting to silence the Christian voice. In a recent letter to the *Washington Post*, which appeared shortly after the Oklahoma City bombing, Charles W. Colson complained that the media was portraying chief suspect Timothy McVeigh as a "creature of the religious right." Colson carefully documented the insinuations of some liberals, and the blatant accusations of others, in linking conservatism and the "religious right" to violence and mass murder. For example, Michael Lind, editor of *Harper's* magazine, wrote an article for the *Post*, published on April 30, 1995, in which he wrote: "The story of Oklahoma City and the militia should not make us forget that the main form of political terrorism in the United States is perpetuated by right-wing opponents of abortion."

Here, of course, the subtle distortion gives way to the gross lie. "Religious Conservatives" (translation: orthodox born-again Christians who accept the historic creedal truths of the faith and the authority of the Scriptures) are murderers and fanatical radicals given to violence and political terrorism. This is a stunning example of what Woodbridge worried would emanate from Christians — warfare rhetoric on a personal and slanderous basis. Disdainful of facts, these critics resort to the "Big Lie." If it's repeated often enough, someone might begin to believe it.

However, it often is not so much what is written about Christians, as the manner in which it is presented and the insinuations seemingly implied in the text. The print media has a way of using words that make them seem dirty and tainted. The "Religious Right" or "Fundamentalist Christians" or "Conservative Right Wing Christian Groups" are all code words for fanatic, extremist, anti-intellectual, and bigot. It has become fashionable to demonize Christians. A recent editorial in the *Wall Street Journal* entitled "Those Troublesome Christians" sympathetically described the increase in deprecatory and uncomplimentary words used to describe Christian activists. Some of these included the following: "homophobic", "unchristian", "McCarthy tactics", "narrow- minded." The editorial concluded with the following observation: "Evangelicals and other Christians have committed the crime of getting into politics to make their views heard." Imagine that! In reality, what all these Christians who the liberal media is so worried about really have in common is their orthodox faith. In a world that hates truth, that really is something to fear. Imagine the consternation when the truth finally becomes vocal.

How Should We Then Fight?

Everyone needs a sense of vision in order to be successful in life, whether it's a vision to start your own business, compose a symphony, or plant a vegetable garden. Without it, few are successful. Vision is nothing more than intelligent foresight or the manner in which one sees or conceives of something. In the Book of Proverbs, it is written, "Where there is no revelation, the people cast off restraint" (29:18). In the King James Version, the Scripture reads, "Where there is no vision, the people perish." Father Theodore Hesburgh, the former president of the University of Notre Dame, once said, "The very essence of leadership is you have to have a vision. It's got to be a vision you articulate clearly and forcefully on every occasion. You can't blow an uncertain trumpet."[18] Robert Schuller, pastor and author, believes that "the world of tomorrow belongs to the person who has vision today."[19]

Vision breeds confidence, and confidence success. Glenn Van Ekeren tells the charming story of a little girl who was drawing a picture with crayons on a plain sheet of paper. Her mother asked her what she was drawing. "I'm drawing God," the child quickly answered. The mother responded, "But honey, nobody knows what God looks like." The child continued drawing and then said confidently, "They'll know when I'm finished."[20]

Faith and determination are required to pursue a vision. Both work within the context of a mission statement. The mission, in turn, is accomplished by devising and executing a practical strategy. America needs to reclaim the land back from the secularists. In our pledge of allegiance, we profess to be a nation under God. That is what our founding fathers intended, but we have wandered far from that goal. We have abandoned the principles of the Judeo-Christian ethic that made us great. We have turned from God and embraced ourselves as gods. In doing so, we have departed from the basic assumption that all human life is sacred. We have denied that right and wrong are essential concepts to live by, preferring instead, to make up rules governing human behavior as we go along. We have refused to admit and accept the consequences of our behavior and to assume personal responsibility for our lives, becoming, in the process, a nation of "victims." We have abandoned the principle of a God-centered education and have removed every trace of God from the classroom, reaping the predictable benefits of academic deterioration and moral irresponsibility, our children addicted to drugs and licentiousness. And we have redefined the family according to our own evil imaginations and have preached tolerance for sin.

It is time to become again what we still profess to be — "one nation under God." If we don't, what is left to restrain the judgment of God from falling on our country? Several psalms repeat the phrase, "He (God) will judge the world in righteousness." Psalm 9 adds "He will govern the peoples with justice" (v.8); Psalm 96 completes the thought with "and the peoples in his truth" (v.13). The meaning is clear; at some future time, God will deal decisively with the wickedness of men and establish his reign of righteousness on the earth. Christians, of course, believe that this prophetic word will find full completion when Jesus returns in glory. But God has proven in human history that He will not long tolerate evil before He causes a nation to fall.

> The wicked return to the grave,
> all the nations that forgot God.

> Psalm 9:17

In order to reclaim this increasingly secular country for God, we need to operate within the guidelines of a defined mission statement, one that will tell us how to behave as we go about the business of reestablishing righteousness in our nation. The prophet Micah provides the prophetic standard for all Godly people:

> He has showed you, O man, what is good.
> And what does the Lord require of you?
> To act justly and to love mercy
> And to walk humbly with your God.

> Micah 6:8

Let's flesh this out in the context of our own national situation.

To Do Justice

We "do justice" when we uphold the righteous standard of a just God. As noted earlier, God's justice is connected to the Biblical notion of judgment and righteousness. Godly righteousness demands goodness and truth. Christians are commissioned to proclaim and commanded to live the righteous demands of God's Holy Word:

> Then Jesus came to them and said, "All authority in heaven and on earth has been given to me. Therefore go and made disciples of all nations, baptizing them in the name of the Father and of the Son and of the Holy Spirit, and teaching them to obey everything I commanded you. And surely I am with you always, to the very end of the age.

> Matthew 28:18–20

• By His Power

To fulfill this command of Jesus adequately and faithfully, Christians must first become sensitized to God's consciousness of holiness. Before Jesus began His earthly ministry, He was baptized by John in the river Jordan (Luke 3:21,22). Jesus was filled with the Holy Spirit from the moment of His conception. He did not receive more of the Spirit in His baptism, but rather His Father's divine approval and empowerment as He began his mission. Thus, full of the Holy Spirit, He is led by the same Spirit into the desert "where for forty days He was tempted by the devil" (Luke 4:1,2).

Similarly, every Christian must labor to fulfill his mission, not under his own power, but by the power of the Holy Spirit. Human power melts away through exhaustion, discouragement, and failure. Godly power perseveres with determination to accomplish the desired goal. The prophet Zechariah reminds us of this, when he writes, " 'Not by might, not by power, but by my Spirit,' says the Lord God Almighty" (4:6). It is the Holy Spirit that enables us to do God's work.

• **Through His Word**

Jesus' encounter with Satan in the desert is instructive for us in that He overcame the temptations of Satan through the Word of God. As He was guided by the Holy Spirit, He resisted every temptation by the power of the Holy Spirit. In turn, the power of the Spirit worked through the Word of God, enabling Jesus, even when weakened and most vulnerable, to remain faithful to His mission.

The Apostle Paul exhorts us to "let the word of Christ dwell in you richly"(Colossians 3:16). We too need to allow ourselves to be led by the Holy Spirit: "Those who are led by the Spirit of God are sons of God" (Romans 8:14). If we are led by His Spirit and filled with His Word, we will always be in that place where God desires us to be and always prepared to meet every obstacle Satan places in our path.

In the Gospel of Luke (22:35-37), Jesus has the following conversation with His disciples:

> Then Jesus asked them, "When I sent you without purse, bag or sandals, did you lack anything?"
>
> "Nothing," they answered.
>
> He said to them, "But now if you have a purse, take it, and also a bag; and if you don't have a sword, sell your cloak and buy one. It is written: 'And he was numbered with the transgressors'; and I tell you that this must be fulfilled in me. Yes, what is written about me is reaching its fulfillment."
>
> The disciples said, "See, Lord, here are two swords."
>
> "That is enough," he replied.

This passage has troubled me for years. On a more natural level, I believe He was telling the disciples that, unlike their first missionary venture (Luke 9:1-7) when they were well received, future efforts would be met with opposition and peril. The disciples misunderstood His instructions to buy a sword and produced two. I'm afraid I would have done the same thing. Clearly, Jesus was dissatisfied with their response. Why? Perhaps they were tired of being ridiculed and believed that Jesus, anticipating danger, had changed His tactics. Doesn't that sound reasonable?

But we all should know better. Jesus never preached the way of sword, but the way of love. He was never inconsistent with what He said before and wasn't in this case. The message of Christ is love for our enemies and it will never change.

> You have heard that is was said, 'Love your neighbor and hate your enemy.' But I tell you: Love your enemies and pray for those who persecute you, that you may be sons of your Father in heaven. He causes his sun to rise on the evil and the good, and sends rain on the righteous and the unrighteous. If you love those who love you, what reward will you get? And if you greet only your brothers, what are you doing more than others? Do not even pagans do that? Be perfect, therefore, as you heavenly Father is perfect.
>
> Matthew 5:43-48

How are we then to interpret his instruction to purchase a weapon? I believe the meaning of the sword Jesus referred to could only be known later through Scriptural revelation. The author of Hebrews writes (4:12,13):

> For the word of God is living and active. Sharper than any double-edged sword, it penetrates even to dividing soul and spirit, joints and marrow; it judges the thoughts and attitudes of the heart. Nothing in all creation is hidden from God's sight. Everything is uncovered and laid bare before the eyes of him to whom we must give account.

Here the Word of God is likened to a double-edged sword. Moreover, it is said to be "living and active." The Apostle Paul fleshes out the point when he writes:

> Finally, be strong in the Lord and in his mighty power. Put on the full armor of God so that you can take your stand against the devil's schemes. For our struggle is not against flesh and blood, but against the rulers, against the authorities, against the powers of this dark world and against the spiritual forces of evil in the heavenly realms. Therefore put on the full armor of God, so that when the day of evil comes, you may be able to stand your ground, and after you have done everything, to stand.

Then, after defining each piece of spiritual armor, he further writes:

> Take the helmet of salvation and the sword of the Spirit, which is the word of God.
>
> Ephesians 6:13, 17

The Sword of the Spirit is the Word of God — the Holy Scriptures. Jesus was telling His disciples then, as He's telling us today: "When you set out to follow Me and fulfill My mission for your life, you will face danger and opposition of every kind. But if you are empowered by My Holy Spirit and armed with My Word, you will overcome. My purposes for you will be accomplished and no one can thwart them. You may suffer, just as I suffered, but the Word I send through you will accomplish the purposes for which I send it. Walk in love, trust My power, use My Word and My Name. The victory is secure."

> Go into all the world and preach the good news to all creation. Whoever believes and is baptized will be saved, but whoever does not believe will be condemned. All these signs will accompany those who believe: In my name they will drive out demons; they will speak in new tongues; they will pick up snakes with their hands; and when they drink deadly poison, it will not hurt them at all; they will place their hands on sick people, and they will get well.
>
> Mark 16:15-18

• Do His Work

So the instruction from Scripture is: by His power, through His Word, do His work. In this, we uphold the righteous standard of God. This is what it means to "do justice" as the prophet commands. Now we need to determine what His work is. Again, we turn to the Scriptures. After Jesus returned from the desert where He had been tempted by Satan, He entered His hometown of Nazareth and on the Sabbath day went to the synagogue. There He stood up, unrolled the scroll of the prophet Isaiah and read:

> The Spirit of the Lord is on me, because he has anointed me to preach good news to the poor. He has sent me to proclaim freedom for the prisoners and recovery of sight for the blind, to release the oppressed, to proclaim the year of the Lord's favor.
>
> Luke 4:18,19

The work of Jesus was first to preach the Good News. The word Gospel in English comes from the Anglo-Saxon "god-spell," translated from the Greek "evangelion" or good tidings. The Good News that Jesus preached and we proclaim is that Jesus came that all might be reconciled to the Father; that He came as Messiah or Savior to deliver us from the power of sin and Satan. We further proclaim that by His life, death, and resurrection, He has secured our salvation; that in Him we have the promise of abundant life here on earth and an eternity with Him in heaven. Paul writes:

> For it is by grace you have been saved, through faith –
> and this not from yourselves, it is the gift of God – not
> by works, so that no one can boast.

> Ephesians 2:8,9

Unmerited favor and forgiving love are the central themes of the Gospel. The Apostle Paul elaborates on this theme and establishes the necessity of faith in Christ:

> But now a righteousness from God, apart from the
> law, has been made known, to which the Law and
> the Prophets testify. This righteousness from God
> comes through faith in Jesus Christ to all who
> believe. There is no difference, for all have sinned and
> fall short of the glory of God, and are justified freely
> by his grace through the redemption that came by
> Christ Jesus.

> Romans 3:21-24

Thus, as Jesus came and announced Good News, we, too, must proclaim the Good News of the Gospel to the world. We do it with the understanding that the Cross is central to the message, that without the Cross we would have nothing to proclaim. With Paul, we announce the Gospel with the firm conviction that He died, was buried, and rose from the dead; that without His dying there is no atonement for sins; and without His resurrection our preaching and faith are useless. We are proud of the Gospel, for it is the Good News of God's grace, salvation, and wisdom. So we take it with us wherever we go, eager to tell everyone what we know and have experienced.

It is also our job (work) to remember that the Good News of the Gospel includes a call to repentance (Matthew 4:17, Mark 1:15). Repentance in the original Greek is "metanoia." Meta means "change," noia "mind." Thus, repentance literally means a change of mind. The Scripture teaches us that this change of mind must be a transforming event that results in a changed life. The Bible instructs us to change our lives and live according to God's righteous standard, His Holy Word. The Scriptures, in turn, reveal God's moral absolutes, and His interpretation of right and wrong.

Repentance forces us to confront our personal sinfulness and mend our ways. Repentance without a change of behavior is counterfeit and betrays our insincerity. Repentance without the conforming sign of good conduct and virtuous living cheapens God's grace. Jesus Himself announced the Gospel by first declaring:

> The kingdom of God is near. Repent and believe the
> Good News.
>
> Mark 1:15

This, then, is our mission to "do justice" by proclaiming God's righteous standards and the truth of His Word; to fulfill His commission to each one of us, announcing the Good News of salvation; and then to do His work in His power through His Word. We are challenged never to compromise the Scriptures, by word or deed, but to live according to our testimony about Him, that He might be honored. We are further challenged to not be ashamed to declare what God is proud to offer. If the Scriptures teach us that abortion is murder, we must teach others. The Word has a power of its own. It is able to cut through truth and half-truth, honesty and deception, sincerity and rationalization (Hebrews 4:12,13). We don't have to embellish it and make it stricter or tone it down to render it more palatable. The teaching of Paul is apt:

> Do your best to present yourself to God as one
> approved, a workman who does not need to be ashamed
> and who correctly handles the word of truth.
>
> 2 Timothy 2:15

As Christians, we must allow the Scriptures to form our opinion about life issues. Knowledge can be acquired by our diligent effort to learn and assimilate information. But wisdom belongs to the Lord. Proverbs says "Blessed is the man who finds wisdom, the man who gains understanding" (3:13). In order to grow in Godly wisdom and understanding, we must be fed and instructed by the Word of God. God communicates himself to man through the Scriptures. Many people have opinions about this or that, but the Bible reveals God's opinion to us. A wise person values God's opinions more than those of man. Often, the ways of God seem foolish to unregenerate man, but Scripture reminds us that "the foolishness of God is wiser than man's wisdom, and the weakness of God is stronger than man's strength" (1 Corinthians 1:25).

We, then, need to be people who diligently read and correctly handle the Word of truth. The values we hold must be birthed by the Scriptures. The Christian's views of life, abortion, euthanasia, mercy, pain, and suffering must reflect what God says about these issues. For this reason, we are never allowed to compromise what God holds sacred, but rather are commanded to hold up His righteous standard. In this way, divine justice is served and we "do justice."

To Love Mercy

The second part of Micah's instruction to us is to love mercy. Mercy is a disposition to be kind and forgiving, forbearing and tender. The prophet tells us that God commands us to be merciful. It is within this standard that we must live our life. The Holy Spirit prompts us and the Scriptures instruct us that part of God's work and ours is demonstrating mercy to others. Let's turn again to Luke to gain further understanding of Jesus' earthly ministry and the manner in which He fulfilled this precept.

We have said that the work of Jesus was first to preach the Good News to the poor (4:18). A second part of Jesus' mission is outlined within the same verse of Scripture and in that following:

> He has sent me to proclaim freedom for the prisoners and recovery of sight for the blind, to release the oppressed, to proclaim the year of the Lord's favor.

> Micah 4:18,19

There are many examples of Jesus fulfilling this mission in the Scriptures. A startling revelation of the Scripture is that we are given the same mission as Jesus and are sent forth with the same goals. Jesus fulfilled the prophesy of Isaiah and announced the intention of His ministry (Luke 4:18,19) before He began it. His instructions to His disciples and us recorded in Mark's gospel (16:15-18) were:

Luke 4:18, 19 (Jesus' Mission)	Mark 16:15-18 (Our Mission)
Preach the Good News (v.18)	Preach the Good News (v.15)
Proclaim freedom to captives (v.18) (captive to sin and Satan)	In my Name, drive out demons (v.16)
• Recovery of sight for the blind (v.18) (those physically and spiritually blind)	[In my Name], place hands on the sick and they will get well (v.18)
• Release the oppressed (v.18) (from illness and torment)	
The Spirit of the Lord is upon me (v.18)	They will speak in new tongues (v.17) (demonstrative of the Holy Spirit which will empower the believer)

Thus, our mission today is to preach the Good News, comfort the afflicted, proclaim freedom to captives, and open the eyes of those blinded to the truth. In another dimension, we are reminded to lay hands on the sick and in the Name of Jesus to pray for healings and to expel demons. It becomes very apparent that the work of Jesus is the work of the church.

Another aspect of "loving mercy" is to treat those who disagree with us with kindness and forbearance. Anything less than this standard is not merciful. If we are faithful to follow God's directive in this regard, God is perfectly able to touch the hearts of those opposed to us and Him. We have the obligation to handle the Word of Truth wisely and to confront the evil in our world with determination. But our attitude must be one of mercy. In this, we follow the advice of Paul who wrote to the Thessalonians:

> And we urge you brothers, warn those who are idle, encourage the timid, help the weak, be patient with everyone.

> 1 Thessalonians 5:14

In the same manner, Paul instructed Titus:

> Remind the people to be subject to rulers and authorities, to be obedient, to be ready to do whatever is good, to slander no one, to be peaceable and considerate, and to show true humility toward all men.

> Titus 3:1,2

Peter's instruction to the Church mirrors that of Paul:

> Live in harmony with one another; be sympathetic, love as brothers, be compassionate and humble. Do not repay evil with evil or insult with insult, but with blessing, because to this you were called so that you may inherit a blessing.

> 1 Peter 3:8,9

While this part of Peter's letter is directed towards believers relating to believers, it, of course, is binding on our relations with others. All of this complements the words of our Lord who commanded us to love our enemies (Matthew 5:44) and to be at peace with each other (Mark 9:50).

In God's economy, there is no place for violence, uncontrolled anger, name-calling, slander, contempt, destruction of property, or pejorative language. All of that is from the devil. But those in whom the Holy Spirit dwells ought to demonstrate "love, joy, peace, patience, kindness, goodness, faithful-ness, gentleness and self-control" (Galatians 5:22,23). Christian character and behavior is formed by the Holy Spirit. Paul makes it clear that hatefulness, fits of rage, dissensions, and factious behavior belong to the sinful nature and Satan (Galatians 5:19-21). In order to complete our work assignment faithfully before God, we must do more than preach the Gospel, we must act the part. One of the toughest verses of Scripture for me personally is found in the first letter of John: "Whoever claims to live in him must walk as Jesus did" (2:6). That is impossible except by the power of the Holy Spirit, yet it is God's direc-tive to us.

The behavior of some in the Church, in our national debates about life and during our Pro-Life rallies and marches, has compromised our message and discredited the Gospel. Every time we scream at those who disagree with us or curse them or carry insulting signs or use vituperative language, we weaken our cause. Our mission is always to show mercy and overcome evil with good. However, we must not be silent when evil is perpetrated; we must actively fight in the political arena against any legislation that will weaken the cause of life; we must vote and work for those who support life, contributing our time and money in the process; we must support those organizations that labor in the public and political domain for the cause of the vulnerable (the fetus, handicapped, elderly, and terminally ill); and we must stay informed and involved, determined to persevere in a righteous cause. Mercy is not a weak-ness or a lowering of God's standards. Rather, it is the attitude of Jesus and must be ours as well. The challenge is to demonstrate mercy in love and, at the same time, fight with great determination for the cause of good. A story, per-haps apocryphal, is told by Erwin Lutzer in an article entitled "The Myths That Could Destroy America."[21]

> A news reporter asked a pedestrian, 'Do you know what the two greatest problems in America are?' 'I don't know and I don't care!' the man responded. 'Then you've got both of them!' was the abrupt reply.

Mercy demands that we keep informed and involved and thus fulfill the commission Christ has given us. We don't have the luxury of being ignorant and lazy.

To Walk Humbly

The third and final part of Micah's directive to us is to "walk humbly with our God." Humility is a virtue that characterizes the man and woman of God. The Bible says of Moses, "Now Moses was a very humble man, more humble than anyone else on the face of the earth" (Numbers 12:3). He was mightily used by God, perhaps less because of his giftedness, than his humility and obe-dience. It is written of Jesus is Paul's letter to the church of Philippi:

> Your attitude should be the same as that of Christ
> Jesus: Who, being in very nature God, did not consid-
> er equality with God something to be grasped, but
> made himself nothing, taking the very nature of a ser-
> vant, being made in human likeness. And being found
> in appearance as a man, he humbled himself and
> became obedient to death – even death on a cross!

Philippians 2:5-8

Jesus put aside His glory and Godly prerogatives and submitted to becoming a man — vulnerable, limited in time and space, and at the mercy of those
He created. Because of His humility and submissive obedience, He has been
exalted and reigns with the Father in heaven. Reverence and worship are His
due. One day, He will return in glory and reign over the earth as the King of
Kings and Lord of Lords to the glory of God, the Father.

Part of Micah's command to us is to walk with the same humility before
God and man. Paul encourages Titus "to show true humility toward all men"
(3:2). Peter urges us "to clothe yourselves with humility toward one another,
because 'God opposes the proud but gives grace to the humble'" (1 Peter 5:5).
The great character traits of Jesus were humility and obedience. Usually, the
two are conjoined. They were in Jesus' life; they ought to be in ours.

As a practical out-working of this command, we ought to remember that
many of us have been rescued out of darkness. Thousands upon thousands of
Christians have a historical memory of living apart from God in a life of desperation, anxiety, and despair. We only have to recall the joy that filled our
hearts when we experienced our spiritual rebirth to find reason to be grateful.
Thus, humility becomes us. It is the required dress code of every follower of
Jesus. Accordingly, we should find it easier to humbly extend mercy to those
who disagree with us.

This, then, is our mission statement as we fight the battle for the cause of life
and righteousness: to uphold the just standard of God, showing mercy to those
who disagree, in an attitude of humility that extends grace into every encounter.
Fight? Yes! But fight the right way — God's way. God is more than able to secure
the victory.

A NATIONAL CALL TO REPENTANCE

*Righteousness exalts a nation, but sin is a disgrace to any
people.*

Proverbs 14:34

The call to repentance, individual and corporate, is one of the most persistent
themes in the Bible. The Old Testament prophets insistently echoed the command

to generations of Jews. John the Baptist began his ministry "preaching a baptism of repentance for the forgiveness of sins" (Mark 1:4). Anticipating Jesus, he announced, "Repent, for the kingdom of heaven is near" (Matthew 3:2). Leaving Nazareth, Jesus began his own ministry preaching everywhere, "Repent, for the kingdom of heaven is near" (Matthew 4:17). Clearly, repentance is the starting point of spiritual change and relationship with God.

It is equally clear that nations, as well as people, require cleansing and a change of heart and attitude. The evil king of Ninevah, challenged by the prophet Jonah, led his people in a time of national humiliation, fasting, and prayer, entreating God to forgive their sins and "turn from his fierce anger" lest they perish (Jonah 3:9). It is telling that the king also exhorted his people individually to urgently call on God and give up "their evil ways and their violence" (Jonah 3:8). A change of heart and a corresponding alteration of behavior have always accompanied true repentance. Several United States Presidents have declared National Days of Prayer and President Abraham Lincoln, on April 30, 1863, issued a Proclamation for a National Day of Fasting, Humiliation, and Prayer.

For our nation in our own time, the hour is growing late. The consequences of sin and rebellion have exacted a near-fatal toll on our country. The words of the prophet speak to our age as surely as it did to his: "Let us examine our ways and test them, and let us return to the Lord" (Jeremiah 3:40). It is obvious that the people of God will have to pray and work for the restoration of our country.

Less obvious to many, is the fact that repentance also needs to begin in the church. The words of Scripture are clear: "*If my people who are called by my name* (emphasis mine) – will humble themselves and pray and seek my face and turn from their wicked ways, then will I hear from heaven and will forgive their sin and will heal their land" (2 Chronicles 7:14).

The church needs to lead the way, not in throwing the first stone, but in humbling ourselves, individually and collectively, and pleading for God's forgiveness. We have been eager to remove the specks from the eyes of our unbelieving countrymen and have ignored the planks protruding from our own. We preach the truth of the Scriptures and then disobey it. We are shocked at the licentiousness of our society, only to fall into moral impurity ourselves. We talk about a gentle and forgiving Savior, while presenting a hard, self-righteous face to our neighbors. We lecture others about values but fail to value highly those things that most please God. We resort to the world's ways to achieve the Lord's purposes, thereby revealing our own lack of understanding and humility. All too many of us are unfaithful to our spouses and the divorce rate among believers nearly equals that of unbelieving society. We often forget the supreme importance of prayer and Scripture reading and then wonder why our plans fail and we feel so exhausted. Indeed, let us search our ways, acknowledge the truth, and turn again to the Lord. Then, and only then, will we be able to lead others to safety and reclaim our country for God. The church has the responsibility, first, to live in a manner pleasing to the Lord and then to speak a life-giving word of correction to all of the people. There is responsibility, as well as privilege, in being a child of God.

> At the end of seven days the word of the Lord came to me: "Son of man, I have made you a watchman for the house of Israel; so hear the word I speak and give them warning from me. When I say to a wicked man, 'You will surely die,' and you do not warn him or speak out to dissuade him from his evil ways in order to save his life, that wicked man will die for his sin, and I will hold you accountable for his blood. But if you do warn the wicked man and he does not turn from his wickedness or from his evil ways, he will die for his sin; but you will have saved yourself.

Ezekiel 3:16-19

FINAL CHARGE

Say Not the Struggle Nought Availeth
. . . .

Say not the struggle nought availeth,
 The labor and the wounds are vain,
The enemy faints not, nor faileth,
 And as things have been they remain.

If hopes were dupes, fears may be liars,
 It may be, in your smoke concealed,
Your comrades chase e'en now the fliers,
 And, but for you, possess the field.

For while the tired waves, vainly breaking,
 Seem here no painful inch to gain,
For back through creeks and inlets making,
 Coming silent, flooding in, the main.

And not by eastern windows only,
 When daylight comes, comes in the light,
In front, the sun climbs slow, how slowly,
 But westward look, the land is bright.

Arthur Hugh Clough (1819-1861)

Arthur Hugh Clough, a Christian 19th Century English poet, saw in his own time a world in spiritual conflict. He appreciated the struggles involved in fighting for the kingdom of God. Further, he knew from personal experience that, at times, obstacles to the advancement of godliness in his increasingly secularized country could seem daunting, and even bring discouragement. But, with the eyes of faith, he believed that the Christian church would triumph, and reminds us that the cause is worth the struggle. It is Clough's brand of muscular Christianity that is needed today.

Life is too precious to abandon to those who devalue it. Abortion and euthanasia are important issues that frame life's beginning and end and deserve our attention. However, they need to be addressed within the broader context of all the many events and experiences between these extremes that color the giant canvas of human existence. Surely, life is about more than the manner of our birth and death. The values and beliefs that frame our time on earth better define us than the length of our days. Indeed, the view that we have of life will, in large part, determine what we believe about its preservation. God values all of life and views it as sacred. He anticipates every birth, invests each life with purpose, desires an abundance in its living, and dignifies each ending with the promise of Himself for those who know Him. Our view of life must try to be as big as His.

Today, life is under attack because some reserve the right to terminate it before it begins. Others claim the right to end it before its time, and many would rob it of its true meaning by devaluing the Creator of life and His rules for living. All of this is of proper concern for every God-fearing person. Atheistic secularization has claimed our country as its own, but it is time for every believer to reclaim it back.

To this end, every Christian needs to take seriously Christ's commission to make disciples of the lost and unbelieving. Like Jesus, we need to see them, not as enemies, but as potential brothers and sisters. It is only by bringing people to Christ that we will win the country back to the Lord, and see people released to live abundant fulfilled lives, free of condemnation and guilt. The mission field, which most of us work in, will be in our own home and neighborhood. Here, we will be judged more by how we live, than by what we say. In imitation of our Lord, we need to remind ourselves that He always seemed more interested in people than in success. He reached out to the lost and lonely with compassion, not condemnation. It is revealing that He never seemed to be as interested in making converts, as He was in touching lives. Our love for the lost must be based on Christ's love for humanity, not on church agendas or theological considerations. And we need to be reminded that more is needed here than zeal and technique. The Christian's commission is to testify by words and deeds to the truth of the gospel message. It is the Lord's job to touch hearts through the Holy Spirit and bring about conversion. Surely, sloganeering, confrontational posturing, angry and pejorative language, and character assassination are poor substitutes for the model Jesus showed us. It is time to take seriously the call and begin the work.

The battle will be arduous and is not for the faint-hearted. Jesus, speaking of the final days, has this to say to his disciples and, through them, to us, "All men will hate you because of me, but he who stands firm to the end will be saved" (Matthew 10:22). The 11th chapter of Hebrews is a great testimony to those who endured with Christ. The author says of these stalwart believers, "These were all commended for their faith, yet none of them received what had been promised. God had planned something better for us so that only together with us would they be made perfect" (Hebrews 11:39,40). In other words, many endured, without experiencing apparent victory over their circumstances, so that we today might share in the blessing of God's triumph. Thus, we persevere that the overall purposes of God might be realized to His glory. We leave it to Him to sort out the winners and the losers. I believe that, many that the world deems victors, will have a different verdict before the judgment seat of God.

Samuel Adams (1722–1803) once said in a speech to his countrymen:

> Let us contemplate our forefathers, and posterity, and resolve to maintain the rights bequeathed to us from the former, for the sake of the latter. The necessity of the times, more than ever, calls for our utmost circumspection, deliberation, fortitude and perseverance. Let us remember that 'if we suffer tamely a lawless attack upon our liberty, we encourage it, and involve others in our doom'. It is a very serious consideration . . that millions yet unborn may be miserable sharers of the event.[22]

The "necessity of the times," today, equally demands fortitude and perseverance. We need to encourage each other to not give in to the ungodly attack upon life, lest we doom countless others who will follow us. The ultimate victory belongs to God, but we need to do our part so that He is free to do His. To paraphrase Samuel Adams, this is no time to give up.

In addition, we need to remember that as in all else, we overcome adversity by our faith. The Apostle John writes, "This is the victory that has overcome the world, even our faith" (1 John 5:4). Just as, in faith, we overcame the sinful patterns of our life and turned to Christ, so too, in our daily struggles, both corporately and individually, we turn to Jesus and trust Him to triumph over the evil that besets us and our world. The Apostle Paul reminds us, "Everyone who trusts in the Lord will never be put to shame" (Romans 10:11). Our confidence needs to be in God who is more than able to win the day. In Christ, we have a tremendous future. We don't need to plea bargain with the enemies of life for better terms. Our trust is in the Lord, as we say with David,

> In God, whose word I praise,
> in God I trust; I will not be afraid.

What can mortal man do to me?

Psalm 56:4

In a time similarly troubled, the prophet Azariah said to Asa, King of Judah, "But as for you, be strong and do not give up, for your work will be rewarded" (2 Chronicles 15:7). These words are appropriate for our time as well: Be strong. Do not give up. Trust in the Lord. Do not be afraid.

Finally, we must not lose our sense of moral outrage. Evil must neither be accommodated nor appeased. In humility, we must continue to hold up God's righteous standard before a country that, in good part, chooses to ignore Him. We must never allow ourselves to be comfortable with anything that dishonors God. Solomon reminds us that "it is to a man's honor to avoid strife" (Proverbs 20:3), but certainly, not at the expense of truth and justice. The cause is worth the struggle.

References

All scripture references, unless otherwise designated, are taken from "The New International Version", Zondervan Publishing House.

CHAPTER 1: IN THE BEGINNING

1. A. Cohen, *Everyman's Talmud* (New York: Schoeken Books, 1949), Chapter 11, *God and the Universe*, pp. 27-66; and *Catechism of the Catholic Church* (Città del Vaticano: Libreria Editrice Vaticana, 1944), Chapter 1, *I Believe in God the Father*, pp. 54-105.

2. G. I. Williamson, *The Shorter Catechism* (New Jersey: Presbyterian and Reformed Publishing Co., 1970), pp. 15-19; A. Cohen, op.cit., pp. 27-66; and *Catechism*, op.cit., pp. 54-105

3. Robert Jastrow, *God and the Astronomers* (New York: W.W. Norton and Company, Inc., 1978), Chapter 6, pp. 111-116.

4. ibid, p. 112.

5. Ronald W. Clark, *Einstein: The Life and Times* (New York and Cleveland: The World Publishing Company, 1971), p. 413.

6. Jastrow, op.cit., p. 14.

7. ibid, p. 116.

8. Alan Moorehead, *Darwin and the Beagle* (New York and Evanston: Harper and Row Publishers, 1969).

9. Somerset Maugham, *The Summing Up* (New York: Penguin Books, 1963), pp. 181-182.

10. Williamson, op.cit., pp. 35-39.

11. A. Cohen, op.cit., pp. 67-120.

12. *Catechism*, op.cit., pp. 92-94.

13. Mortimer Adler, *The Great Ideas: A Lexicon of Western Thought* (New York: MacMillan Pubishing Company, 1992), Chapter 48, p. 443.

14. A. Cohen, op.cit., p. 67.

15. ibid, pp. 76-78.

16. Paul Veyne, *A History of Private Life: From Pagan Rome to Byzantium* (Massachusetts and England: Harvard University Press, 1987), Chapter 1, *The Roman Empire*, pp. 9-14.

17. Kermit L. Hall, ed., *The Oxford Companion to the Supreme Court* (New York and Oxford: Oxford University Press, 1992), pp. 739-742.

CHAPTER 2: THE VALUE AND DIGNITY OF LIFE

1. Colin Chapman, *The Case for Christianity* (Grand Rapids, Michigan: Wm. B. Eerdman's Publishing Co., 1981), pp. 217-226; Gordon H. Clark, *Thales to Dewey* (Boston: Houghton Mifflin Co, 1957), pp. 498-53.

2. Thomas V. Morris, *Making Sense of It All* (Grand Rapids, Michigan: Wm. B. Eerdman's Publishing Co., 1993), p. 21.

3. Harry Blamires, *The Christian Mind* (Ann Arbor, Michigan: Servant, 1963), pp. 67-85.

4. Peter Singer, "Sanctity of Life or Quality of Life?", *Pediatrics*, 72(1), July 1993, p. 129.

5. Glenn Van Ekeren, *Speaker's Sourcebook II* (Englewood Cliffs, N.J.: Prentice Hall, Inc., 1994), part of a quotation attributed to Leo Rosten, p. 237.

6. J. I. Packer, *Knowing God* (Downers Grove, Illinois: Intervarsity Press, 1973), p. 56.

7. William G. Storey, *Bless the Lord* (Notre Dame, Indiana: Ave Maria Press, 1974), p. 74.

8. John R. W. Stott, *Basic Christianity* (Downers Grove, Illinois: Intervarsity Press, 1971), p. 81.

9. John Bartlett, op.cit., (Quote attributed to Tertullian, Apologeticus, 17), p. 126.

10. ibid, (Quote attributed to St. Jerome, Letter 82), p. 126.

11. Kenneth Scott Latourette, *A History of Christianity: Beginnings to 1500* (New York, N.Y.: Harper and Row, 1975), Vol 1, p. 91.

12. *Catechism of the Catholic Church* (Città del Vaticano: Libreria Editrice Vaticana, 1944), Chapter 1, *The Profession of Faith*, p. 64.

13. ibid., p. 64.

14. ibid., p. 65.

CHAPTER 3: THE DILEMMA OF ABORTION

1. *The World Book Encyclopedia*, s.v. "birth control."

2. Lawson, HW, A. Frye, HK. Atrash, JC. Smith, HB. Shulman, M. Ramick, "Abortion Mortality, United States, 1972 through 1987," *American Journal of Obstetrics and Gynecology*, 171 (5), November 1994, pp. 1365-72.

3. *Roe.v.Wade*, 410 US 113, 151 (1973).

4. *The Merck Manual*, 15th Edition, Merck Sharp and Dohme Research Laboratories (Rahway, New Jersey, 1987), p. 1760.

5. Mike W. Martin, *Everyday Morality* (Belmont: Wadsworth Publishing Company, 1995), pp. 187-188.

6. See Colin Chapman, *The Case for Christianity* (Grand Rapids: Wm B. Eerdman's Publishing Co., 1981), pp. 217-226.

7. *Griswold.v.Connecticut*, 381 US 479 (1965). For a summary of this piece of legislation, see Michael W. McCann, "Griswold.v.Connecticut," in *The Oxford Companion to the Supreme Court of the United States*, ed. by Kermit L. Hall (New York: Oxford University Press, 1992), pp. 351-353.

8. *Oxford Companion*, p. 351.

9. ibid., p. 352.

10. ibid., p. 352.

11. D. J. Leyshon, "Abortion in Search of a Constitutional Doctrine," *Medicine and Law*, 10, October 1991, p. 158.

12. ibid., p. 158.

13. *Webster v. Reproductive Health Services*, 492 US 490 (1989).

14. ibid., II A. This material found in Webster pertains to a provision stated in Roe.v.Wade.

15. ibid., Justice Scalia's statement, concurring in part.

16. "Planned Parenthood of Southeastern Pennsylvania v. Robert P. Casey," quoted in Daniel C. Maguire, *The Ethics of Abortion* (Buffalo, New York: Prometheus Books, 1993), pp. 60–85.

17. Robert H. Bork, "Again a Struggle for the Soul of the Court," quoted in *The Ethics of Abortion*, pp. 86–88.

18. F. K. Beller and C. A. deProsse, "Confusion of Trimester and Viability, Consequences for Abortion Laws in the United States and Abroad," *Journal of Reproductive Medicine*, June 1992, 37(6), pp. 537-540.

19. Sheldon B. Korones, M.D., "Must Life be Weighed on a Scale?", hand-out at Neonatal Conference at the University of Tennessee, Memphis, Regional Medical Center, Newborn Center.

20. ibid.

21. Roger Wertheimer, "Understanding the Abortion Argument" in *The Problem of Abortion*, ed. Joel Feinberg (Belmont: Wadsworth Publishing Company, 1984), pp. 43-57.

22. Alan Zaitchik, "Viability and the Morality of Abortion," in *The Problem of Abortion*, pp. 58-64.

23. D. J. Leyshon, "Abortion in Search of a Constitutional Doctrine," *Medicine and Law*, 10, October 1991, p. 162.

24. L. W. Sumner, "A Third Way," in *The Problem of Abortion*, pp. 71-101.

25. D. J. Leyshon, op.cit., p. 162.

26. Leyshon, op. cit., pp. 161–64.

27. Theodore Ooms, "A Family Perspective in Abortion" in *Abortion: Understanding Differences*, (New York and London: Plenum Press, 1984), p. 90.

28. ibid., p. 90.

29. Bernard Nathanson, *Aborting America* (New York: Doubleday, 1979), pp. 256–257.

30. Charles J. Sykes, *A Nation of Victims* (New York: St. Martin's Press, 1992), p. 180.

31. Christine Smith Torre, et. al., Amicus Brief filed in the Supreme Court of the United States: Jayne Bray, et. al., v. Alexandria Women's Health Clinic, in *Studies in Prolife Feminism*, 1(1), winter 1995, pp. 72-73.

32. ibid., pp. 74–77.

33. ibid., pp. 78–79.

34. ibid., p. 81.

35. Rosalind Pollack Petchesky, *Abortion and Women's Choice: The State, Sexuality, and Reproductive Freedom* (Boston: Northeastern University Press, 1984), p. 2.

36. Sykes, op.cit., pp. 182-183.

37. ibid., p. 181.

38. ibid., p. 183.

39. ibid., pp. 183–190.

40. *Christianity Today*

41. Barbara R. Gottlieb, "Abortion - 1995," *The New England Journal of Medicine*, 332 (8), 23 February 1995, pp. 532-533.

42. R. I. Goldenberg and L.V. Klerman, "Adolescent Pregnancy — Another Look," *The New England Journal of Medicine*, 332 (17), 27 April 1995, pp. 1161-1162.

43. Christine Smith Torre, et. al., op.cit., p. 70.

44. ibid., p. 66.

45. ibid., p. 66.

46. D. J. Leyshon, op.cit., p. 168.

47. George A. Maloney, S.J., *Mary: The Womb of God* (Denville, New Jersey: Dimension Books, 1976), p. 15.

48. D. J. Leyshon, op.cit., p. 168.

49. ibid., p. 169.

50. ibid., p. 170.

51. Rosalind Pollack Petchesky, op.cit., p. 351.

52. *Early Christian Writings* [translated by Maxwell Staniforth] (New York, New York: Penguin Books, 1981), p. 228.

53. J. B. Lightfoot, *The Apostolic Fathers* (Grand Rapids, Michigan: Baker, 1986), p. 154.

54. Plato, *Republic*, 5.9

55. Paul B. Fowler, op.cit., p. 16.

56. William A. Jurgens, *The Faith of the Early Fathers*, 2 vol. (Collegeville, Minnesota: The Liturgical Press, 1979), 2: 7.

57. Michael J. Gorman, *Abortion and the Early Church* (Downers Grove, Illinois: Intervarsity Press, 1982), pp. 47-73.

58. Frances and Joseph Gies, *Marriage and the Family in the Middle Ages* (New York: Harper and Row, 1987), pp. 295-306.

59. John A. Harden, S.J., *The Catholic Catechism* (New York: Doubleday and Company, Inc., 1973), p. 336.

60. Karl Barth, *Church Dogmatics*, English ed. G.W. Bromiley and T.F. Torrance (Edinburgh, England: T&T Clark, 1961), vol. 3, The Doctrine of Creation, p. 415.

61. John A. Harden, S.J., *The Catholic Catechism* (New York: Doubleday and Company, Inc., 1975), p. 341.

62. John XXIII, encyclical "Mater et Magistra," III, p. 194.

63. Paul VI, "Declaration on Procured Abortion" in *Congregation for the Doctrine of Faith*, III, 12, December 1974.

64. John Paul III, "Evangelium Vitae," rpt. in *The New York Times*, 31 March 1995.

65. Norman L. Geisler, *Christian Ethics* (Grand Rapids, Michingan: Baker Book House, 1989), pp. 148-152.

66. Stanley Haueerwas, "Why Abortion is a Religious Issue," in *The Ethics of Abortion* [ed. by Robert M. Baird and Stuart E. Rosenbaum] (Buffalo, New York: Prometheus Books, 1993), pp. 149-169.

67 Paul B. Fowler, *Abortion: Toward an Evangelical Consensus* (Portland, Oregon: Multnomah Press, 1987), p. 14.

68. Daniel C. Maguire in *The Ethics of Abortion*, op.cit., p. 146.

69. ibid, pp. 147-148.

70. Paul D. Simmons in *The Ethics of Abortion*, op. cit., pp. 170-186.

71. Mary Ann LaManna in *Abortion: Understanding Differences*, op.cit., pp. 2-5.

72. ibid, p.4.

73. Material excerpted from a bulletin announcement in the column "Rounds" published in *Physician*, March-April 1995, p. 3.

74. Albert S. Lyons, "Hippocrates," in *Medicine: An Illustrated History*, ed. Albert S. Lyons, M.D. and R. Joseph Petrucelli, II, M.D. (New York: Harry N. Abrams, Inc., Publishers, 1978), p. 214.

75. ibid., p. 214.

76. Edmund J. Pellegrins, "The Metamorphosis of Medical Ethics: A Thirty Year Retrospective, "*Journal of the American Medical Association*, 3 March 1993, 269(9), pp. 1158-1162.

77. ibid., p. 1158.

78. R. James McKay, "The Fetus," in *Textbook of Pediatrics*, ed. Waldo E. Nelson, Victor C. Vaughan III, and R. James McKay (Philadelphia: W. B. Saunders Co., 1992), p. 347.

79. American Medical Association Council on Ethical and Judicial Affairs, *Code of Medical Ethics: Current Opinions with Annotations*, 1994.

80. ibid., p. 2.

81. ibid., p. 2.

82. Christine Smith Torre, op. cit., p. 72.

83. Roe.v.Wade, op. cit.

84. Christine Smith Torre, op. cit., p. 72.

85. ibid., p. 72.

86. Norman L. Geisler, *Christian Ethics* (Grand Rapids: Baker Book House), p. 149.

87. Sir Thomas Browne, M.D., *Religio Medici*, The Classics of Medicine Library (1642; rpt, Alabama: Leslie B. Adams, Jr., 1981).

88. I consulted the following sources in compiling this graph: R. K. Creasy and R. Resnik, *Maternal-Fetal Medicine*, 3d ed. (Philadelphia: W.B. Saunders and Co., 1994); J. E. Dimmick and D. K. Kalousek, *Developmental Pathology of the Embryo and Fetus* (Philadelphia: J. B. Lippincott Co., 1992); F. G. Cunningham, P. C. McDonald, K. J. Levens, N. F. Gant, L. C. Gilstrap, *Williams Obstetrics*, 19th ed.(Norwalk, Conn.: Appleton and Lange, 1993).

89. Dr. A. Liley, quoted in J. C. Wilke and B. Wilke, *Abortion Questions and Answers* (Cincinnati: Hayes, 1955), p., 59.

90. Warburton, D., Fraser, FC, "Spontaneous Abortion Risks in Man: Data From Reproductive Histories Collected in a Medical Genetics Unit," *American Journal of Human Genetics*, 16, 1964, p. 1.

91. Nicholson J. Eastman, *Williams Obstetrics* (New York: Appleton-Century-Crofts, Inc., 1956), p. 1077.

92.   William Droegemuller, Arthur L. Herbst, Darnell R. Mishell, Morton A. Stenchever, *Comprehensive Gynecology* (St. Louis: The CV Mosby Co., 1987).

93.   Table 2 is excerpted from Steven G. Gabbe, Jennifer R. Niebyl, and Joe Leigh Simpson, *Obstetrics*, 2d ed. (New York: Churchill Livingston, 1991).

94.   See Michael D. Volk and Melvin D. Morgan, *Medical Malpractice: Handling Obstetric and Neonatal Cases* (Colorado Springs, Colorado: McGraw Hill Book Co., 1986), pp. 112-23.

95.   Richard E. Behrman, *Neonatal-Perinatal Medicine: Diseases of the Fetus and Infant* (St. Louis: CV Mosby Co., 1977), p. 175.

96.   Richard E. Behrman, Robert M. Kliegman, Waldo E. Nelson, and Victor C. Vaughn III, *Nelson Textbook of Pediatrics (Fourteenth Edition)* (Philadelphia: W. B. Saunders, 1992), p. 298.

97.   Norman Geisler, op.cit., p. 152.

98   Helen Dewar, "Senate Debates Limits on Late-Term Abortions," *The Washington Post*, 8 November 1995.

99.   Helen Dewar, "Senate Votes to Ban Rare Procedure for Late-Term Abortions," *The Washington Post*, 8 December 1995.

100. ibid.

101. Jennifer Ferranti, " 'D and X' Abortion Ban Faces Presidential Veto," *Christianity Today*, 11 December 1995, p. 69.

102. ibid., p. 74.

103. Helen Dewar, op.cit., *The Washington Post*, 8 November 1995.

104. Dewar, op.cit., *The Washington Post*, 8 December 1995.

105. Norman Geisler, op.cit., p. 141

106. William Osler, *Counsels and Ideas and Selected Aphorisms* (Boston and New York: Houghton, Mifflin and Company, 1905).

107. Gina Kolata, "Doctors Isolate a Common Cancer-Related Gene," *The New York Times*, 23 June 1995.

108. Department of Health and Human Services, Public Health Service, National Institutes of Health, NIH Publication Number 95-3897.

109. Elizabeth Mensch and Alan Freeman, *The Politics of Virtue: Is Abortion Debatable?* (Durham: Duke University Press, 1993), p. 126.

110. ibid., p. 126.

111. Jerry Gray, "Issue of Abortion is Pushing Its Way to Center Stage," *The New York Times*, 19 June 1995.

112. National Right to Life Committee, "States Which Have a Woman's Right to Know Law," *State Legislation Committee Bulletin*, February 1995.

113. National Right to Life Committee, "Parental Involvement Laws: The Minnesota Success Story," *State Legislation Committee Bulletin*, March 1991.

114. Elizabeth Mensch and Alan Freeman, op.cit., pp. 126-52.

115. D.J. Leyshon, op.cit., pp. 223-34.

116. Abraham Lincoln, *Lincoln's Yarns and Stories*, ed. Colonel Alexander K. McClure (Toronto and Philadelphia: The John C. Winston Company), p. 332.

CHAPTER 4: EUTHANASIA: THE DEBATE INTENSIFIES

1. Derek Humphry, *Final Exit* (New York: Dell Publishing Company, 1993).

2. Fyodor Dostoevsky, *The Brothers Karamazov*, trans. Richard Pevear and Larisca Volkhonsky (New York: Vintage, 1991), p. 263.

3. *The American Heritage Dictionary* (Boston: Houghton Mifflin Company, 1982).

4. Albert S. Lyons, MD, "Hippocrates" in *Medicine: An Illustrated History*, ed. Albert S. Lyons, MD and R. Joseph Petucelli, II, MD (New York: Harvey N. Abrams, Inc., Publishers, 1978), pp. 210-14.

5. Robin Lane Fox, *Pagans and Christians* (New York: Alfred A. Knopf, Inc., 1987), pp. 342-343.

6. Peter Urbach, *Francis Bacon's Philosophy of Science* (LaSalle, Illinois: Open Court, 1987), p. 146.

7. Ezekiel J. Emanuel, MD, "Euthanasia: Historical, Ethical, and Empiric Perspectives," *Archives of Internal Medicine*, 154 (12), September 1994, p. 1892.

8. Samuel D. Williams, *Euthanasia* (London, England: Williams and Northgate, 1872).

9. See the following editorials, "Euthanasia," BMJ, 1, 1906, pp. 638–639; "Euthanasia — Degenerated Sympathy," *Boston Medical Surgical Journal*, 154, 1906, pp. 330-31.

10. Michael Burleigh, *Death and Deliverance: Euthanasia in Germany 1900-1945* (Cambridge, England: Cambridge University Press, 1994), pp. 1-42.

11. ibid, p. 27.

12. Karl Dietrich Bracher, *The German Dictatorship* (New York, Washington: Preger Publishers, 1970), translated by Jean Steinberg from the German, pp. 420-431, section entitled "The Murder of the Jews."

13. Eugene Davidson, *The Trial of the Germans: Nurenberg 1945-1946* (New York: The McMillian Company, 1966), pp. 7-9.

14. Proctor, "Atrocity Begins at Home," book review for *The New York Times Book Review*, 5 February 1995, p. 3.

15. See G.E. Pence, "Do Not Go Slowly Into That Dark Night: Mercy Killing In Holland," *American Journal of Medicine*, 84, 1988, pp. 139-41; Ezekiel J. Emanuel, op.cit., p. 1896; Peter Singer, *Rethinking Life and Death* (New York: St. Martin's Press, 1994), pp. 143-44.

16. Daniel Callahan, *The Troubled Dream of Life* (New York, Simon and Schuster, 1993), pp. 112-13.

17. See JKM Gevers, "Legislation on Euthanasia: Recent Developments in the Netherlands," *Journal of Medical Ethics*, 18, 1992, pp. 138-41; Ezekiel J. Emanuel, op.cit., p. 1897.

18. "The Remmelink Report," *Health Policy* (State Commission on Euthanasia, The Netherlands), 22, 1992, pp. 1-262.

19. J. Keown, "On Regulating Death" (Briarcliff Manor, New York, Hastings Center Report) 22, 1992, pp. 39-43.

20. Ezekiel J. Emanuel, op.cit., p. 1898.

21. See Daniel Callahan, "When Self-Determination Runs Amok," *Hastings Cent Rep*, 22, March–April 1992, pp. 52-5; Alex Capeon, "Euthanasia in the Netherlands: American Observations," *Hastings Cent Rep*, 22, March–April, pp. 30-33.

22. Daniel Callahan, *The Troubled Dream of Life*, op.cit., p. 114.

23. Quinlan, In re, 70 New Jersey 10 355 A.2d (1976).

24. Peter Bernardi, "Dr. Death's Dreadful Sermon," *America*, 30 April 1994; reprinted in *Christianity Today*, 15 August 1944, pp. 30-32.

25. Peter Singer, *Rethinking Life and Death* (New York: Simon and Schuster, 1993), pp. 133-35.

26. Peter J. Bernardi, op. cit., p. 30.

27. ibid., p. 30.

28. See Marcia Angell, M.D., "Prisoners of Technology: The Case of Nancy Cruzan," editorial in *The New England Journal of Medicine*, 332(17) 26 April 1990, pp. 1226-1228; Case 4a "Cruzan v. Director, Missouri Department of Health," presented in publication *Moral Controversies: Race, Class, and Gender in Applied Ethics*, [edited by Steven Jay Gold] (Belmont, California: Wadsworth Publishing Company, 1993), pp. 175-79.

29. R. J. Blendon, U. S. Szalay, R. A. Knox, "Should Physicians Aid Their Patients in Dying?" *Journal of the American Medical Association*, 267, 1992, pp. 2658-62.

30. J. S. Cohen, M.D., M.P.H., Stephan D. Fihn, M.D., M.P.H., et. al., "Attitudes Toward Suicide and Euthanasia Among Physicians in Washington State," *The New England Journal of Medicine*, 331(2), 14 July 1994, pp. 89-94.

31. ibid., p. 89.

32. See Philip Yancey, *Where Is God When It Hurts* (Grand Rapids, Michigan: Zondervan Publishing House, 1990), pp. 25-58.

33. William H. McNeill, *Plagues and Peoples* (New York: Anchor Books, 1977), p. 128.

34. Fielding H. Garrison, MD, *History of Medicine* (Philadelphia: W.B. Saunders, Co., 1929), p. 64.

35. Philip Yancey, op.cit., p. 31.

36. C.S. Lewis, *The Problem of Pain* (New York: MacMillian Publishing Co., Inc., 1976), p. 93.

37. Albert Einstein, "Overview of Cancer Pain Management," in *Pain Management and Care of the Terminal Patient*, ed. Judy Kornell (Washington: Washington State Medical Association, 1992), p. 4.

38. See "Cancer Pain," in *The Merck Manual*, ed. Robert Berbow, MD, (Rahway: Merck Sharp and Dohone Research Laboratories, 1987), pp. 1342–47; Burke J. Balch, JD, and David Waters, *Pain Control* (Medical Ethics Department, National Right to Life Committee, May 1994), pp. 7–8.

39. Daniel Callahan, *What Kind of Life* (Washington, DC: Georgetown University Press, 1990).

40. ibid, p. 27.

41. ibid., pp. 103–34.

42. Jerome P. Kassirer, MD, "Managed Care and the Morality of the Marketplace," *The New England Journal of Medicine*, 333 (1), 6 July 1995, pp. 50–52.

43. Daniel Callahan, op. cit., p. 269.

44. James H. Brown, Paul Henteleff, Samia Barabat, and Cheryl J. Rowe, "Is It Normal for Terminally Ill Patients to Desire Death?", *American Journal of Psychiatry*, 143 (2), February 1986, p. 10.

45 Burke J. Balch, JD, and Randall K. O'Bannon, MA, "What About the Terminally Ill?", *Why We Shouldn't Legalize Assisting Suicide, Part III*, Medical Ethics Department, National Right to Life Committee, May 1994.

46. Norman Geisler, op. cit., pp. 162–63.

47. Daniel Callahan, op. cit., p. 232.

48. ibid., pp. 231–237.

49. ibid., p. 237.

50. Norman Geisler, op.cit., pp. 157–71.

51. Burke J. Balch, et.al., *Pain Control*, p. 8.

52. *New International Version*, op.cit., citation from footnote explaining text.

53. The text that follows is the result of my personal study of the Scriptures, but owes much to several other sources, especially Geisler's work, *Christian Ethics; The Catechism of the Catholic Church*, and the *Shorter Catechism*, all of which have been previously cited.

54. A. Cohen, *Everyman's Talmud* (New York: Schoeken Books, 1949), p. 75.

55. *Catechism of the Catholic Church*, Città del Vaticano: Libreria Editrice Vaticana, 1944), pp. 550-51.

56. Chuck Colson, "The Volunteer at Anschwitz," in *The Body* (Word, Inc., Dallas, Texas), 1992.

57. The text is the result of my personal study of the Scripture. I am also very indebted to the following sources, cited previously: J. I. Packer, *Knowing God*, pp. 138-47; Bruce M. Metzger and Michael D. Coogan, *The Oxford Companion to the Bible*, pp. 655-56; and John L. McKenzie, SJ, *Dictionary of the Bible*, pp. 465-69.

58. Franklin G. Miller, et.al., "Regulating Physician-Assisted Death," *The New England Journal of Medicine*, 331 (2), 14 July 1994, p. 119.

59. Bernard Lo, MD, Fanella Rouse, JD, and Laurie Dornbrand, MD, "Family Decision Making on Trial: Who Decides for Incompetent Patients?", *The New England Journal of Medicine*, 322 (17), 26 April 1990, pp. 1228-31.

60. See Peter Singer, *Rethinking Life and Death*, op.cit., pp. 106-107; John Lantos, MD, "Baby Doe Five Years Later: Implications for Child Health," *New England Journal of Medicine*, 317 (7), 13 August 1987, p. 444.

61. John C. Moskop and Rita L. Saldanha, "Baby Doe Rule: Still a Threat," in *Moral Controversies*, op. cit., p. 180.

62. ibid., pp. 180-86.

63. *Code of Medical Ethics* (American Medical Association, 1994 Edition).

64. ibid, pp. 50, 55.

65. ibid, pp. 50, 55.

66. ibid, pp. 50, 55.

67. ibid, pp. 51, 52.

68. ibid, pp. 51, 52, 58, 59.

69. Darrel W. Amundsen, "The Physicians Obligation to Prolong Life: A Medical Duty Without Classical Roots," *Hastings Center Report*, August 1978, pp. 23-30.

70. Marcia Angell, MD, "Euthanasia," *The New England Journal of Medicine*, 319 (20), 17 November 1988, pp. 1348-50.

71. See Christine K. Cassel, MD, and Diane E. Meier, "Morals and Moralism in the Debate Over Euthanasia and Assisted Suicide," *New England Journal of Medicine*, 323 (11), 13 September 1990, pp. 750-52.

72. Franklin G. Miller, op. cit., p. 122.

73. ibid, p. 121, 122.

74. ibid, p. 122.

75. Ezekiel J. Emanual, op. cit., pp. 1898-1899.

76. Survey cited in *Physicians Magazine*, 6(5), September-October 1994, p. 3.

77. Jonathan S. Cohen, MD, MPH, Stephan D. Fehn, MD, MPH, Edward J. Boyko, MD, MPH, Albert R. Jonsen, PhD, and Robert W. Wood, MD, "Attitudes Toward Assisted Suicide and Euthanasia Among Physicians in Washington State," *New England Journal of Medicine*, 331 (2), 14 July 1994, pp. 89-94.

78. ibid., p. 94.

79. Jerald G. Blachman, Ph.D., Kirsten H. Alcser, Ph.D., David J. Doukas, M.D., Richard L. Lichtenstein, Ph.D., Amy D. Corning, M.A., and Howard Brody, M.D., Ph.D., "Attitudes of Michigan Physicians and the Public Toward Legalizing Physician-Assisted Suicide and Voluntary Euthanasia," *The New England Journal of Medicine*, 334(5), 1 Feb 1966, pp. 303-309.

80. Melinda A. Lee, M.D., Heidi D. Nelson, M.D., M.P.H., Virginia P. Tilden, R.N., D.N.Sc., Linda Ganzini, M.D., Terri A. Schmidt, M.D., and Susan W. Tolle, M.D., "Legalizing Assisted Suicide — Views of Physicians in Oregon," *The New England Journal of Medicine*, 334(5), 1 Feb 1966, pp. 310-315.

81. ibid., p. 311.

82. ibid., p. 312.

83. ibid., p. 313.

84. ibid., p. 313.

85. ibid., p. 312.

86. David A. Asch, M.D., M.B.A., "The Role of Critical Care Nurses in Euthanasia and Assisted Suicide," *The New England Journal of Medicine*, 334(21), 23 May 1966, pp. 1374–1379.

87. ibid., p. 1375.

88. ibid., p. 1376.

89. ibid., p. 1376.

90. See Robert H. Curtis, MD, "The Ancients and Pain," in *Triumph Over Pain* (New York: David McKay Company, Inc., 1972), pp. 8–13; Albert Lyons, "Ancient Egypt," in *Medicine: An Illustrated History*, op. cit., p. 97; Fielding Garrison, *History of Medicine*, op. cit., p. 30.

91. Fielding Garrison, op. cit., p. 30.

92. Amir Halevy, MD and Baruch Brody, *Annals of Internal Medicine*, 119 (6), 15 September 1993, p. 519.

93. Harrison's *Principles of Internal Medicine* [11th Edition] (New York: McGraw-Hill Book Company, 1987), p. 120.

94. Peter Singer, *Rethinking Life and Death* (New York, St. Martin's Press, 1994), pp. 133–135.

95. Amir Halevy, M.D. and Baruch Brody, op. cit., pp. 519-20.

96. Daniel Callahan, *The Troubled Dream of Life*, op.cit., pp. 37–40.

97. See Alan Meisel, *The Right to Die* (New York: John Wiley and Sons, 1989), pp. 311–428; Daniel Callahan, What Kind of Life, op.cit., pp. 226-31.

98. Marion Danis, MD, et.al., "A Prospective Study of Advance Directives For Life-Sustaining Care," *The New England Journal of Medicine*, 334, 28

March 1991, p. 882.

99. Louis L. Brunetti, MD, JD, Stephanie D. Carperos, MD, and Ronald E. Westlund, MS, MBA, "Physician's Attitudes Towards Living Wills and Cardiopulmonary Resuscitation," *Journal of General Internal Medicine*, 6, July-August 1991, pp. 323-27.

100. Michael Rie, MD, "The Limits of a Wish," *Hastings Center Report*, July-August 1991, pp. 24-25.

101. Julien S. Murphy, "Should Pregnancies Be Sustained in Brain-Dead Women? A Philosophical Discussion of Postpartum Pregnancy," in *Moral Controversies*, op. cit., pp. 158-75.

102. ibid., p. 161.

103. ibid., p. 163.

104. Jody A. Charnov, "AIDS Specialist Says Physician-Assisted Death May Be Appropriate in Late-Stage Disease," *Infectious Disease News*, 8 (5), May 1995, p. 3.

CHAPTER 5: RECLAIMING THE LAND

1. Qtd. in *The Rebirth of America* (Arthur S. DeMoss Foundation, January 1986), p. 151.

2. *The Rebirth of America*, op.cit., p. 21.

3. Catherine Drinker Bowen, *Miracle of Philadelphia: The Story of the Constitutional Convention May to September 1787* (Boston: Little, Brown and Company, 1966), pp. 125-26.

4. William Barclay, "The Salt of the Earth," *The Daily Study Bible Series* (Philadelphia, PA: The Westminster Press, 1975), pp. 118-22; *The Eerdmans Bible Commentary*, ed. D. Guthrie and J.A. Motyer, 3d ed.(Grand Rapids: Wm B. Eerdmans Publishing Co., 1970), p. 822.

5. Francis A. Schaeffer, "The Mark of the Christian," reprinted in *Christianity Today*, 6 March 1995, pp. 27-33.

6. ibid., p. 28.

7. ibid., p. 31.

8. John D. Woodbridge, "Culture War Casualties," *Christianity Today*, 6 March 1995, pp. 20-26.

9. ibid., p. 25.

10. H. Dermot McDonald, "Marcion," in *Eerdmans' Handbook to the History of Christianity*, ed. Tim Dowley (Grand Rapids: WM. B. Eerdmans Publishing Co., 1977), pp. 102-103.

11. Everett Ferguson, "Athanasius," in *Eerdmans' Handbook to the History of Christianity*, p. 136.

12. James Dobson, "Why I Use 'Fighting Words': A Response to John Woodbridge's 'Culture War Casualties,'" *Christianity Today*, 19 June 1995, pp. 27-30.

13. *The Eerdmans Bible Commentary*, op.cit., p. 829.

14. J. Gresham Machen, "The Good Fight of Faith," in *25 of the Greatest Sermons Ever Preached*, ed. Jerry Falwell (Grand Rapids: Baker Book House, 1983), p. 193.

15. John W. Whitehead, "Freedom of Religious Expression: Fact or Fiction," in *The Rebirth of America*, op.cit., pp. 133-39.

16. *The Rebirth of America*, op. cit., p. 135.

17. Justice John Paul Stevens qtd. by Justice Harry Andrew Blackmun in his dissenting opinion in "Webster v. Reproductive Health Services," in *Moral Controversies: Race, Class, and Gender in Applied Ethics*, ed. Steven Jay Gold (Belmont, California: Wadsworth Publishing Company, 1993), p. 49.

18. Fr. Theodore Hesburgh, qtd. in *Speaker's Sourcebook II*, ed. Glen Van Ekeren (Englewood Cliffs: Prentice Hall, Inc., 1994), p. 375.

19. Robert Schuller, qtd. in *Speaker's Sourcebook II*, p. 376.

20. Glen Van Ekeren, qtd. in *Speaker's Sourcebook II*, p. 380.

21. Erwin Lutzer, "The Myths That Could Destroy America," in *The Rebirth of America*, op.cit., p. 81.

22. Samuel Adams, qtd. in John Bartlett, <u>Familiar Quotations</u>, ed. Emily Morison Beck, 15th ed. (Boston: Little, Brown and Company, 1980).